Latin American International Politics

Latin American
International Politics

Ambitions, Capabilities, and the National Interest of

Mexico, Brazil,

and

Argentina

CARLOS ALBERTO ASTIZ
Editor

with Mary F. McCarthy

UNIVERSITY OF NOTRE DAME PRESS
NOTRE DAME   LONDON

Library of Congress Catalog Card Number: 68-30668
Manufactured in the United States of America

Foreword

This book is an attempt to bring to the attention of English-speaking scholars engaged in the study of international politics some considerations which enter into the making of foreign policy in some of the Latin American countries. The literature in this field is extremely scarce in any language, and it is hoped that this collection of articles will encourage others to look into the foreign policy of specific Latin American countries, taking into account as much as possible the point of view of those whose foreign policy is studied. If this objective is achieved, I will be fully satisfied.

The role played by Mary F. McCarthy in the preparation of this volume deserved recognition on the title-page; she worked tirelessly on the translation of many of the articles. I also wish to express my deepest appreciation to the staff of the Main Library, State University of New York at Albany, who assisted me with infinite patience in obtaining elusive materials. Finally, my thanks to Patricia Caracci, John McCarthy, Marco Poletto, Frances Weisenfelder, and Christina Zawisza, student assistants of the Center for Inter-American Studies, State University of New York at Albany, who at various times contributed physically and intellectually to the production of this book.

Contents

SECTION IV. THE FOREIGN POLICY OF ARGENTINA

Section I

The Overall View

The Latin American Countries in the International System

Carlos Alberto Astiz

It is not unusual today to visualize the international political system as being loosely bipolar, with emphasis on the word "loosely." The role of France within the Western world and Rumania and Czechoslovakia within the Eastern European bloc is conclusive evidence of the growing inability of the two superpowers to impose their will in many fields on some of the countries with which they have recently had very close political ties.[1] The military move against Czechoslovakia by Warsaw Pact members led by the Soviet Union, which took place in 1968, would seem to have been an attempt to indicate firmly the outward limits of permissible dissent within that organization; in a way, it could be considered a recognition of the fact that covert pressures by the superpowers are not as effective as they once were. Within this framework the twenty independent nation-states of Latin America show varying degrees of commitment to either side: Cuba became aligned with the Soviet bloc in this decade, and the other nineteen countries have been on the side of the United States, at least since World War II.

It has always been interesting to this writer that in spite of the fact that some of the Latin American countries are quite large both in territory and population (that is, Brazil) or show relatively high levels of development (Argentina and Uruguay), they have been and continue to be ignored in the field of international politics. What is perhaps more interesting, with the possible exception of Cuba under the Castro regime, they have come to accept that position, if not in words, certainly in fact.

3

Realistically speaking, the smaller Latin American countries cannot be said to have a foreign policy; to be sure, they have the institutions traditionally responsible for conducting foreign affairs, but even the most superficial inspection of their foreign ministries indicates that they place rather low in the priorities of the national bureaucracy. All the Latin American countries are prolific in regard to embassies and consulates, but in view of the procedure employed in the selection of those who occupy such offices, it is proper to assume that these positions often exist (or are created) to provide attractive rewards for the faithful of limited means and satisfactory exile for politicians and military officers who do not get along with the government of the day.[2] This use (or misuse?) of diplomatic appointments is perhaps the best evidence of the lack of interested involvement on the part of those Latin American countries which resort to them as a matter of course.

On the other hand, there are other Latin American countries, such as Mexico, Argentina, Brazil, Cuba, Chile, Colombia, and a few others, which see themselves as playing a role not only in inter-American affairs but also in the international political system as well. Yet even those countries which try to participate actively in the international political system are quite often unwilling or unable to assert their presence and their national interests in many instances. For there seems to be a substantial reservoir of isolationism among the politically active citizenry (which need not be the majority) and among the leadership and the ruling sectors. This hypothesis should immediately be qualified by stating that this political isolationism is set aside when their economic interests dictate, and that, as private citizens, many of these politically active individuals would rather travel to one of the more advanced countries of the world than within their own country or to neighboring countries, with the exception of the large, gay metropolis.

It would seem, then, that this latter group of countries is willing to interact within the international political system only to the extent of insuring their survival and the economic benefits which come from abroad, but one is hard pressed to find concrete efforts directed to the enhancement of their power, prestige, and influence on the international scene or, even less so, to extending their ideological values and social systems as the more active participants in world politics have traditionally done.

THE DETERMINATION OF THE NATIONAL INTEREST

As Professor Aspaturian has written, the concept of national interest

> must have as its reference point the concrete interests of people, either as individuals, as groups, or as aggregates of groups in some ordered structure of a concentrically radiating consensus. The policies of the state, external and internal, register unevenly upon the interests of various individuals and groups in society, and represent in effect a societal distribution of power reflecting either an informal or a formal consensus pattern or a nonconsensual structure of active and passive coercion.[3]

The situation here described is often more evident in Latin America than in those more advanced countries where one finds varying degrees of counterbalancing political forces which even cancel each other out in a pluralistic fashion. The overwhelming amount of political power held by extremely small groups such as the traditional upper class, the new industrialists, the military establishment, and others, or a combination thereof, and the immediate problems of social and economic improvement faced by the large majorities who belong to the lower class (exacerbated by the revolution of rising expectations) leave the conduct of foreign relations to a very small number of individuals and groups with the time and knowledge to engage in it and the interest in doing so. Thus it can be said that the foreign policy of these Latin American countries (1) is, or tries to be, a continuation of domestic policy; (2) sponsors policies which are a function of the interests of internal elites; and (3) serves more as a way of preserving the social order and the interests of its ruling elites than of the state or the national well-being in the abstract.

It is not surprising, then, that when one of the Latin American countries active in international politics articulates a specific interest, it usually coincides with or at the very least does not contradict the individual or group interests of its ruling elites. Thus, the concrete objectives of most foreign policy moves made by Argentina and Brazil are intended to maintain and increase the market for their traditional exports, and only under special circumstances have their own policy makers been interested in finding markets for their industrial products. On the other hand, when a regime sensitive to the interests of the industrial sector gains power, the country's foreign policy shifts to the protection of its infant industries, the search for nations willing to purchase industrial goods, and the downgrading of its "traditional markets" for raw materials. An example of this type of foreign policy is that followed in Argentina by the Frondizi regime, particularly in the period 1958–1960 (see Section IV of this book).

Generally speaking, the perception of the national interests of the countries of Latin America has remained extremely static in the face of numerous changes in personnel at the top, as well as of the new conditions in the international system. The only radical alterations in recent times have been the neutralist foreign policy followed by the Quadros-Goulart administration in the period of 1960–1964 (discussed in Section III) and the change effectuated by the Castro regime after it took power in 1959. With these two exceptions, the Latin American countries have refused to introduce innovations into their foreign policies not only in regard to their most important partners, such as the United States, Great Britain, Germany, and France, but also in regard to their petty regional jealousies and rivalries as well. In most cases these static foreign policies are the product of unimaginative policy makers, lack of power, and isolationist sentiment. But the stability tends to indicate that the same power elites have maintained control of the countries in question, and since their interests have not changed, their countries' foreign policies have remained unchanged.

By the same token, it is to be expected that when profound

political changes take place in a Latin American country and a new power elite enters the scene, these changes will be reflected in the nation's foreign policy, as they have been in Cuba, Bolivia, and, to a certain extent, Mexico. The trend has been and will tend to be away from submission to the United States and from sole reliance on the Organization of American States, and toward a more noncommittal position, with emphasis on the United Nations. The realization of these tendencies has prompted the United States to look with disfavor upon basic sociopolitical changes in Latin America and to suspect those who truly favor such changes. As one observer put it,

> The preference for order, which is confused with immobility, also creates difficulties for Washington's diplomacy or, once more, for its various diplomacies. The element of order is generally a strong man or an army, more stable interlocutors than a series of organizations which have rivalries or fight among themselves.[4]

This role of the United States, often disclaimed by its officials but confirmed by its deeds, constitutes at the present time the most important external limitation to the political processes involved in the making of foreign policy in the nations of Latin America. I shall be dealing with this limitation later in this article.

LATIN AMERICAN DIPLOMACY

Different authors have already emphasized that a nation's role in international affairs depends upon the quality of its government, its diplomatic service, its intelligence-gathering operations, and all other elements which make up a nation's foreign policy. With one or two possible exceptions, true career diplomats have existed and exist in Latin American countries only by accident and in spite of the procedures employed in their selection, promotion, and assignment. As indicated above, this is a reflection of the low level of priority awarded to international relations by these countries. At the same time this situation downgrades even more the conduct of foreign affairs and further reduces whatever confidence important interest groups or the population at large may have in their diplomats. The best evidence that one can provide of this deterioration is the fact that when important negotiations are to be conducted, influential groups whose interest is at stake either will make sure that capable individuals are appointed special representatives or will send such special representatives on their own, even though their government may have the best intentions of protecting these groups' interests. Anyone who wants to assess the situation for himself has only to walk into Latin American consulates and embassies at random and question the staff about their background, training, language ability, and mode of appointment; he will probably get no answer, an indication of the interviewees' inability to provide what they know are the right answers.

In the conduct of international relations today the possession of accurate information has been recognized as a must. Information relevant to foreign policy making is gathered in many ways and through many sources, but most advanced countries rely heavily on intelligence organizations of one type or another. Most of the Latin American countries have imitated the other nations with international involvement by setting up such agencies, usually under the jurisdiction (officially or unofficially) of the military establishment. Although their specific activities are a more or less guarded secret, the surprising fact is that most of the efforts and resources of these intelligence organizations are directed toward gathering information within their respective countries, so that they play the role of a supersecret police, while producing relatively little that can be used in foreign policy making.[5]

This misdirection of the efforts and resources of the intelligence organizations, when coupled with the unreliability of the information produced by the diplomats, forces the making of policies on the basis of personal impressions, which are often nothing more than guesswork; this process cannot be conducive to an effective role in international politics. If one adds to this the dominance of military personnel both in the intelligence agencies and in the diplomatic corps and their tendency to fear nearly every type of basic economic, social, and/or political change and to brand as Communist those who subscribe to programs whose objective is to revise the status quo, it is easy to visualize the handicaps under which the foreign policy of the Latin American countries is made and implemented.

In the last few years some of the larger Latin American countries have made attempts to professionalize their foreign services and to develop career staffs immune to changes in political leadership. Foreign service schools or academies were created or revitalized; new laws and decrees were issued to reactivate old statutes or outline new admission and promotion requirements. While only an impressionistic opinion can be given, since most Latin American foreign offices are as reluctant about disclosing personnel data as their military establishments are about theirs, it seems that very little, if anything, has been accomplished. The most popular and effective method of entering the foreign service continues to be personal or political "pull," and the same rule applies to assignments within the service. Thus, assignment to the large, cosmopolitan capitals is reserved for those who carry the most weight; the rest are sentenced to the out-of-the-way places or, even worse, to stay at home. This latter alternative is feared because it means regular civil service salaries (which are generally low) instead of the diplomatic benefits and the cost-of-living allowances given to those outside their own country.[6]

In regard to the intelligence services, very little of their recruitment procedures is known. Nevertheless, it can be stated that in practically all countries they are led and heavily staffed by military officers, either retired or in active service. Civilians tend to be hired solely for technical positions and even then only when military personnel is not available. Furthermore, because of their domestic political involvement, it would seem that political reliability is more important than training, skill, or background. Low salaries and budgetary limitations narrowly limit recruitment possibilities and facilitate corruption. In fact, there are indications that the United States Central Intelligence Agency and American military missions have access to the information gathered by the Latin American intelligence services.[7] This situation, as well as that which exists in the diplomatic corps, undoubtedly limits the quality of these countries' foreign policy.

THE LATIN AMERICAN COUNTRIES AS PENETRATED SYSTEMS

In a recent essay, Professor Rosenau brought forth a concept which appears to be relevant to Latin American countries, both in the management of their domestic affairs and in the conduct of their foreign policy. I am referring to a *penetrated political system* "in which non-members of a national society participate directly and authoritatively through actions taken jointly with the society's members, in either the allocation of its values or the mobilization of support on behalf of its goals."[8] Close scrutiny indicates that all the Latin American political systems have been and are subject to varying degrees of penetration, mostly by the United States, but also by the European countries. This penetration is quite evident in the economic sphere, where crucial investments in important sectors of the economy are dominated by one or more outside investors (such as the chemical and automobile industries throughout the area). Penetration is also quite evident in the military establishment of most of the countries which rely on outside missions, training centers, and manufacturers for their equipment and technical preparation. Penetration in the cultural and political areas is much more subtle and difficult to pinpoint, but it undoubtedly exists as evidenced by the reluctance of any of the Latin American countries to adopt publicly a foreign policy position which would contradict that of the United States. In fact, since the Onganía regime took over in Argentina in mid-1966, the weekly magazine *Confirmado*, which communicates the thinking of one of the factions within the government, has been making a deliberate effort to give its readers the impression that certain foreign policy actions, which obviously constituted a reiteration of the United States position, were in fact an expression of defiance and contradiction of that position.

The case of Cuba is a very interesting one because it is a

country which shifted from being very highly penetrated by the United States to being penetrated, although substantially less so as recent events have demonstrated, by the other superpower. Naturally, this is not a case in which penetration has determined domestic and international changes, but a situation in which domestic and international changes (especially the former) have altered the source of penetration. To make the point very clear:

> The foreign policy of Castro differs substantially from that of Batista because the nature of the social order and the threats which its dominant groups perceive are correspondingly different, not because Cuba has been transported geographically or because its population has been replaced or its history altered.[9]

It would appear that the American penetration of Cuba, while an extreme example, does not stand alone. What has confused the picture in Latin America has been the fact that the non-members participating directly and authoritatively, or causing that participation, have not always been American diplomats. In most cases American investors have provided the energy and have been the main beneficiaries of penetration sometimes *at the expense* of American long-range foreign policy objectives. The American involvement in a proposed land-reform law of 1962 in Honduras, in which some United States Senators prodded the State Department into action at the request of the United Fruit Company,[10] provides an enlightening example of the nature and mechanics of this penetration. The events which took place in Guatemala in the 1950's and culminated in the overthrow of the reformist administration of Jacobo Arbenz by an invasion force sponsored by the United States Central Intelligence Agency provide another overt case of penetration.[11] But, after all, many Latin American scholars have subscribed to the seldom-avowed assumption that American domination of the small Caribbean and Central American countries was a fact of geopolitical life, although it is clear that Castro does not subscribe to that particular school of thought.

It may be more important, in terms of international politics, to identify the level and mechanics of penetration in the larger and internationally more active countries of Latin America. Without attempting a detailed study, which is badly needed, it is possible to say that American penetration seems to rely the most heavily on the rapport developed between the United States military and their South American counterparts and is reflected in the mutual defense agreements and in the programs of military assistance. Commenting on the Argentine-United States Mutual Assistance Pact subscribed in 1964, Professor Veneroni concluded (perhaps too legalistically) that,

> We reiterate in this regard what was said before in the sense that there do not exist in the agreement "reciprocal and equal" obligations for both parties. One of them, the United States, is only the supplier of defense equipment and services, as the owner who grants the use of such equipment and services under specific conditions, who has the right to the constant control of such use and to the return of the equipment and services. The other party, our country, is the receiver of those services and equipment, as a depositary who will only have the right to have them, but not to use them except in such a manner as established by the agreement (determined by an American law), who must allow the control—by citizens of the other party—of the use to which said equipment and services are put, who should pay the expenses of those who perform such control, who should protect the equipment and services and return them to the other side.[12]

This relationship between the military establishments is supplemented by heavy investments in certain key aspects of the countries' economic activities and by close ties with the local power elites, be they traditional, industrial, or a combination of these. This economic penetration acquires paramount importance in Mexico, where the armed forces have not played a significant political role for some time (see Section II, Introduction).

THE LATIN AMERICAN SUBSYSTEM

Most students of international politics tend to concentrate their attention on the affairs of the two superpowers and of the group of second-ranking actors which provide most of the headlines. To these observers the countries of Latin America, committed in general to the American side, have not engaged in international politics. Their sporadic appearances have been directed mostly to lobbying for the acceptance of principles of international law with which the proponents hoped to protect their interests. Their efforts produced the Drago, Estrada, and Calvo doctrines which not surprisingly refer to the use of military force to recover public debts, the recognition of governments, and the treatment of foreign investors, respectively; hence the impression, conveyed explicitly or implicitly by most writers, that the Latin American countries "stood outside the mainstream of world politics."[13]

If the "mainstream of world politics" is composed of Europe and the United States, the view that the Latin American countries have been, and probably still are, marginal cannot be refuted. If, on the other hand, one recognizes that Latin America *is* a part of the world, then this view is undoubtedly erroneous, inasmuch as almost since independence most of the countries of Latin America have engaged in the game of international politics, primarily vis-à-vis their neighbors. They have also become entangled, although less frequently, in conflicts with those countries which "moved in" in attempts to fill the power vacuum left by the Spaniards. Great Britain, the United States, France, Holland, and Germany thus came into contact with the countries of Latin America, mostly in the latter's territory.

Without attempting here to review the history of Latin American diplomacy, it is possible to affirm that tradition and undetermined national boundaries gave rise to a continuous flow of relations which have existed throughout the nineteenth and twentieth centuries and which, by and large, remain a key element of the foreign policies of the Latin American countries to this day. These sets of relations, which are reflected in the regional international organizations of the area, include the traditional rivalry between Argentina and Brazil, apparent in their relations with Paraguay and Uruguay; the boundary disputes between Argentina and Chile, which exploded again in 1967–1968; the conflicts between Chile, on the one hand, and Bolivia and Peru, on the other, which were exacerbated by the War of the Pacific (1879–1883); the Chaco War, fought between Bolivia and Paraguay (1932–1935); and finally, the conflicts between Ecuador, Peru, and Colombia, which culminated in various armed struggles. Similar rivalries have existed among the countries of Central America and, in the Caribbean, between Haiti and the Dominican Republic.

A consequence of these rivalries has been the tacit acceptance of a balance of military power, particularly among the South American countries. This balance, which has not been spelled out anywhere, seems to call for a one-to-one ratio between Argentina and Brazil, at least in regard to major war items such as modern planes, tanks, or naval vessels.[14] Chile and Peru tend to follow at a level of from one-half to two-thirds of the "big two," with Venezuela and Colombia constituting the third level, not too far behind the second echelon. The other countries are financially unable to participate in this competition, but quite often weapon purchases by their more powerful neighbors trigger rounds of acquisitions among them. This balance is not necessarily reflected in the size of the armed forces at a given moment, but it can be clearly perceived over a period of time in the purchase of war materiel.

The balance of military power and the correlated role played by the countries involved in the Organization of American States and the Latin American Free Trade Association, as well as in some of the universal international institutions, outline the boundaries of what can be called the Latin American international subsystem. Another major regional international organization, the Central American Common Market, has so far played a marginal role in spite of its apparent success; this situation may be explained by the minute political weight carried by its five members and by the overwhelming influence exercised by the United States over them and over the organization.[15]

The traditional rivalry between Brazil and Argentina has set the tone of the relations within the Latin American subsystem. Mexico's aloofness, particularly evident since the Mexican Revolution (see section II), has increased the significance of foreign policy moves by either country. While Brazil tended to identify its national interest within the inter-American system and acted in close alliance with the United States, Argentina looked toward Europe and the universal international organization, when one existed. Unquestionably, both countries hoped to exercise some sort of leadership over the rest of South America, while their policy makers considered Central America, the Caribbean, and Mexico within the sphere of influence of the United States and thus beyond their jurisdiction.

Argentina felt that the most effective way of gaining recognition as South America's leader was to offer an alternative to United States influence by becoming the spearhead of passive and sometimes active opposition. Brazil, on the other hand, tried to convince both the United States and the other South American countries that it was the natural intermediary between the region and the "Colossus of the North." This traditional competition was altered in 1961 when the Frondizi and Quadros administrations for a time succeeded in coordinating their countries' foreign policies, at least institutionally, along the lines of the Uruguayana agreement.[16] The coordination broke down after Quadros' resignation and Frondizi's overthrow, and was explicitly rejected by the military regime of Castelo Branco, which took over the Brazilian government in 1964, and that of Onganía, which assumed control of Argentina in 1966. Although the two military governments showed points of agreement, such as their interest in creating an inter-American military force, by and large they have gone back to their traditional suspicion of each other.

The other South American nations active in international politics, such as Chile, Peru, Colombia, and Venezuela, often preferred to remain aloof from the struggle for regional power, although occasionally they would indicate preference for one or the other, depending on the specific situation and the issue. Recently, the opposition of these countries to the inter-American military force and to the regional economic policies sponsored by Argentina and Brazil, often with Mexico's concurrence, led them to the formation of the Andean bloc, whose future seems to be in doubt.[17] It would seem, however, that moves of the type just described are reactions to the positions taken by the "big two" and, needless to say, the United States. As a recognition of this fact of political life, as well as of the special role played by Mexico, Sections II, III, and IV attempt to deal in greater detail with some aspects of these countries' foreign policies, with the understanding that their positions will determine, or at least heavily influence, the positions of the rest.

NOTES

1. This point is very well treated by Morton A. Kaplan, "Some Problems of International Systems Research," in *International Political Communities: An Anthology* (Garden City, N. Y.: Doubleday and Company, Inc., 1966), pp. 468–501. See also his "Bipolarity in a Revolutionary Age," in Morton A. Kaplan (ed.), *The Revolution in World Politics* (New York: John Wiley and Sons, Inc., 1962), pp. 251–66.

2. See, for instance, the complete lists of Peruvian diplomatic and consular officers on assignment abroad and the uproar caused by its publication, in the July and August, 1965, issues of the weekly magazine *Oiga* (Lima, Peru).

3. Vernon V. Aspaturian, "Internal Politics and Foreign Policy in the Soviet System," in R. Barry Farrell (ed.), *Approaches to Comparative and International Politics* (Evanston, Ill.: Northwestern University Press, 1966), p. 215.

4. Luis Mercier Vega, *Mecanismos del Poder en América Latina* (Buenos Aires: Editorial Sur, S. A., 1967), p. 128.

5. For an interesting account of the various roles and priorities of the Argentine intelligence agency, see *Primera Plana* (Buenos Aires), July 19, 1966, pp. 44–9; specific activities have been reported in *Confirmado* (Buenos Aires), Sept. 15, 1966, p. 17; Oct. 20, 1966, p. 17; and Aug. 3, 1967, p. 16.

6. Cost-of-living allowances are very generous (or perhaps civil service salaries are too low), increasing net salaries three or four times; thus, a low-ranking foreign service officer may earn the equivalent of two hundred dollars when stationed in his country, but his salary jumps to seven hundred dollars or eight hundred dollars as soon as he is transferred to a foreign post. Furthermore, upon his return home, he is allowed to enter a number of household items and an automobile duty-free.

7. For an obvious case of this type of penetration see the episode described by Víctor Villanueva, *Un Año bajo el Sable* (Lima: Empresa Gráfica T. Scheuch, S. A., 1963), pp. 58–61.

8. James N. Rosenau, "Pre-theories and Theories of Foreign Policy," in R. Barry Farrell (ed.), *Approaches to Comparative and International Politics* (Evanston, Ill.: Northwestern University Press, 1966), p. 65.

9. Vernon V. Aspaturian, "Internal Politics and Foreign Policy in the Soviet System," in Farrell, *op. cit.*, p. 218.

10. The details have been reproduced in Marvin D. Bernstein (ed.), *Foreign Investments in Latin America* (New York: Alfred A. Knopf, 1966), pp. 186–208.

11. The Arbenz administration and the Castillo Armas invasion and its aftermath have been discussed by Kalman H. Silvert, *A Study in Government: Guatemala* (New Orleans: Tulane University Press, 1954); Ronald M. Schneider, *Communism in Guatemala, 1944–1954* (New York: Frederick A. Praeger, 1959); Mario Monteforte Toledo, *Guatemala; Monografía Sociológica* (México, D. F.: Universidad Nacional Autónoma de México, 1959); Ezequiel Ramírez Novoa, *La Farsa del Panamericanismo y la Unidad Indoamericana* (Buenos Aires: Editorial Indoamericana, 1955); and Gregorio Selser, *El Guatemalazo* (Buenos Aires: Iguazú, 1961). The role of the CIA is outlined in David Wise and Thomas B. Ross, *The Invisible Government* (New York: Random House, 1964), pp. 165–83.

12. Horacio Luis Veneroni, *La Asistencia Militar de los Estados Unidos* (Buenos Aires: Talleres Gráficos Buschi, S. A. I. C. I., 1964), p. 39. For an attempt to institutionalize this military penetration through a multinational facade, see the recent proposals for a permanent inter-American military force; for a well-researched discussion consult Veneroni, *Fuerza Militar Interamericana* (Buenos Aires: Talleres Gráficos Buschi, S. A. I. C. I., 1966).

13. W. Friedmann, *An Introduction to World Politics*, 5th edition (New York: St. Martin's Press, 1965), p. 305.

14. A relatively recent example of this balance is the series of acquisitions caused by the addition of an aircraft carrier to the Brazilian navy in the early 1960's. Argentina immediately matched the unit, and Chile and Peru added lesser ships to their fleets.

15. In regard to the Central American Common Market see J. S. Nye, "Central American Regional Integration," in Joseph S. Nye, Jr. (ed.), *International Regionalism; Readings* (Boston: Little, Brown and Company, 1968), pp. 377–429.

16. Uruguayana, a Brazilian town located near the Argentine border, was the place where Presidents Frondizi and Quadros met in 1961.

17. For the development of the Andean bloc, or Bogotá group, see the *New York Times*, Aug. 20, 1966, p. 8; June 25, 1967, p. 32; and Aug. 20, 1967, p. 22. For recent moves by the various groups see Mariano Grondona, "Perspectivas Regionales," *Primera Plana*, May 21, 1968, p. 11.

The "Latin American Crisis" and Its External Framework*

Espartaco

Latin American development is taking place in an international context which is conditioning it decisively. We will not deal here with the economic aspects of the matter, though there are many and all are important,[1] but concentrate on matters of a political nature that have generally been neglected or submitted to analysis from a narrow sectarian point of view.

In the first place we are interested in stressing the persistence of the old pattern of the Cold War in this hemisphere, the possible causes of this anachronism, and its implications for the Latin American countries. We will then examine briefly some prerequisites or efforts necessary to deal with these implications.

PART ONE

THE PERSISTENCE OF THE OLD PATTERN OF THE COLD WAR

In Latin America, as a result of massive political propaganda, the basic fact has almost been overlooked that during the last few years there have been changes of substance in the operation of the Cold War and in the world projection of the struggle among the superpowers.

* This article was originally published in Spanish as " 'La Crisis Latino-americana' y su Marco Externo," in *Desarrollo Económico*, 6:319–353, July–Dec., 1966. Translated and printed by permission.

On the one hand we have the general fact of the relatively peaceful coexistence of the United States and the Soviet Union, which involves a certain freezing of their positions, since any substantial modification could bring on the dreaded atomic confrontation.[2] It is, as has been said, a balance of terror.

On the other hand (and to a certain extent as a result of the aspect just noted, but also because of other factors), instead of the trend toward polarization becoming accentuated, an opposite tendency toward disassociation or, we might say, toward "de-satellization"[3] has prevailed.

We need not review in detail all that has happened within the spheres of the two poles. In the case of the USSR the dispute with China has been accompanied by an unmistakable weakening of the former's position as guardian of the surrounding states. In the case of the United States the affirmation of independence by France is the conspicuous feature of a larger reality: the strengthening and increasing integration of Western Europe. At the same time other regional alliances of the Western bloc in Asia and the Middle East have fallen apart or barely exist on paper. In short, then, the monolithic aspect of the blocs is a thing of the past.

But rather than in the events which have taken place within the two poles or which have affected them, we are interested in noting what has happened outside those areas, primarily in a large part of the underdeveloped world.

Most people thought until recently that the new nations, despite their proclamations of neutrality and of an uncompromising attitude toward the superpowers, in the long run would gradually orient themselves toward one or the other pole, strengthening and completing a supposedly inevitable polarization on a worldwide scale.

Actually, such a process has not materialized; on the contrary, an "interpolar" situation has developed, in which, even though the foreign or domestic policies of the new countries tip the scales in the direction of one or the other center of power, there does not seem to be any increasing advance toward full affiliation, that is, toward satellization.

However, this pluralistic picture of the international situation does not apply to what has taken place in the Latin American area, or more properly in the Western Hemisphere (with the exception of Canada). In this case, the forms of the old pattern of the Cold War, instead of becoming weakened, have been reaffirmed. Both the United States and, generally, the ruling groups of almost all Latin American countries have succeeded in maintaining their foreign policies within the anachronistic framework of the Cold War. The independent attempts of some countries in the recent past have ceased, and the isolated gestures of others are looked upon with suspicion, if not with animosity, in spite of not involving any break with or challenge to the basic status which prevails in inter-American relations. In short, any deviation from the rules in regard to total allegiance to the hegemonic superpower is branded as a transgression or a sign of a very definite change of allegiance, that is, of adherence to the rival bloc.

On the other hand, we must remember that other Latin American groups, such as those linked to the official left, have an opposite point of view, but one equally adapted to the old pattern of the conflict abroad. For them the essential objective at the moment is to harass the United States and to break with it, and they wish to join the ranks of the other center of power, although they frequently avoid or deny the inference. Of course, in this case the problem has become complicated by the schism within the socialist world.

To what do we owe this exception to the general trend? Why has this part of the "third world" not been able to relax its position of dependence and affirm an autonomous personality as others have done?

To begin with, one should refute simplistic explanations such as those that only emphasize the weaknesses and inconsistencies of the governing sectors of the region or the wickedness of the powerful neighbor to the north. It seems clear that there are countries more dependent and defenseless, as least from the economic point of view, that are yet more independent. On the other hand, the United States, like any other great power, will exercise as much influence as it can (or is allowed to) within its sphere of influence. What is important is to establish the reasons why in this region its force is so overwhelming and why it has been oriented toward freezing the old patterns of the Cold War.

THE REASONS FOR THE FREEZING

To begin with, in this connection we must remember two very obvious and well-known facts. The first fact, a political one, is that a large segment of the underdeveloped world gained its independence from declining powers or from powers greatly affected by World War II.[4] In contrast to this, Latin America is within the sphere of the most powerful nation of the world, whose economic system has demonstrated in the last few years a vitality and a renewal that few people would have imagined some time ago.

The second aspect is of a geographic nature and can be summed up by paraphrasing the old saying attributed to Porfirio Díaz: "Latin America is very far away from God and too close to the United States." This is intensified by the fact that the possible competitors of the dominant power, including those not antagonistic to it, are located too far away to counterweigh its influence. The differences with other underdeveloped areas are obvious from both points of view.

But we must go much further in the analysis. In making it, we must take into consideration other factors that have determined the internal changes within both poles and, also, the nature and spread of the Cold War in the corresponding spheres.

Let us begin by examining the process in the Soviet sphere.

THE THAW IN THE SOVIET AREA

The first thing that becomes apparent is that the Soviet camp has suffered a wider schism than the capitalist alliance, contrary to what was assumed in the last writings of Stalin. The disagreements between the United States and France, for instance, seem almost academic beside the disagreements that have separated the USSR and China, at least on the political level. Without going into the nature of this schism, its importance for the understanding of the problem of "power politics" (that is, the type of interpower struggle that goes beyond or is not strictly identified with imperialist rivalries of an *economic nature*) should be emphasized. The idea that once these causes are eliminated—for example, in the relations between socialist powers—the conflicts would disappear has been shown to be wrong.

Be that as it may, what is certain is that the dispute has aroused the tendencies toward independence of the so-called USSR satellites. Now, when this superpower negotiates with Rumania or Poland—and also with countries outside its orbit—it has to consider, among other things, that the shadow of China also hovers over it, not only that of the United States.

On the other hand, those tendencies are reinforced by the undeniable fact that the nations on the Soviet periphery are "attached," physically and historically, to the Western European complex, with which they also maintain old economic ties. The capitalist alternative, which is today dynamic and prosperous, lies just beyond their doorstep; and obviously the conditions that would allow the lowering of an iron curtain like the one that surrounded and protected the Soviet experiment and the first years of the peoples' republics no longer exist.

It might be thought that these circumstances would create a situation of potential insecurity for the USSR that might have driven it to enforcing extreme control instead of acquiescing in its relaxation. However, we must consider other aspects that lead to an opposite conclusion.

One of the most significant is that between the USSR and its affiliated states the bonds of a common sociopolitical organization exist. The Communist parties, while instruments of power more or less rooted in the masses, are also valuable agencies for bringing about controlled changes leading to new situations. In Poland or Hungary, where the orthodox hierarchy was incapable of controlling events, it was possible to replace the old leaders with forces that were more flexible and had greater insight with respect to what adjustments could be introduced without modifying the foundations of the system internally or externally.

Another aspect that is not always recognized is that the Soviet military presence in their area is a decisive factor that undoubtedly increases the possibility of transition to new patterns.

In this connection we cannot avoid bringing up the 1956 Hungarian crisis. In that episode the political agency, the Communist party, manifestly failed, but the Red Army, *which was there*, was able to maintain control over events (without the necessity of sending Marines). Also, and wisely, a new political pattern was set up immediately, one capable of reforming what was nonessential while retaining what was essential within the system.

Nor should one forget the existence of a supranational bond in the Soviet area which is not always adequately evaluated. This bond has been forged by memories of World War II and by fear of German revenge, which now appears much more threatening because of the possibility of United States support. For the countries that have more than once suffered the "expansion to the East" of German power this is not a trifling question, and it is certainly a cohesive force that can surmount many reservations against other aspects of Soviet influence in the countries affected.

Finally, we must emphasize that despite all the criticism of the rigidity of the foreign policies of the USSR, the truth is that its leaders have not shown themselves shortsighted in understanding the realities of the world situation. Clear examples are to be found in the way they have adjusted to the problems of Poland, East Germany, Hungary, and Rumania. And this is true not only within its own orbit. Its policy toward the underdeveloped world bears witness to this, and another outstanding example is Finland. In regard to this country, which upon cursory examination might seem to be as, or more, vital to Russia than Cuba is to the United States, the Soviets have maintained a type of conduct that has allowed an essential degree of independence for the Finns, the latter accepting several unavoidable limitations arising from their strategic geographic location.

Since the preceding paragraphs are intended to explore the "whys" of the relaxation of the Cold War in the Soviet area, they are merely an introduction and a point of reference for leading up to the matter that is of most interest to us—the reason why in this hemisphere there has been a freezing of the antiquated idea of "either you are with me (100 percent) or you are against me."

THE AMERICAN SCENE

Without forgetting the general elements previously emphasized—the power of the United States and its geographical location—we must now consider other elements more pertinent to the complex relations between the United States and Latin America, and especially to the unknowns implied by the so-called "prerevolutionary condition" of Latin America.

In order to place and evaluate this general problem, all we need do is examine the case of Cuba as a point of reference. There, when one of the most corrupt "establishments" of the area was overthrown, not only did *a transformation of a socialist character take place in the system of power and property but a change of alignment in the pattern of the Cold War also occurred.*

An examination of the origin and nature of this historic Latin American episode is not pertinent here. What does matter is its hemispheric repercussions, which by analogy could be compared with what theoretically would have taken place in the Soviet sphere if the Hungarian uprising had terminated in a victory for the opponents and the admittance of the new government to NATO. In short, the shock from the Cuban experience has caused the United States and also the dominant groups of Latin America *to identify the Latin American revolution with a given pattern of general change: a socialist Marxist-Leninist ideology in the domestic field, with an orientation toward the Soviet pole in the international area.*

As it must be obvious, the above does not imply any judgment on the Cuban phenomenon, nor does it imply a justification of the attitudes or reactions of the United States and its supporters. It only attempts to emphasize an aspect which is essential for the understanding and analysis of the problem under discussion, which is the freezing-in of the antiquated pattern of the Cold War.

THE PREREVOLUTIONARY CONDITIONS

We must examine with more care the nature of the prerevolutionary conditions in Latin America. On this matter the general or global interpretation has obscured certain differentiations that are basic for understanding the subject and its outlook.

One could say that in reality *there are various prerevolutionary conditions*, in the sense *that not just one regional type or "establishment" becomes involved in a crisis*. At least two must be mentioned, still at a very abstract level. One type is the oligarchical republic characteristic of the most underdeveloped countries in the area. The other type is the country with a greater relative development which includes the sociopolitical pattern of a "mesocratic" coalition based upon the middle classes, certain sections of business, and the wage earners integrated into the "capitalistic" pole of their economy; this sociopolitical pattern is also in crisis.

Our analysis will concentrate on this second type, for the reason, among others, that such countries have already experienced in their own way the crisis of an oligarchical society, and so can be used to illuminate and serve as contrast to the corresponding phenomenon that countries of the other type now face, even though we reject any mechanical analogy.

Recalling the collapse of the traditional patterns in the most diversified economies (such as Mexico, Brazil, Argentina, Uruguay, and Chile), we can see that nowhere did a smooth or constitutional transition take place in the direction of the new pattern, except, in part, in Batlle's Uruguay.* In a few countries such as Mexico an extensive and profound revolution was neces-

---

* Translator's note: The author apparently refers to José Batlle Ordoñez, who occupied the presidency of Uruguay briefly in 1889 and in the periods 1903–1907 and 1911–1915.

sary; in others, various interregnums and extralegal formulas were needed. Nevertheless, aside from the violent case of Mexico, it is evident that the convulsions were not too intense. Various reasons can be given to explain these relatively peaceful transitions.

The principal one is that the previous evolution of those countries—despite all the limitations on their external growth—had produced certain diversifications in the social structure, especially in the urban centers, so that different groups and strata had appeared that were capable of displacing the oligarchical clan and of taking a part (but only a part) of the political power into their hands. These civilian forces usually were not able to realize their task by themselves, but in almost all places found a decisive ally in the young officers of the armed forces, who shared a similar social background. *It was this alliance, whether formal or informal, of middle class and military groups, with the urban wage earner serving as support in the rear guard, that served as the historic agent in the transfer to the new mesocratic political system.* And let us add in passing that the simultaneous or later development of new types of industry and the increase of complementary services and of those of the public sector constituted the economic platform that for a long time justified and maintained this juxtaposition of interests.

The second aspect to be considered (in reality an extension of the first) is the fact that the political and institutional transformations undertaken at the time were not revolutionary, at least in the strict sense of the word. In Marxist terms one might say that they corresponded to an incipient phase in the bourgeois-democratic changes and that only in the case of Mexico did they cause a liquidation of the traditionally powerful agricultural sector and hence a substantial transformation in the distribution of power.

The third element worth stressing is that the downfall of the oligarchical establishments did not have great external consequences or implications (again with the exception of Mexico). They were essentially local phenomena. In some countries, such as Brazil or Argentina, in a more or less advanced stage of the process some reflections of the conflict between fascists and democrats may be found, but they did not greatly influence the content or the origin of the process.

THE CRISIS IN THE MESOCRATIC ESTABLISHMENT

The contrasts become apparent when we compare the above conditions with those that appear in times of crisis in the mesocratic establishment and the transition toward a new general pattern, not yet defined, in the relatively advanced countries of the region.

Before beginning the comparison, we should run through some theories about the origin of that crisis, whose intensity is difficult to assess but is evident from the instability of the present situation and the uncertainties concerning future prospects (again some exceptions must be made in the case of Mexico).[5]

We think that behind that reality lie two crucial and related facts.

On the one hand we have the arrival on the political scene of the large urban mass and of part or all of the rural mass, that is, of those relatively or absolutely kept out of political life up to fifteen years ago or less. The various populist movements, almost always invincible when conditions for free elections exist, are the most visible expression of the phenomenon.

On the other hand we have the delay in the process of development, in relative terms (or, rather, in the face of increased social pressure), or the decrease in the rate of growth, which can be attributed, by another gross oversimplification, to the difficulties encountered in advancing toward or along the road of heavy industrialization. This is particularly true when it was not possible in the previous stage to solve agricultural problems and those of the foreign sector and when the domestic market is also substantially restricted.[6]

The interplay and disassociation of these two factors seem to be the principal causes of the dislocation of the mesocratic conglomerate. In practice the coalitions among the middle sectors represented by the center parties and the organized or "integrated" wage earners broke up or became inoperable in different ways and degrees. The pressure from the right and from the left (in this case the peripheral masses and not the official parties) broke the base and the viability of the scheme.

Circumstances are now very different from those we have already discussed as existing at the time the oligarchical power was overcome.

In the first place, in almost all areas it is difficult to conceive of any coalition, either within or outside the existing parties, capable of replacing the old one and so serving as an agency of transition toward a new social pattern. It seems clear that a viable combination suited to the present circumstances would at least have to join some of the middle sectors and "integrated" workers to the main portion of the urban and rural peripheral masses. It is not at all easy to formulate a common political platform for such heterogeneous segments (for example, factory workers from São Paulo and farmers from Northeastern Brazil; bank employees and unskilled construction workers; etc.).[7] This is shown by the many difficulties that both the progressive parties and those of the official left have encountered in extending their influence to the populist and rural masses. It is not only a matter of the deficient political education of the latter and of its reverse, the ideological load, habitually alienated, of the former. There are also other factors, such as the conservatism of the more or less leftist forces which keeps them within the pattern of the redistributive politics of the old type, which is always advantageous for small organized sectors, but which cannot serve as a common platform when the interests of the majority are to be taken care of.

The forces that favor or demand change do not have the backing of the military this time, a condition opposite of what it has been in the past.[8] On the contrary, the bulk of the uniformed establishment holds a conservative position, although apparently the attitude of the young officers is more radical than that of the old.

A basic reason for this change of position may be found in the external variations of the phenomenon, which we will examine later, but it is also possible to detect a few internal motivations. In this connection one could suggest the following hypothesis:

in the breakdown of the oligarchical pattern the military, as a body, join the reforms because they feel or know that the overthrow of the status quo will open up to them opportunities for upward social mobility in a broad sense. But now the outlook is quite different: the pressures from below and the slowing down of economic expansion (not to mention other related phenomena resulting to some extent from this maladjustment, such as inflation) make them think, with some reason, that instead of gaining, they may find their status and their opportunities diminished. They therefore lean toward the maintenance of the existing establishment and against change; what is more, they tend consciously or unconsciously to turn toward those measures that lessen or overcome the disquieting pressure of the great mass.

The crisis of the mesocratic establishment and its economic platform (light and import-substitution industrialization) does not necessarily imply a revolutionary alternative of a socialist nature. Much imagination would be needed to support the case that what is being attacked in Latin America is the capitalistic system as a whole. More defensible is the postulate that, in orthodox terms, the more advanced phases of the democratic-capitalistic process (probably characterized by the integration and organization of the peripheral mass, the widening of the scope and responsibility of state authority and ownership, and the changing of the structure and functioning of the agricultural sector) are being attacked by the antistatus quo groups. We should note that for the countries under analysis our outline has little to do with the anti-imperialistic agrarian revolution. Yet such an approach may be more or less adequate for understanding the situation in other more backward communities, those having more influential agricultural sectors, but lacking developed and decisive urban-capitalistic poles, and having more direct foreign intervention and a less diversified social structure.

In any case, although the historical task of today may not seem to be revolutionary in the strict sense, it could well become so if there are no social forces and political instruments capable of controlling the transition toward a new pattern.

At first glance one might think that this has been a constant in the development of society. In spite of Marx's optimism in several of his early works,[9] the truth is that there has been no synchronization between the exhaustion of a given state and the maturing of conditions for its replacement.

However, in general there has been in the great revolutionary processes a relative degree of association, with varying appraisals of situations, between the crisis of an establishment and the existence of some substitutive social mechanism. Upon the relation and weight of those factors the viability of the change and its consolidation and cost to the community have depended.

Without discussing how sharp the crisis of the status quo is when there are no replacement forces, or very weak ones (as they appear to be in these mesocratic countries), the process tends to get out of hand, and may lean toward the left or toward the right because the political, or power, vacuum must be filled.

In that eventual overflow, or even under its immanent threat, the more cohesive and aggressive conservative minority often has more opportunities for victory, both because it includes, or revolves around, the armed forces, and because it can also find support or tolerance in the middle sectors and even among some "integrated" wage earners, not to mention support through Cold War and anti-Communist slogans. (Any similarity between this speculation and the recent history of Brazil, for example, is not a mere coincidence.)

It is worth pointing out the possibility of a reactionary alternative, because in some circles the somewhat naive idea has prevailed that any crisis in an establishment necessarily tends toward popular-revolutionary solutions; this is a carry-over from the historical optimism of the eighteenth century!

The last point has already been presented, and of course is that of international relations and how they can be decisive in the short-term or secondary approach.

Contrary to what happened in the crisis of the oligarchical system, any change is now indissolubly tied to external variables because domestic readjustments can to some extent affect Cold War affiliations. In view of this and with the specter of Cuba in mind, the hegemonic power looks with distrust or hostility upon any change in the existing establishments. This attitude has grown stronger as the Vietnam war has become a large-scale commitment of the United States.

SOME REMARKS ON THE PRESENT OLIGARCHICAL PATTERNS

Having touched upon these contrasts, it might be useful to digress here to glance at the present crisis of the oligarchical establishments in the region. Their crisis differs appreciably from that faced earlier by the more developed countries and instead bears some similarity to the picture we have already presented in connection with the decline of the mesocratic coalition.[10]

In the first place, in the crisis of the oligarchical establishment in the less advanced nations, such as Nicaragua, Honduras, or the Dominican Republic, there are no social forces available to replace the present system, *precisely because of the meagerness and abnormality of its previous development and the little change it has made in the pyramidical class structure.* Because of that vacuum, the fall of the top of the pyramid almost inevitably brings about either a revolutionary or a reactionary shift, in which case the military is generally more in favor of preserving the status quo than of changing it. Finally, because of the international implications and the strong bonds of the military with the United States, the facts and the pretexts of the Cold War have a major effect on the situation.

In summary, then, the crisis of both establishments has at the present time many aspects in common. One aspect, perhaps the dominant one, is the internationalization or, if you will, the inter-Americanization of the process of domestic change.

THE SOCIOPOLITICAL "STRINGERS"* OF THE UNITED STATES

The problem we have already discussed, that is, that of substitute social forces to replace the establishments under

---

* Translator's note: The word "stringer" is used here in the sense employed in the news media, meaning a part-time representative in certain areas.

attack, can and ought to be looked at from another angle which is very important to the hegemonic power and which has to do with what we might call the sociopolitical "stringers" in Latin America.

It seems clear that the United States has an enormous economic and geopolitical gravitation with respect to Latin America. Nevertheless, taking as a point of comparison what we stated earlier* about such bonds in the socialist world, we can easily find some appreciable differences.

On the one hand, in a political sense the United States has in Latin America relatively precarious bases and agents, or social "stringers," usually restricted to the top of the social pyramid, to the so-called "consular" bourgeoisie and to the officer corps of the armed forces.

The value of such assets should not be underestimated; however, it seems clear that where the minimum rules for the formal democratic game have prevailed or been maintained, those elements have been overcome by populist or center coalitions, usually by combinations of middle class groups (including part of the managers and entrepreneurs) and the working class.

We might wonder why part, or even the majority, of those middle class groups does not under the new conditions join the conservative front, thus to establish a platform sufficiently broad and solid to bring together a group that could both support the domestic establishments and present itself as the "natural stringer" for the United States.

The first objection to this possibility is that, despite the size and strength of such a coalition, it would still not be sufficient to support the establishment where the masses have already been incorporated into the political process. Anyway, quantitatively we are dealing with a minority coalition. An example of this is to be found in what happened in Chile in 1964 to the so-called Democratic Front made up of radicals, liberals, and conservatives. Despite its apparent and real strength, it could not even present itself as a viable alternative in the elections of that

---

* Pages 22–23 above.

year. The later example of Brazil is also thought-provoking. Although the military had (especially on the occasion of the April
coup) valuable civilian endorsement, the latter gradually melted
away, and in the first electoral confrontation, despite all the
restrictions on freedom of expression by the opposition, the
weakness of the support for the government became so evident
that the latter then chose to "close" the system more rigorously.

Other elements should be pointed out which up to now have
made difficult or prevented a more massive endorsement of the
United States by the middle sectors and by the "integrated."

One must not think that these elements are distinguished by
the prevalence among them of an anti-imperialistic consciousness or sentiment. In reality, they are generally the social sectors
that are most receptive and most committed to that caricature
of the affluent society which is popularized in Latin America.
This to some extent binds them together and lends prestige to
the image of the United States and its way of life. Let us add
that all the surveys we have seen on this subject have confirmed
this view.

It seems to us that more important than this aspect is the fact
that such middle-class and "well-placed" groups have little or
nothing to do with, and in practice are opposed to, the ideology
and methods of the free enterprise system which the United
States displays as a flag or goal in Latin America (and elsewhere).[11] Furthermore, the relative and the absolute advantages
in the socioeconomic structure which these strata have attained
vis-à-vis the traditional oligarchy and the peripheral masses
have resulted from policies and changes that contradict or are
completely foreign to the basic tenets of the American creed.

In this way, as it has already been shown in several events,
every time a political development is translated into the application of orthodox prescriptions pleasing to the official and financial circles of the "great neighbor," they bring about economic
upheavals which have not spared the interests of the privileged
groups, although they may have affected the lower income and
more disorganized sectors more severely.

These and other similar significant realities apparently have been understood by a limited number of politico-intellectual groups in the United States; the original philosophy and terms of the Alliance for Progress were an example of this. Essentially, as politico-economic strategy, the initiators of that program envisaged the broadening of the base for social support for their country within the region through action that would promote the interests of the middle and popular groups.

The diagnosis may have been correct, but very little time was required to show the difficulties in carrying it out. It is not our purpose to analyze the ups and downs and the progressive anemia of the Punta del Este project. We only want to point out those elements which are significant for our analysis.

On the one hand, it became apparent that, except for a few countries (perhaps Mexico, Venezuela, and Chile), it was almost impossible to count on civilian "social stringers" who were more or less representative of a nonoligarchical coalition. Futhermore, both the traditional forces and some middle class organizations were not willing to carry on a serious campaign of reforms that might endanger their interests and upset the political balance. Third, the pressure for change in many places means the abandonment of safe backing for the foreign policy of the United States and the creation of uncertainty as to what would take its place. Fourth, influential American private investors in Latin America did not want to have anything to do with the new policy and preferred to maintain their alliance with the conservative groups. And, finally, the new administration in Washington, having survived the Cuban trauma and other international responsibilities, also tended to avoid risks.

To sum up, for one reason or another the sociopolitical "stringers" of the United States continue to be in the minority, and while this fosters the uncertainty and fear of change in the balance of power, it also exerts pressure toward a narrower but safer democratic system, at least in terms of short-run risks. And it matters very little that this greater security may turn out to be a mere illusion or mirage in the long run.

THE WEIGHT OF BUSINESS

Interference on the political level by private North American business groups undoubtedly constitutes another major problem in this connection, and *one in which the contrast with the Soviet Union and the relations within her sphere stands out with exceptional clearness.*

As we pointed out on another occasion,[12] this aspect has a very special significance for Latin America, because in none of the regions of the world to which North American political influence extends do its private companies have comparable weight. While the latter are not a principal or decisive factor in areas where their investment is not considerable (for example, in Asia) or where general political considerations are paramount (for example, in Western Europe), in Latin America they have enormous weight, often surpassing that of the political evaluation of the interests of the United States as a whole or as a nation. Naturally, in these matters much depends upon the particular circumstances. If at a given moment the United States faces a crisis (as it did during World War II or the first phase of the Cuban revolution), the macropolitical considerations acquire greater relative force. Inversely, in more normal circumstances *the private microvision* tends to predominate. Also, of course, much depends on the amount and the nature of the investments in each country. We will deal with this aspect later on.

The relevance of this to the general problem we are considering is obvious. Many of the movements in Latin America (including Cuba during its initial stages) may or may not have had an anti-Yankee character in the macropolitical, or Cold War, sense, but certainly they did so insofar as they affected private interests. These movements have been, and will continue to be, represented, not as merely opposed to given investments, but rather as actions of enemies of the United States and of potential or actual deserters to the other side in the Cold War. Obviously, those forces which seek nationalization or control of a given foreign asset, not on the merits of the specific case, but rather as part of a general anti-American strategy, will make excellent allies in furthering this impression.

Real or assumed implications for the Cold War are used as a shield for their affairs not only by private foreign interests but also by national consortiums that feel threatened by reform or development policies. In this way another link is established between the two groups, and this is exaggerated by both domestic and foreign propaganda media.

Here lies one of the great differences in the situation and in the relations of the other superpower. In contrast, the Soviet Union can guide its foreign policies exclusively by the light of its national advantage and its ideological orientation. This certainly allows it a degree of coherence and stability in its lines of action not available to the Department of State, since the latter is always under pressure from private interests and is always striving to reconcile the microperspective of those interests with the general vision of a superpower.

PART TWO

IMPLICATIONS AND LINES OF ACTION

One important fact stands out clearly from the above, that is, that, for a variety of reasons, at this historical juncture the internal transformations that are incubated and tend to erupt in most of our countries are indissolubly connected to the external situation because of their actual, hypothetical, or fictitious effects on the Cold War and, more specifically, on the hegemonic superpowers.

It hardly seems necessary to emphasize that this adds new obstacles and complications to a process or task in itself difficult. In fact, even when considered in a strictly domestic context, the problems of transition from one to another pattern corresponding to and establishing a different sociopolitical reality and other perspectives and ways of development are very great. As we have seen, in spite of the crisis of the present establishments, it would be a grave mistake to underestimate the power of those interested in perpetuating them, especially when it is clear that the forces that struggle for substantial change are not very solid or very well organized. If to the internal obstacles we add the restrictions and even threats that originate outside the country, the conclusion seems clear that the challenge that radicals or revolutionaries face is of enormous magnitude.

Nevertheless, one cannot, or rather one should not, be pessimistic in this connection. On the one hand we have the movements and changes taking place *urbi et orbi* which, while subject to the fluctuations of the general situation in the mid-sixties, do seem to move toward a more democratic and socialized society in the broad sense of these words.[13] There is nothing inevitable about this, nor should one be too optimistic about the time element (Franco and Salazar are there to remind us of this). Nevertheless, to underestimate the general trend of the historical process would be equally, or perhaps even more, mistaken and at the same time dangerous. It might be well to recall in this connection what happened in the Dominican Republic, that is, not the intervention itself, but rather its failure to impose the "world of yesterday."

Next we should consider that the future opportunities that may develop or be created to supersede the present Latin American situation will depend to a great extent upon the conscious and resolute action of those who attempt the task. First of all, an accurate appraisal of our situation and a thorough discussion of possible alternatives is needed. Finally—and perhaps most important—one must keep in mind the fact that millions of persons in Latin America, especially among the young, do not seem disposed to live with the status quo and that they must be guided and helped in their search for the new community that they long for. A mere heroic attitude or a belief that after the deluge or the catastrophe comes the dawn is a very unsatisfactory foundation, for numerous reasons which cannot be discussed now, but which lead to the conclusion that the processes and the perspectives must be analyzed.

THE DISASSOCIATION OF THE POLITICAL GROUPS

Keeping in mind the above essential implication, let us look at some lines of action or objectives that would permit facing it.

The first is for the most part self-evident: as in other areas or countries it would seem advisable to disassociate the process of domestic change from affiliation with the Cold War. Faced with the de facto internationalism of the phenomenon, we must seek what we might call its "internalism."

It is obvious that such a statement only has significance in a relative sense. Apart from the different conditions prevailing in Latin America as compared to other places (for example, Egypt or Algeria) where transformations of a revolutionary nature did not require a change of alignment in the superpower struggle, we have the undeniable fact that in any case *some* connection does exist between domestic orientation and foreign policies. The problem lies in tracing these ties, which will be different for each country and will be modified as domestic and foreign situations vary.

In order to continue the analysis, let us suppose that in a given country domestic conditions favorable to substantial changes that will undeniably affect its foreign policies develop. *The question is whether this change necessarily involves or leads to breaking with the hegemonic superpower of the moment and turning to the other.*

To examine existing alternatives we must lower the level of abstraction and introduce some more specific elements. Although some important aspects of this matter were dealt with in another work,[14] repetition cannot be avoided if we are to complete the outline.

We must first single out those of an economic nature.

In certain countries—not necessarily in all—pursuing a policy of substantial change requires decisions that might affect certain foreign interests which for the sake of simplicity we will identify with those of the United States. As we have already seen, under these circumstances those that are affected will tend to identify their particular problem with that of the United States as a national entity. Whether they are successful or not will depend on various factors which may work separately or in unison.

It depends, in the first place, on the importance of those interests in the United States and their ability to bring pressure to bear. Secondly, on the importance of the investments to the United States for present or future supplies. We need not stress that the expropriation of a beverage plant or a textile factory will not have the same repercussions as an attempt to nationalize the oil fields of Venezuela or the copper mines of Chile. Finally, on the methods used to transfer foreign assets to national control, that is, whether by confiscation, some form of expropriation, or by simple purchase.

Let us look now at some political variables.

Here we might classify the possibilities into two large groups. In one, which could be called nationalist-developmental, action for or against foreign enclaves would be governed basically by an evaluation of their importance for the tasks involved in the economic and social development of the country. In the second, measures to be taken would principally be determined by ideological considerations, that is, by the logic of anti-imperialistic action and by the final objective of harassing or injuring the hegemonic power.

Obviously, it is almost impossible to find these two types or alternatives in pure form; nevertheless, the greater or lesser degree of one or the other motivation has a decisive bearing on our analysis.

Since it would be very difficult to analyze hypothetical situations for the region in a general outline, it might be well to take the case of some specific nation in order to evaluate and identify the elements already mentioned.

Proceeding from north to south, let us take Mexico as our first example. Without for a moment forgetting the background of its Revolution, we will look at its experiences in the last decades.

The contrasts of the Mexican case are fascinating. On the one hand, for many on the official left the country of Cárdenas and of Díaz Ordaz represents the archetype of "surrender to imperialism" and "loyalty to the United States." Nevertheless, in the sphere of domestic economy Mexico has during this period gradually transferred to national ownership the key sectors that were under foreign control and placed basic industries and activities under state control or under that of mixed domestic enterprises. At the same time, although it has permitted and at times even stimulated foreign investment in important areas of the secondary sector (for example, durable consumer goods) and in commerce, it has not relaxed the pressure for the coparticipation of national private interests and has maintained general control over the process.

In the area of foreign relations Mexico seems to have established a status vis-à-vis the United States which is reminiscent of Finland's with Russia. Mexico has not adhered to or initiated any action that could be considered an open defiance of the United States but yet has persevered in maintaining a certain significant degree of independence. It did not agree to the inter-American military plan; it did not break relations with Cuba (in spite of the fact that its policy toward Havana is cold and even hostile); it has criticized all violations of the principle of nonintervention; and so on.

It is true that in the very original course followed by Mexico no disassociation of the domestic and the foreign sectors is to be found, but rather something more complex, which is rather a special congruence between the two areas combining a certain degree of moderate reformism and a certain restrained independence.

Of course, this unique arrangement could not be understood without keeping in mind two key points: on the one hand, that it has been a long time since Mexico achieved some of the structural changes proposed in other countries; and on the other, that at this stage there does not seem to be any conflict between the pursuit of its economic and social development and its foreign interests. In our judgment these are the objective foundations of its special situation which cannot be generalized but which nonetheless have significance for an analysis of the region or of various countries.

Although it is an old episode and had an unfortunate ending, we might do well to pause to recall the well-known experience of Guatemala. In our opinion that situation presented a clear example of a deliberate ideological association between the two sectors just considered. Up to the time of Arbenz, largely because there were no large North American interests involved (it must be remembered that the principal lands affected by the agrarian reform were German property), it was possible to keep the domestic process detached from foreign factors. Subsequently, however, the official left, by a suicidal and even puerile deviation, forced the process into a foreign context by implicating the government almost officially in campaigns as preposterous as that of the Peking bacteriological war charges. It is just as well not to go into the regrettable results.

It might be thought essential to examine how these questions were handled in the case of Cuba. However, this could only be done in a special study; besides, we must confess that our ideas are not sufficiently clear in this respect. In general we are inclined to think that the internationalization of the Fidelista revolution was, on the whole and in its inception, a consequence of pressure from the private interests affected and from Washington's solidarity with them,[15] but at the same time it seems certain that subsequently there was a certain domestic intention to emphasize that aspect; for example, in the quixotic definition of the process as Marxist-Leninist. Finally, although Cuba is the most dramatic example of the problem that concerns us, the truth is that such is the emotional involvement in this case that it would be easier to select other cases for the somewhat abstract analysis we are making.

Let us now take as points of reference the two largest countries of South America, Brazil and Argentina. How does the possibility of eventual disassociation between a policy of essential changes and the conventional Cold War pattern appear in those countries?

The first thing to keep in mind is that in neither of the two has there been a serious or organized attempt at structural transformations. Whoever has known at first hand the critical period of the Goulart administration would agree with this point of view. So we can only put together a few hypotheses. However, both countries in recent times have lived through an attempt at an independent foreign policy which is relevant to our topic and which is worth analyzing.

Let us first examine the general subject in the light of the categories or factors we have presented before.

Without taking into account the "specific gravity" and the significance of these two nations within the regional community, one salient fact is apparent: that North American investments in these countries are neither great nor have strategic significance, either from the point of view of the domestic economy nor from that of their importance for supplying the present or future needs of the United States. To this is added the fact that these are two relatively diversified economies, with a high degree of self-sufficiency in basic goods and with a capital goods sector which constitutes a valuable support for a relatively autonomous development. We may add that all these factors are usually disregarded in many conventional analyses of these countries, so that often the impression is left of dealing with a very underdeveloped and dependent community.

From these basic facts we may arrive at a working hypothesis (it is no more than that) to the effect that these countries might be able to undertake very radical social and economic policies without necessarily having to confront foreign private interests. Also, it would be reasonable to think that owing to these circumstances they might be able to adopt a more independent orientation in their foreign policies without this necessarily implying or requiring a break in relations with the United States or an affiliation with the other rival bloc.

Actually, as we have indicated, about 1960 both nations under the direction of Jânio Quadros and Arturo Frondizi—with some cooperation between them—attempted a break toward an independent policy. As everyone knows, the experiment ended in failure. This has been attributed basically to foreign pressure, namely, that of the United States and its domestic "stringers," especially the military.

However, in our opinion the phenomenon is not so simple as

it has been pretended. What has been overlooked is that the frustration of those efforts was due just as much, or even more, to the fact that they did not have appropriate minimum domestic support as to foreign interference. In the Brazilian case, for example, the progressive coalition was never able to reach an understanding with Quadros—not even for the purpose of supporting his foreign policy. Partial proof of this is to be found in the fact that it accepted with indifference, and even with joy, the resignation and fall of that eccentric statesman from São Paulo. As to Argentina, the Frondizi movement was also unable for many reasons, which it would take too long to enumerate, to consolidate an agreement with Peronism that would have given it a domestic base when it was feeling its way toward an independent policy.

In summary, then, it seems to us that such experiences are far from confirming the supposition that it had been, was, or would be, practically impossible to escape from the conventional pattern of the Cold War because of restrictions established by the hegemonic superpower. And this hypothesis—because of the basic situation of the above countries—might even be extended to cover a parallel process of basic reform should such arise. In the final analysis the decisive variable would seem to be the domestic sociopolitical circumstances, to which we will have occasion to refer later.

Although they have different structures and degrees of general development, Chile and Venezuela have many points in common within the context that concerns us. In both, the strategic nexus of the foreign sector is owned by foreign interests, and in addition the production of materials is of critical significance in itself and for supplying the region of the Western superpower, especially in case of external emergencies. Therefore, in these two cases the private and public interests of the United States are considerably fused, with the result that any policy designed to restrain or to force those foreign interests out would have direct and serious foreign repercussions. Under such circumstances one can take for granted that the powerful private interests affected will move heaven and earth to prove that any developing situation would not be purely domestic, but that actually or potentially it would alter the equilibrium abroad, an argument to which Washington would be receptive. Once such a situation would develop, one can indeed assume that the mere weight of events or some degree of ideological deliberation would lead the country in crisis to seek some support for its policy by a change of its Cold War alignment, although this may not have been its original intention.

Before speculating on the possible social cost of such a development, on the viability of the enterprise, on the possibilities of an intervention "*a la Santo Domingo*" or of Soviet support "*a la Cuba*" and on other similar basic themes, it would be useful to look at the matter from other angles that present more pertinent aspects for our study.

For example, it is essential to make clear whether in these or other countries in a similar position the nationalization of the strategic holdings is a *sine qua non* requisite for starting or carrying through a policy of structural changes. In this respect—and without being guilty of eclectic acrobatics or of priding ourselves on satisfying or appeasing the opposing sides—it seems to us that what matters is to ascertain the future outlook. On one hand, it could well be argued that many substantial advances and much progress could be made in those countries even while foreign ownership of the key export sectors is retained. In any case the export sectors are subject to a variety of controls of major or minor importance. On the other hand, however, it seems equally evident, or perhaps more so, that in the long run (which may mean a few years or many, according to circumstances) such holdings constitute an anachronism and a basic restriction upon national development, that is, development governed by the exclusive consideration of the country's own interests. Obviously we are not dealing here with ordinary foreign investments. On the contrary, these are in a way the heart, or as it has been said, "the keystone" of these economies. And it is absurd that in the main they are managed from abroad in accordance with considerations that may be perfectly legitimate, but do not always necessarily coincide with national evaluations and needs. Paraphrasing Lincoln, we could say that we cannot have a nation half independent and half controlled from abroad by foreigners.

After having presented these two aspects of the problem, we feel it would be well to examine the tactical aspects of a general strategy having as its objective the full integration of these basic holdings into the economies and the realm of national decisions.

At the risk of repeating what has already been mentioned, we must insist that the success of the objective will to a great extent depend upon disassociating any action with reference to foreign private consortiums as completely as possible from the political relations between the country and the hegemonic power, and also making it clear that the new status in no way will affect the present or future flow of exports to the American market—at least as a result of considerations of a foreign political nature. Logically, the procedures for expropriation should be added to this. In this connection, it seems quite improbable that countries like Chile or Venezuela can follow the Mexican example of plain, smooth, commercial acquisition. In other words, although they might not be able or might not want to resort to confiscation, they would have to find workable formulas for compensating the investors.

It is obvious that these and other directives might not suffice to achieve the basic condition of separation of private and foreign policy levels. But at least they would create an opportunity for such separation, or, stated another way, if action is not taken along these lines, the internationalization of the quarrel would be little short of inevitable, with all that implies and which it would be foolish to underestimate. In either case, one should keep in mind that there is another basic requirement for any line of conduct in this regard: it is the absolute necessity of being able to count on a broad and solid domestic front. Such a condition is taken for granted in the "heroic" or "catastrophic" approach, but it is far from assured, since it depends on the existence of certain sociopolitical conditions which we will have occasion to discuss later.

Needless to say, the above remarks do not warrant any general or specific deductions as to the problem of disassociating the political levels, nor do they pretend to do so. They are merely intended to point out some factors and to foster discussion of some cases so as to reach a more objective and fruitful approach to the problem.

ALTERNATIVE POLITICAL FRAMEWORKS

The second point to be examined is implicit in the first part of this work. As we have seen, the crisis of the mesocratic coalition has left a void that must be filled if we wish to achieve a decisive and controlled change toward a more just and dynamic general pattern.

The main lines of the new establishment can be discerned with relative clarity despite the important differences inherent in the various national versions. *Basically, what we are trying to do is to establish some form of association between the marginal masses and the other groups essential to a forward-looking political coalition, that is, the integrated wage earners and the middle sectors.* We need not point out that we seek, not a conglomeration of the total of each of these groups (which in any case do not have clear lines of demarcation), but rather a joining of the major parts of those groups which together will constitute a decisive majority sociopolitical base.

Although it will take us away from our central theme, it would be well to stop here and fix more precisely the content and scope of what is set forth in the preceding paragraph.

It should at once be made clear that such a social scheme differs substantially from the Bolshevik or Leninist vision of the revolutionary vanguard or minority that assumes power, imposes the dictatorship of the proletariat, and in some distant future becomes "democratized." Regardless of any inclination or preference, the truth of the matter is that we think that this "traditional" road has little or no future in the type of country we are analyzing, although who knows whether it might have a chance in those economically more backward countries having little social diversification and closed or oppressive systems. Naturally, the opinion expressed refers to a given present situation, that is, to actual or assumed circumstances, which might change in many ways in the future.

Next, it should be made clear that the situation outlined differs substantially from the old formula transplanted to Latin America, which envisaged the need and possibility of an alliance between the progressive bourgeoisie and the wage earners. Without denying the validity of that method for very specific situations (for instance, if the basic problem at a given time is the reestablishment of a minimum degree of formal democracy, and not even a minimum in some cases), it seems clear that it does not correspond to the essential reality derived from the crisis of the mesocratic establishment. Under the new conditions a different platform is needed, the outlines or components of which have been discussed before.

On the other hand—complementing what has already been said—it would be well to point out that the new sociopolitical mechanism does not presuppose a deliberate radical antagonism against private ownership, because, as we have said, it would be foolhardy to forecast the collapse of the capitalist system per se or, the opposite, the viability of a total socialist reorganization of the community. Many different points of view on this subject can be justified, especially when we examine specific situations in various countries; however, from a general point of view and upon evaluation of all the domestic and foreign factors, it seems certain that the radical hypothesis is closer to wishful thinking than to the objective reality of this immediate phase.

For these reasons we cannot discard the possibility or necessity of united action or commitments with segments of the world of private enterprise, although they may differ substantially from the plan we have analyzed. This is so both because we do not work with that somewhat mythical social category, the progressive bourgeoisie, and because the new alliance does not include it, but rather relies on other social groups.

We are not going to repeat or elaborate on what has already been said about the difficulties of cementing the ties between the vital parts of the marginal mass, the integrated wage earners, and the middle classes.[16] It would hardly be worthwhile to emphasize the drawbacks and the lack of realism inherent in generalized judgments when dealing with such heterogeneous social structures as those that characterize Latin American countries and which reflect their disjointed development. Seemingly clear-cut and commonly employed categories such as "working class," "middle class," and, of course, "the marginal masses" often obscure differences of substance in such a way that it is necessary to break them down not only as a means of analysis but mainly to describe the political movements.

Continuing the examination in the same way as in the previous section, we will relate the general topic to corresponding situations in some of the relatively developed countries of the area.

Let us again begin with Mexico.

As we suggested more than once in the course of the first part of this paper, Mexico is a very special case. Paraphrasing Orwell, we could say that while it is true that "all cases are different, some are more different than others." This is true of Mexico.

If we think in terms of the crisis of the mesocratic establishment, which is more or less common or acute in the countries of greater relative development, we are immediately beset by doubts as to whether the Mexican plan can be equated to their sociopolitical model. This is so for a very clear reason: we are certainly dealing with the only country where the dominant political apparatus in some way and to some degree includes a substantial fraction of the marginal mass, that is, of the rural contingent. We can argue all we want about the actual significance of such participation, but the fact remains that the *Partido Revolucionario Institucional* (PRI) has not disintegrated, or, if you prefer, that the internal tensions or contradictions among its integrants have not come to the point where some main branch has had to break off from the trunk.

It seems evident that distintegration will have to occur in time as a consequence of development itself and the resulting diversification of the social structure. It would be useless to speculate about possible alternatives. Instead, one should not underestimate the actual or potential reserves of the existing system. In outline form we might bring out the following: (1) Mexico still has ample opportunity to duplicate two old phenomena which have almost disappeared from the countries in the southern tier: the increase of public spending and a redistribution of wealth by this and other means in favor of the middle sectors and organized wage earners; (2) foreign demand, including tourism, constitutes a support that to a certain extent compensates for the limitations of the domestic market due in part to the very unequal distribution of income; (3) the agricultural sector, both because of its dynamism and because of the landholding system established by the agrarian reform, still accounts for a very high percentage of the population (62.5 percent according to the 1960 census); this has consequently had the effect, among others, of preventing the aggravation of the problem of marginal urban masses to the degree it has elsewhere; (4) aside from the evident agility and political finesse of the regime, in few countries is there a more incompetent and alienated left than in Mexico. At this late date and under present conditions it still continues to work on the theme of "national liberation"!

Let us next look at Brazil. There is little doubt that the crisis that led to the April, 1964, coup is one of the clearest cases of erosion and collapse of a mesocratic establishment. What some Brazilian sociologists called the national front constituted in reality an association mainly of middle classes, industrial management groups, and employed workers. Their political organ was the alliance of the Social Democratic party and the Brazilian Workers' party, supported and sustained ideologically from the rear by the Communist party. It would take too long and lead us too far afield to go over the factors that led to the breakup of that coalition. However, it does interest us to show that, as elsewhere, the mesocratic establishment neither paid attention to nor succeeded in establishing ties with the marginal urban and rural masses, despite the warning represented by Jânio Quadros and the strength of other populist redoubts like that of Ademar Barros. In the end, increasing inflation and political disintegration drove that mass away from the regime and disrupted even its mesocratic base, thus permitting the entrance of the military.

Although it would be idle to shuffle hypotheses about what might happen in Brazil in the near future, it seems clear that an essential condition is the reconstitution or establishment of some political instrument (or group of instruments) capable of reuniting or bringing together alternate social forces, both from the power regime and from what is as, or even more, important, the outworn national front.

The task is not at all easy in the Brazilian case not only because of the existence of a military dictatorship but because of other factors as well. The continental extent of that country, the structural diversity of its economy and its society, the absence of traditional parties that are more or less homogeneous as to ideology and class composition—all present an equal number of difficulties for the organization of the nuclei or movements that could bring together part of the middle classes, the organized wage earners, and key sectors of the marginal masses. In order to attain this objective it would probably be better to approach the problem regionally rather than nationally, to leave national integration until later.

In our opinion the Argentine situation constitutes a very special case for two main reasons. First, the crisis of the mesocratic pattern dates from some time ago, perhaps from the more distinctly populist Perón government. Second, while we are dealing with a country which is considerably integrated, a substantial fraction of those relatively or absolutely marginal found a political refuge in Peronism. In a way this is a novel movement in Latin America, since it incorporates the bulk of the organized workers and the more or less peripheral urban-rural mass.

At first glance these seem to be the basic conditions most favorable for resolving the problems under discussion. However, other serious difficulties appear in the way. One of them seems to be that the sum of the "Peronist trauma" and the economic stagnation of the last decade (interrupted in more recent years) opened up a wide breach between the Peronist world and the large majority of the middle and managerial classes who also have the military behind them. Another hurdle, perhaps, is to be found in what might be called the primitivism of the Peronist movement that is still inspired by its old leader and its even more anachronistic distributive populism. Paradoxically, while elsewhere ideological baggage represents a major impediment for certain forces of the left, in Peronism one has the impression that it errs precisely because of its ideological vacuum, that is, the lack of an up-to-date, practical, modern vision of the realities of the country.

The overwhelming victory of the Christian Democrats has transformed Chile into a passionate arena for discussion of the issues at hand. The mesocratic establishment suffered its first "earthquake" in 1952, with the overwhelming victory of Ibáñez over the traditional parties of the right, center, and left. It later gave the impression of returning to conventional ways. However, what was happening was a most significant rise and regrouping of the marginal urban and rural masses made possible by the electoral reforms that practically doubled the electorate in a few years. In the elections of 1964, immediately after a process which cannot be reconstructed here, that mass, as it were, found an available political agent in the Christian Democratic party, and especially in its leader, President Frei.

One of the most significant facts is that the success of that union did not damage the position of the official left, but rather was achieved at the expense of the traditional sectors. In this way an exceptional political base emerged which served to coalesce the alternate forces that were to take over from the prevailing establishment, especially because of the coincidence of many positions and objectives of the two large reform blocs.

The Chilean political process is in full swing and at this writing (latter part of 1965) still undefined, so that it would be very risky to speculate about its eventual tendencies. Nevertheless, a fact is evident which has considerable importance for our analysis. In effect, the political dispute seems to have been more bitter among the forces favoring change than between the latter and the traditional agglomerate. The diverging opinions as to the United States and foreign investors stand out as one of the reasons for the conflict, but behind them lie other no less important factors. One of them is the crude problem of "power politics," that is, the logic of the power struggle, stimulated on the left by the conviction (probably unfounded) that the failure of the Christian Democratic attempt will necessarily mean a chance for the left.[17]

Be that as it may, one could say that, at least potentially, in Chile alternate nuclei exist for the typical mesocratic establishment. But whether this latent possibility is going to, or can, become a reality is a horse of another color. Needless to say, if they do not arrive at certain basic agreements among themselves, and if, on the contrary, both groups weaken each other in the struggle, giving way to some reaction, the responsibility would certainly be laid to some sinister "gorilla" or to some telephone call from the Pentagon, both undoubtedly real possibilities, but ones which generally become realities only when the civil-democratic system falters.

We cannot draw definite conclusions from this superficial examination of some national situations related to the problem. We have indeed made evident the complexity of the subject and various possible approaches to making a deeper concrete and operational analysis of it.

RELATIONS AMONG LATIN AMERICAN NATIONS

The third and final aspect to be considered is that of the relations between the Latin American countries and, by inference, the relations of the whole or a part with the United States.

Going straight to the point, the matter could be expressed as follows: transcending the old Cold War pattern in the hemisphere, affirming an independent position on the international level (derived from the first point, which does not mean antagonism or necessarily breaking off relations with the United States), and making the internal changes which present development and social problems demand would be more feasible if some degree of consensus existed among the Latin American nations or at least among a good many of them.

Conversely, each and every one of these objectives becomes more difficult because of the disunity of Latin American nations and because of the system of bilateral ties with the hegemonic power, although the latter are camouflaged by the Pan-American system.

We should emphasize that present conditions have deep historical and economic roots. The phase of outward development which occurred in Latin America connected each of these countries separately with the industrial centers of the world. Since domestic development took place within the monopolistic framework mentioned by the Economic Commission for Latin America (CEPAL), it did not change the situation. Of course, the change in the international scene made the United States the "sun" of the system, because it had become either the principal buying and selling market or the financial and political arbiter of the area.

In summary, at present the bonds that connect each Latin American republic with the United States are more powerful than the ones that associate any one of them with any of the sister republics that share the same traditions and cultures.

In the abstract, very few or none in Latin America dispute that from many angles it would be highly advantageous to correct this historical situation; the preoccupation with Latin American integration is the most visible proof of this. However, it seems equally certain that there has not been much progress. Many explanations are possible, but of course it is still strange —and it is also a good index to the mental confusion of progressive elements in this area—that while some maintain that the United States is to blame for the slow pace, others (and sometimes the same ones on different occasions) allege that integration is merely a new imperialist trick.

For our part we would like to call attention to what is quite obvious and indeed almost a truism. More than to foreign factors or interference, the scant progress of Latin American integration can be attributed to the fact that there are no domestic interests or forces in each country that are convinced that steps toward integration are imperative.

At least from the economic point of view they are not far from right, especially in view of the difficulty of systematizing and carrying out long-range plans. In fact, who could or should be the natural economic agents charged with this task? In a private-enterprise society there is no doubt that such a role would fall to the businessmen. However, the latter, whether because they are not doing badly in their domestic "game preserve," or because they fear the risks of foreign adventures, or because they are not prepared for them, do not show great enthusiasm, except in very rare cases such as those of industries that have been established for export (for example, those of the paper and cellulose industry in Chile). Besides, in some countries like Brazil or Mexico those interests have available the much less complicated alternative of bringing the considerable peripheral mass into the market economy.[18]

Because of these difficulties, the problem must necessarily be handled at the political or state level, since it is at that level that an alternate force might be found; in fact, the little that has been done has been accomplished by this means.

But it is obvious that on this level another set of requisites and obstacles looms up. They cannot be analyzed properly here, but we would still like to call attention to a seldom-noticed aspect.

In attempting to classify the impulses or motivations that animate or guide the conduct of nations, we might separate them into two groups. Within the first would fall direct pressure from various interests and problems, all a reflection of social existence. Within the second (rooted in the first, but without direct causal relationship) would fall those motivations that have become materialized and incorporated in the social conscience.

For our purpose here it is the second type of motivation that interests us, since the first does not constitute, at least not yet, a principal factor. In other words, since there are no immediate interests or problems forcing Latin America toward integration, it could only be achieved by a degree of awareness that might induce or compel the necessary decisions.

It seems reasonable to suppose that such a level of awareness is very far from having been attained, although preoccupation with the problem of integration is undoubtedly greater than in the past, and it has been assimilated into current basic ideas.

One main and obvious reason why we have not attained this level of awareness is the survival of Latin American "parochialism," manifested in the most various ways, the most evident being the lack of knowledge, of contacts, and even of mutual interests among Latin American countries. Instead, it is clear that each of them is open or exposed to the powerful and multifaceted pressures from the major external centers of influence, and especially to those from the United States. It is obvious that both facts are related, and in a way both are interdependent. Because we have not been able to forge bonds among ourselves, we are left defenseless before the foreign tide and hence tend toward alienation. At the same time these phenomena are transformed into obstacles to integration in the wide sense we are discussing.

In our judgment this situation presents the Latin American intelligentsia with a tremendous responsibility, and, indeed, not only the intelligentsia but also all key nuclei of society: political parties, cultural and industrial associations, entrepreneurs, and so on. While the disunity among these living forces is almost complete, a cynic might point out that the only institution that seems to be "integrating" is the military one, although in this case by inter-Americanization under a sponsorship only too well known.

In concluding these comments we might well focus on a more limited aspect of the matter, that of the possibility (and of course the necessity) of mutual support among some or several Latin American countries for an independent foreign policy that would also entail an opportunity for more autonomous domestic development.

At this time we are not interested in stressing what has already been said in commenting on the Brazilian-Argentine experience during the period of the Quadros-Frondizi governments, that is, on the importance of a domestic front and support. Here we would like to emphasize that there is no doubt that any progress in the direction indicated will have to come from the initiative and backing of one or more of the large countries of the region, that is, Mexico, Brazil, or Argentina. It would otherwise appear quite unlikely.

Looking at things on this quite elementary level, we can easily see the various difficulties which loom up. Mexico's foreign policy has always avoided any tendency toward regional leadership; it has not even, as Brazil has, tried to play a role as intermediary between the "Colossus of the North" and the disunited countries of the south. It seems to feel sure that a stance of relative "splendid isolation" is best for it. As for Brazil and Argentina, after that fleeting "orbital encounter," not only have they drawn apart but they have also (at least temporarily) buried any yearnings for an independent policy. Moreover, the leadership of one or the other of these nations will have to overcome both the old nationalistic attitudes a la Perón and also the parochial distrust of the other countries, who at times think more about local squabbles or disagreements than about the prospects for an inter-Latin American or regional policy.

NOTES

1. "America Latina y la Conferencia de las Naciones Unidas sobre Comercio y Desarrollo," *Revista de la Facultad de Ciencias Económicas y de Administración* (Montevideo, Uruguay, Oct., 1964), pp. 1–344.

2. The by-products of the Vietnam war are not considered in this work because it is of necessity temporal or "topical."

3. A term which is here used in a metaphorical sense.

4. Powers, we might add, that have developed more vigorously without colonies than with them for the basic reason that the social transformations caused by war, as well as interchange among the industrialized nations, have had more stimulating effects than the old exploitation of their dependencies.

5. Celso Furtado, "Reflexiones sobre la pre-revolución brasileña," *El Trimestre Económico*, Vol. 29, No. 115 (July-Sept., 1962), pp. 373–84.

6. Anon., "The Growth and Decline of Import Substitution in Brazil," *Economic Bulletin for Latin America* (March, 1964), pp. 1–60.

7. "The more developed a country is, the greater tends to be the area

of agreement in regard to its principal objectives. The development already achieved forms a base for the standardization of the situation of people, since social projects and the prospects of each individual tend to draw closer together in proportion to the greater or lesser similarity of their respective patterns of participation in society. In contrast to this, the backwardness of underdeveloped countries considerably reduces what there is in common in the situation of people, their methods of participation in the community being highly differentiated." Helio Jaguaribe, *Desenvolvimento econômico e desenvolvimento político* (Rio de Janeiro: Editora Fondo de Cultura, 1962).

8. An interesting and important fact is the opposite tendency in another basic institution, the Church. While generally in the past it was associated with the oligarchical establishment, in the new circumstances it seems inclined to open the way to change. Naturally, there are substantial differences among the different countries (for example, between Chile and Argentina) and even within countries (like Brazil) and also in the attitude of ecclesiastical orders: in general, although not always (viz., Colombia), the Jesuits are the major advocates of change.

9. Karl Marx, Preface to *Capital, A Critique of Political Economy* (New York: The Modern Library, 1906).

10. This analysis does not pretend to include the status of intermediate nations like Venezuela, Colombia, or Peru. Each one of them is of a particular type that would have to be considered in any model-building attempt.

11. Celso Furtado, "United States Hegemony and the Future of Latin America," *World Today*, 22 (September, 1966), pp. 375–85.

12. Espartaco, "Crítica del modelo político-económico de la izquierda oficial," *El Trimestre Económico*, Vol. 31, No. 121 (Jan.-March, 1964), pp. 67–92.

13. Ibid.

14. Ibid.

15. In this connection we might consider the following penetrating observation by Herbert L. Matthews, "Dissent Over Cuba," *Encounter*, Vol. 23, No. 1 (July, 1964), pp. 82–90.

> In United States policy there is no objection in principle to the idea that revolutions are sometimes necessary and unavoidable.
>
> The trouble comes when an individual dissents against specific, strongly held popular opinions, or when a revolution means, for instance, seizing American property. A revolution in Bolivia, including nationalization of the tin mines [locally owned], aroused little emotion or interest in the United States in 1952. Few Americans knew that a revolution was taking place in Bolivia and they would not have cared if they did know.

The Cuban revolution hurt; it still hurts. Therefore, it is resented.

16. See above, Part One, "The Crisis in the Mesocratic Establishment."

17. The great politico-electoral changes in Chile have given unusually clear evidence of a sort of duality of power that seems typical in the phenomenon of the incorporation of the marginal masses, or, if you wish, of populism. On the one hand is the power arising from the presidential elections, which is repeated less effectively on the parlamentary level. On the other stands the present power system made up of the traditional parties from the right to the left: the business organizations, the associations of integrated workers and employees, the state bureaucracy itself, and so on. While the first level or stratum of power expresses itself intermittently, for example, through periodic elections, and does not have greater opportunities, precisely because it is disorganized, to make itself felt as a pressure group in daily political life, the second group does have all the conditions and means for doing so.

18. It is idle to note the differences in the European case, in which the majority of the large private interests supported integration, principally because they knew that they had much to gain in the process in the immediate future.

The OAS in the Inter-American Political System*

Estanislau Fischlowitz

I

Three years ago, on May 29, 1958, the Operation Pan America program was launched by President Juscelino Kubitschek. It is unlikely that anyone would question the *raison d'être* of this great program, essentially designed, as everyone knows, to raise the low socioeconomic level of the Latin American area of the Western Hemisphere speedily and fully by mobilizing the resources of the three Americas to that end. Yet from the beginning there were some who raised objections to Operation Pan America because they would have preferred us to concentrate our attention exclusively on what could be termed "operation Brazil" instead of on a program of wider scope.

Nevertheless, an enterprise covering such a great area seems justified to us, since it would still be possible to (1) guarantee, not just a nominal, but a real, implementation of the program on the broadest possible scale; (2) assure maximum utilization by Brazil of the advantages of inter-American regional development; and (3) secure full appreciation of our active contribution to continental progress through Brazil's effective exercise of the directing role she is undeniably entitled to play within the community of twenty sister republics.

* This article was originally published in Portuguese as "A OEA no Sistema Político Interamericano," in *Revista de Direito Público e Ciencia Política*, 4(2):62–80, May–Aug., 1961. Translated and printed by permission.

No one will deny the advantages Brazil can derive from the greater socioeconomic integration of the region to which it geographically belongs. In view of world conditions in 1961, which include great economic blocs such as the two West European trade associations and the Communist group, we cannot face the growing power of those organizations alone without forming a collective body of Western Hemisphere countries, closely associated through gradual elimination of customs barriers. Fortunately, as we will explain later, we are already following such a course. Obviously, what is achieved along these lines, while necessarily modest and limited, may still in the future offer new and much more promising opportunities for the industrialization of Brazil.

There seems to be no objective foundation for what we could call, with intentional overstatement, Brazilian extracontinentalism, a phenomenon apparent throughout her diplomatic history, with but few exceptions. This is true despite its indisputable contribution not only to some program proposals but also to isolated Pan-American achievements closely associated with the name of our great national statesman, Joaquim Nabuco.

The fuller and more rapid development of this region is becoming a particularly relevant and urgent task in view of the obvious deterioration of its whole economy within the last three years. As the result of various very unfavorable experiences in Latin America—among them the increasing population explosion taking place at a rate not matched elsewhere, the export crisis in traditional agricultural products, and the tremendous decline in the flow of private investment capital (especially in American capital) destined for Latin America—we have recently witnessed a considerable decline in the economic expansion of this region. The annual increase in gross national product fell[1] from 6 percent in 1955 to 4 percent in 1958, to less than 3 percent in 1959, and to an even lower percentage in 1960, not even equal to the increase in the birth rate (more than 2.5 percent per annum!).

Contrary to the views held by superficial observers, when we consider the region as a whole, it is the common denominator of the twenty republics that must predominate, and undue importance should not be attached to the corresponding variable numerators related to their individual typology.[2]

We believe that this fully justifies undertaking regional development collectively. Incidentally, parallels are to be found with similar projects carried out, with highly profitable results, by the democratic sector of Europe within the community created during the last postwar decade. We hasten to add that they have done so with a thoroughness and scope incomparably greater than those achieved by Pan-Americanism.

The weak and insignificant organizational universalism institutionalized in the United Nations (Chapter 8 of whose Charter expressly permits regional orientation) tends inevitably to give greater emphasis to entities of a regional type. This happens especially when, as in this case, there is an appreciable degree of interdependence among the countries making up the Western Hemisphere, also manifested by intraregional commercial and financial relations.

Three years after the formal promulgation of our dynamic program, it does not seem premature to inquire whether the optimistic expectations associated with the proclamation of Operation Pan America (OPA) have been justified.

Is there really anything that can reasonably be considered a practical fulfillment of OPA? Or has the program represented by those three letters remained an abstract slogan, divorced from reality, a mere symbolic device without appreciable influence on events in this turbulent area, which in 1961 is undergoing its gravest crisis, a crisis surely no less serious because it is one of growth and feverish transformation of its infrastructure?

The answer to this question depends upon an objective and impartial assessment of inter-American activities designed to aid us in translating into practical accomplishments the general ideas contained in the program of Operation Pan America.

The implementation of such an ambitious, complex, and far-reaching program requires maximum efficiency in the functioning of all existing organizations for Pan-American cooperation because without a properly planned and well-structured administrative base the achievement of the goals of President Juscelino Kubitschek's program cannot be conceived. We may add that this program has been approved by President Jãnio Quadros, and is logically complemented by the new social-action program of the Alliance for Progress launched in 1961 by President John Kennedy.[3]

II

Within this context, we must attempt a concise analysis, as brief as possible, of the history of the principal instruments of American regional organization. In doing this, we must especially stress reform because in the last three years it has been undertaken in order to adapt the organization to the new requirements of the two programs Operation Pan America and the Alliance for Progress, the first being economic and the second, social.

We want to make it very clear that in preparing the following evaluation we rely not merely on acquaintance with the proper documents and pertinent international juridical literature[4] but also, and to an even greater degree, on personal experience derived from working with the Pan American Union (PAU) (up to March, 1961) in the capacity of specialist in socioeconomic affairs. The impression made by the facade of that institution differs greatly from the conclusions to be drawn from an intimate "inside" knowledge of how programs are prepared which are later offered for adoption at inter-American meetings.

As everyone knows, the inter-American organization, after going through a long "prehistoric" phase of preliminary planning, both theoretical and intellectual (1815–1889), in 1889 entered into a period of more concrete accomplishments through the creation, on April 14, 1890, of the International Union of the American Republics. Therefore, chronologically it is undoubtedly the first regional organization of an institutional character.[5] During its seventy-one year history it has achieved some isolated victories but has also encountered numerous difficulties in its attempt to integrate a great continent, at present comprising twenty-one republics,[6] with 305 million inhabitants speaking

English, Portuguese, Spanish, and innumerable native dialects.

Nothing would justify too detailed an examination of the hundreds of conferences convened and the thousands of resolutions approved during that time, most of them without appreciable effect on the course of events in the three Americas. We will only point out that all that has happened and is happening in that sector is first of all the result of the natural political dichotomy of the Western Hemisphere. This is what causes the difference in orientation in the symbiotic relationship between the major American power, the United States, and the community of Spanish American nations of North (Mexico), Central, and South America and the Caribbean.

Therefore, once the last vestiges of European colonialism had been almost completely eradicated,[7] the threat of which inspired the earliest Pan-American efforts, and aside from ideological and doctrinal issues,[8] the degree of unity and cohesion of the Americas reflects, on the one hand, the changing course of United States inter-American policy. This vacillating policy has included successive stages of isolationism, "big stick" and "dollar" diplomacy, the Good Neighbor Policy proclaimed by F. D. Roosevelt on March 3, 1933, and, finally, the Alliance for Progress launched by John F. Kennedy on March 13, 1961. On the other hand, the degree of unity and cohesion of the Americas is a consequence of the reaction of the countries "south of the Rio Grande" to the various policy directives of the United States. Such degree of unity is affected especially by the choice, to be made by these nations, of either hemispheric regionalism in a broad sense (that is, including the United States) or mere strengthening of the ties that link the Latin American republics to each other, excluding our great neighbor to the north (Ibero-Americanism).[9]

In the history of inter-American institutional cooperation the following three consecutive periods stand out clearly:

1. that of progressive unification, the work of eight international conferences of the American states (1890–1948);

2. that of advanced regional integration, especially by the creation of the Organization of American States (OAS) at the

conference held in Bogotá on April 30, 1948, an organization maintaining a center of gravity obviously oriented toward the juridical, parajuridical, diplomatic, and political aspects of inter-American cooperation (1948–1958).

3. the last, that of "constructive neo-Pan-Americanism," initiated in 1958, designed (so far with not very encouraging results) to extend the orbit of the Pan-American symbiotic relationship to include the key problem, that of the substantial and immediate socioeconomic development of Latin America, so that she can take her place fully within the circle of materially advanced civilizations in the second half of the twentieth century.

The programmed development of this extensive and potentially rich region could, if successful, some day surpass regional achievements in other economically developing areas such as that of the famous Colombo Plan in Asia.

This most recent phase in the evolution of the OAS permits striving at the same time toward an almost unlimited increase in its field of action, which so far has almost excluded the economic and social aspects. In this about-face (more de facto than de jure since the broad constitutional provisions of the OAS do not exclude such an extension of its orbit) this organization is attempting to assume the functions of the UN, the United Nations Educational, Scientific, and Cultural Organization (UNESCO), the Food and Agricultural Organization (FAO), the International Labor Organization (ILO), and the World Health Organization (WHO) within the inter-American area, an ambitious multifunctional objective, hard to put into practice.

III

First of all, it still remains to be seen whether the inter-American organization encountered by Operation Pan America when it was founded in 1958 is really capable of forming the organizational base for such an enormous and difficult undertaking.

We should first point out that the Organization of American States, though representing what is most important, the administrative machinery for Pan-American collaboration, is not the only organization with specific attributes in this area. In fact, various other entities coexist with the OAS and have functions closely related to the implementation of our dynamic program. In some cases their practical achievements have been superior to those that can now be credited to the great Washington-based organization.

Now we must take up the thorny question of the divergence of the two plans, UN and a regional grouping such as OAS, for international organization, since we know that an inadequate solution to this divergence continues to be their true Achilles' heel. On the one hand, in a regional grouping there is a horizontal design based on territorial criteria, with special attention to regional peculiarities. On the other, there is a vertical structure aiming at *ratione materiae* discrimination in international administration, as a result of the diversification of some large sectors. This has found expression in the creation of the so-called "specialized organizations" of the United Nations: ILO, UNESCO, FAO, WHO, and so on.

Let us then see how this delicate question is being answered in relation to the international activities carried on within the boundaries of the Western Hemisphere.

In accordance with Article 63 of the United Nations Charter sanctioning the functioning bases of regional economic commissions subordinate to the Economic and Social Council (ECOSOC), the Economic Commission for Latin America (CEPAL, or, according to the initials derived from its name in English, ECLA) was created. Continuously directed by the eminent Argentine economist, Professor Raúl Prebisch, this organ, unlike the Economic and Social Department[10] of the Pan American Union (which is subject to supervision and control by a whole series of supervisory organizations), in practice enjoys a much greater degree of autonomy, contributing greatly to the healthy orientation of the economy of that region.

ECLA is in reality an organ of Latin American cooperation, not subject, up to a certain point, to the disturbing influence of participation by the United States. Consequently it more adequately reflects the genuine economic thought of Latin Americans. ECLA fathered the promising project dealing with the commercial unity of Latin America, actually started by the two free-trade associations.[11] Deserving of special mention is the work of numerous technical advisory missions sent by ECLA to various Latin American republics; the economic studies produced by that commission according to the highest scientific standards; and its interesting contribution to the formation of panels of the economic elites, without which it is hard to conceive of the possibility of perfecting the economic and financial administration and the other subsidiary activities of ECLA (some of them discreet, indirect, and semiofficial) designed to accomplish the great work of economic development.

Under these circumstances, Operation Pan America cannot achieve anything without closer association with the implementation of this ECLA program and without its being closely geared to the functions performed by ECLA in the parallel activities of the OAS—which, be it said in passing, always involve lower technical levels.

It is to be regretted that coordination between the OAS and ECLA should have been inexplicably delayed until the beginning of 1961.[12] Unfortunate also is the undeniably inadequate coordination with the Inter-American Development Bank, which recently was added to ECLA and OAS. It must be noted that results up to now have not been what we might logically expect from such biparty or triparty interplay.

This account would still be incomplete if we failed to make some slight reference to (1) the excellent record of the Pan-American Health Organization (the former Inter-American Sanitary Office, also a regional branch of the World Health Organization), led by Dr. Abraham Horwitz; (2) the intensive activities in the Latin American field of the International Labor Organization (seven conferences of the American member states of the ILO, the last held in Buenos Aires in April, 1961), directed from two centers located in Mexico City and Lima, respectively; (3) the similar activities and achievements incorporated in the concept of regional administrative decentralization of the FAO, UNESCO, and even of various other public and semipublic organizations of a universal territorial character.

Finally, we must point out the strict functional interdependence between Operation Pan America and the numerous important duties of the ICA, the International Cooperation Administration of the United States. ICA benefits the Latin American countries to an increasing degree and in the near future will assume new responsibilities in the Kennedy social program, thus to fill in the gaps left open in the activities of the OAS, the latter being relegated to second or third place in the planning of OPA.

Observers of inter-American cooperation cannot fail to note the inexplicable, self-defeating, and complete (despite some misleading and hardly representative appearances to the contrary) lack of coordination of international and inter-American activities closely connected with the objectives of Operation Pan America. This lack of coordination results in inevitable gaps and duplications.

The lack of unity in the direction and coordination of the activities carried on by all these organizations (unity being necessary for the mobilization of the maximum technoadministrative resources that this great program requires) affects the efficiency of all the efforts subordinated to this objective, especially because of the obviously limited availability of such resources in the OAS itself.

IV

After this digression, which we thought essential to properly delimiting the position of the OAS, let us go on to explain briefly the Pan-American organizational chart.

What becomes apparent at first glance is the extreme proliferation both of the collective representative organs of the OAS and of the administrative organs proper (most of them embodied in the structure of the Pan American Union) and, finally, of the diverse organs of opinion and consultation having specific duties. This tangle of organizations is even further complicated by the existence of various official institutes *sui generis*, the number of which constantly increases, like mushrooms springing up after the rain, and of numerous private and semiprivate inter-American groups which enjoy a special privileged status within the OAS.

What are the representative organs of the OAS as provided in its Charter?

The principal representative organs are four. Beyond this, Specialized Conferences may be organized (with participation by all or some of the member states) for the purpose of handling specific technical matters. Since 1890 there have been more than 270 conferences of this kind.

1. The Inter-American Conference is the highest representative organ of the organization. Generally it meets every five years in one of the twenty-one capitals, sets the guidelines for action by the OAS, and determines the structure and functions of its various administrative organs. Up to a certain point it may be compared to the United Nations General Assembly.[13]

The repeated postponement of the date of the Eleventh Conference, to be held in Quito, is a clear symptom of the grave political crisis that Latin America is undergoing at present.

2. The Meeting of Consultation of Ministers of Foreign Affairs is called, on request, for the purpose of studying urgent political problems of common interest to all the American states.

3. The Council is the permanent executive organ of the OAS. It is composed of a representative from each member state, and it meets regularly at the seat of the organization, which is the Pan American Union Building in Washington, D. C. The Council takes cognizance of matters referred to it by the Inter-American Conference or by the Meeting of Consultation, and in emergency cases acts as a temporary consulting body.

It is comprised of three auxiliary entities: the Inter-American Economic and Social Council, the Inter-American Council of Jurists, and the Inter-American Cultural Council.

Because of the very special interests represented, as viewed through the prism of Operation Pan America and the Inter-American Economic and Social Council, it should be noted that the functioning of that slow-moving body (composed in great part of representatives not very familiar with matters within its jurisdiction—an organ which meets in permanent and almost uninterrupted sessions and little geared to the Council of the OAS) did not succeed in discharging its tasks in a satisfactory manner, or in a manner that justifies the "reform" recently put into effect.

In compliance with the provisions of the Act of Bogotá,[14] approved by the third session of the Committee of Twenty-One, a Special Meeting of High Level Government Representatives for the Strengthening of the Inter-American ECOSOC was called and held in Washington from November 28 to December 9, 1960. This meeting, without accepting the much more radical suggestions formulated by the ad hoc Consulting Committee, limited the functioning of said organ to only two annual meetings of short duration and granted the Secretary General full powers to restructure the socioeconomic services of the Pan American Union; hence, it is unanimously felt that the special meeting did not fulfill the hopes that had been entertained when it was called.

4. Lastly, the permanent administrative Secretariat of the OAS should be mentioned; the Pan American Union (PAU) is directed by the Secretary General,[15] with broad responsibilities (although these do not include all the functions entrusted to the Secretary of the United Nations), who is elected for the surprisingly unduly long term of ten years.

The present structure of the Pan American Union, after partial revision by the Secretary General, includes, among various other technical and administrative units, the economic and social departments. The total showing to date of the Department of Economic and Social Affairs (divided in 1961 into two separate and divorced departments, a solution open to justifiable criticism) is still not very impressive.

Because of largely inadequate selection of the personnel for its services, without many fully qualified economists and highly regarded social scientists on its staff, and because of the not very convincing orientation of its programs of action, this department has not been able to carry out tasks of greater significance and importance.

For some unknown reason, absolute priority has been given in recent years to the preparation of "by country" studies, intended to produce the scientifically precise economic profile of each one of the countries of this region. It would not be possible to complete these studies, a sort of national census of very doubtful practical value, the level of which varies considerably from case to case, before 1964, by which time the first of them would already have become largely obsolete. It seems to us that in any case the possible value of these studies to the program of raising the low economic standards of the region is limited even at best. And except in this area nothing has been done by this department which could be considered to have contributed in any appreciable way, even indirectly, to the success of the OPA.

It would be a flagrant injustice to deny the contribution of the OAS to the creation of the Inter-American Development Bank, (IDB), under the direction of the eminent Chilean statesman, Sr. Felipe Herrera. Brazil is very brilliantly represented on the Bank by Sr. Cleantho de Paiva Leite, whose recently inaugurated credit activities can certainly contribute to the financing of the economic development of the Latin portion of this continent.

The first annual statement submitted by the President of the Bank to the Assembly of Governors[16] held in Rio de Janeiro in April, 1961, casts much light on the first accomplishments of the IDB, based on a capital of 850 million dollars (capital available: 400 million) destined for normal operations, besides the Special Operations Fund of 150 million dollars.

The auspicious beginning of the credit and technical assistance operations of the Bank and the new opportunities now available to it, in view of the fact that the loan techniques and related operations of the new social program are to be concentrated in its hands, justify the most optimistic expectations for its participation in the processes of regional development. However, this is obviously an autonomous institution whose future is independent of the success or failure of the OAS, to whose salutary initiative it owes its existence.

It is not our purpose to attempt a total evaluation of the PAU, particularly in the sectors which are only indirectly related to the OPA.

Still, it should be pointed out that the social aspects of economic development were almost totally neglected. The study project on the financing of agrarian reform achieved no success whatever.[17] So far it has not been possible to give any practical application to the interesting conclusions of the seminars called by the PAU, the first (Mexico, April 18–22, 1960)[18] covering production, and the second, (Bogotá, May 9–15, 1960)[19] labor-management relations. For instance, the Inter-American Production Institute suggested by the first of these two seminars has not been set up yet.

Aside from a few studies started for the modest purpose of collating the legislation which governs social security in Latin America (be it said, in passing, a self-defeating duplication of functions, since the same ground is covered by no less than four highly specialized international organizations!), the Division of Social Affairs, whose first chief was the eminent Brazilian specialist Dr. Luiz Carlos Mancini, accomplished nothing, or almost nothing, in the seven years of its existence! . . .

Contrary to Resolution Twenty-three, approved by the Seventh International American Conference (Montevideo, December 3–26, 1933), up to now it has not been possible to create the Inter-American Labor Institute. In notable contrast to the interesting activities developed in this field by ECLA,[20] the OAS remains way behind with regard to its programs for developing a qualified work force, the inadequacy of the latter being one of the principal obstacles in the way of regional economic progress.

The results of the labors of the Planning and Housing Center, located in Caracas, also continue to be very scanty, even though ten years have elapsed since its organization.

To attempt an objective evaluation of the accomplishments in the sectors of cultural exchange, educational programs, juridical activities, and so on would divert us too much from the subject matter of this work.

However, because of its closer connection with the problem of the economic progress of the Americas, we cannot fail to mention the greatly expanded programs for technical cooperation which absorb approximately half of the budget of the PAU and whose success is due to the administration of the department by an illustrious Brazilian administrator, Dr. João Gonçalbes de Souza.

The OAS is carrying on three programs of great importance for the continent: the Technical Cooperation Program, the Scholarship Program, and the Technical Assistance Program, a critical evaluation of which is also beyond the scope of this work.

The Pan American Union is represented in twenty capitals of the Latin American republics by national bureaus, the majority of which are still nothing more than mere intermediary bureaucratic organs for contact between the PAU and national government services. The understaffing of these bureaus led to the creation in 1960 of a second network of local representatives with functions related to the carrying out of the "country-by-country studies" program. Incidentally, this project too has shown no greater practical accomplishments.

In this brief review we shall try to deal fairly with the occasional highlights and the frequent shadows in the accomplishments of the PAU.

In view of the considerable financial resources of this organization (an annual budget of about 7 million dollars for the past few fiscal years) and the great increase in its personnel (almost five hundred employees), it is hard to find results at all commensurate with the operations.

Over and above the increase in the number of internal organizations we have already mentioned, there is a superstructure of specialized organizations carrying out specific functions of a *sui generis* technical character. These include the Inter-American Statistical Institute (led brilliantly by an excellent statistician and fellow countryman, Dr. Tulo Hostílio Montenegro), the Inter-American Institute of Agricultural Sciences (Turialba, Costa Rica), the Inter-American Women's Commission, the Inter-American Infants' Institute (Montevideo), the Pan-American Institute of Geography and the Inter-American Indigenous Institute (both located in Mexico City), and various others.

After this unavoidable digression, let us return to the examination of the functional aspects of Operation Pan America. We were faced with the apparent failure of the various organs of the OAS having economic and social responsibilities. Therefore, how could the inadequate operations of the OAS be revitalized and how could a concrete plan for intensifying collective efforts to accelerate the harmonious economic development of member nations be directed? It was deemed necessary to create two specific extraconstitutional organizations exclusively devoted to this objective, that is, the Committees of Nine and Twenty-One.

Chiefly composed of the cream of the economists of this continent, especially as regards the Brazilian members, these two emergency organizations became another addition to the already ample and diversified network of the permanent organization of the OAS, without a clear delineation of their respective responsibilities in relation to the duties corresponding to the constitutional organizations. This lack of a clear delineation greatly affected the outcome of their activities. Add to this that it would be unrealistic to view the OPA as an isolated operation of limited duration, capable of transforming the economy of this continent overnight at the touch of a magic wand in such a way as to make possible a substantial increase in the living standards of its inhabitants. On the contrary, it is a long-range development program which requires, not the creation of temporary ad hoc organizations charged with this task, but rather the adaptation of the permanent structure of the OAS for this purpose.

V

If it were still necessary to prove the almost wholly irrelevant role played by the OAS in the most critical phase of the vigorous, but unbalanced and disjointed, development of the Western Hemisphere, it would be enough to point out that it will remain almost wholly outside the framework of the organization entrusted with the execution of the new United States social program for Latin America mentioned above, which will adequately supplement OPA.

We are not overlooking the fact that on the occasion of the launching of this program there was no lack of criticism directed not only against the relatively modest amount destined to satisfy the practically infinite social needs of Latin America but also against its very purpose. Contrary to current opinion, it does not seem wise to us purposely to relegate to a secondary position the measures capable of directly attacking the grievous aspects of the social panorama of this region in the futile and unrealistic hope of an automatic solution resulting from the unilateral promotion of economic progress.

However, it does seem to us that despite its precarious initial resources the Alliance for Progress can serve as a powerful catalytic agent, especially through the diverse facilities—credits, subsidies, technical assistance services, and so on—concentrated in some specific programs. This is a great pilot program, whose success would lead to future use on a greater scale of the experience thus gathered. In the final analysis this program would constitute a challenge to the social conscience of the governments of the recipient countries, whose actions are not always inspired, as we might wish, by the principles of distributive social justice.

As we have already mentioned, the Inter-American Development Bank (IDB) will assume duties of major importance in carrying out this program, being in charge of granting "easy," flexible, and ultraliberal (394 million dollars) social loans, since the other collateral services (based on the amount of 100 million dollars) will be carried out by the United States International Cooperation Administration. The OAS will receive no more than 6 million dollars, without any more important responsibilities than those assigned to it within the mechanics of that program.

Obviously, it would not have been necessary to have recourse for this purpose to the joint participation of a governmental department of the United States if the Pan American Union organization were considered capable of taking on responsibility for the operation of the Alliance for Progress through various techniques, that is, aside from the credit activities which fall exclusively within the jurisdiction of the IDB.

It seems to us that it is absolutely clear from the above exposition that the dense cloud of smoke created by bombastic and high-sounding resolutions, issued at a constantly increasing pace by innumerable meetings, can hardly conceal the unhealthy emptiness of the OAS with regard to the socioeconomic core of the development programs. Obviously in this failure there must be many factors involved, not just one.

We cannot deny the disintegrating impact on inter-American cooperation of the sharp political conflicts that have occurred unexpectedly in recent years (especially in the case of Cuba— which, in its broader implications, goes beyond our continent— but also, in connection with problems related to the continuance of some dictatorial regimes, the boundary dispute between Ecuador and Peru, and so on). These conflicts have repercussions which inevitably lead to a breakdown of continental unity.

Various structural and functional defects which do not stand up under critical scrutiny from the point of view of the elementary principles of international administration must in turn have contributed to the obvious failure of the OAS in the socioeconomic sector also. Other factors involved have been the excess of organs of the most diverse types; their insufficient coordination, both internally and externally; a lack of long-range and even medium-range planning; deficiencies in the supreme command; little discernment in the recruitment of personnel for its service; and various other defects of equal importance.

Even so, it is conceivable that the technoadministrative efficiency of the OAS, and particularly of its executive organization, the Pan American Union, would be different if in practice they could count upon the active and diligent collaboration of all the governments of the member states in their various activities.

In what is said about the inadequate showing of the activities connected with the OPA, a certain responsibility should be assigned to the unproductive internal struggles between the "Moralista" group (Dr. Cecilio Morales, former director of the Department of Economic and Social Affairs) and the "Morista" group (Dr. José A. Mora, secretary general), which have no great significance[21] except insofar as they have continued (especially during the second half of 1960) to paralyze the functioning of the Pan American Union, depressingly known, with some justification, as the "Pan American Disunion."

Therefore, a total organizational reform, top to bottom, is required in the highest entity of inter-American cooperation, this reform to include both its structure and its operational methods.

President Jânio Quadros rightly pledged unlimited support of all the aims of Operation Pan America. However, it will not be possible for OPA to fulfill its lofty purposes without making use of an organization fully adapted to its philosophy.

It is therefore to be hoped that, in the spirit of wholesome realism which has characterized the international and inter-American policy of Brazil in 1961, it will be possible to communicate to the OAS (once it has been thoroughly overhauled in its entirety and its constitution has been purged of the numerous defects we have pointed out) the dynamic quality which it so lacks at this time.

NOTES

1. See Seventh Conference of American States Members of the ILO, the Director General's report, pages 37 and 38, Geneva 1961 and Economic Tendencies of Latin America in 1959 (Economic Bulletin of Latin America, ECLA, No. 2, October, 1960).

2. For the elements which separate the countries of this region from each other see the original study, under the authorship of Professor Roger Vekemans, S.J., entitled "Síntesis de la tipología socio-económica de los países latinoamericanos," presented to the Interorganizational Group to Work on the Social Aspects of Economic Development in Latin America meeting under the patronage of UNESCO, in Mexico, December 12–21, 1960 (UNESCO docum. /SS/SAED/LA/A 6, November 28, 1960).

3. See the Minutes of the Meeting of the Committee of Twenty-One (Special Committee to Study the Formulation of New Measures for Economic Cooperation), CECEIII-70 of September 11, 1960, which contains "Measures for Social Improvement and Economic Development within the Framework of Operation Pan America"; this program was reinterpreted in President Kennedy's message of March 14, 1961. See also the first analysis of said program in Estanislau Fischlowitz, "The New Social Program for Latin America," *Economic Development and Cultural Change Review*, No. 2 (1961).

4. See George Langrod, "Les Problèmes Administratifs du Regionalisme International," in *Histoire et Realisations du Panamericanisme*

(Athens, 1958), as well as numerous works by such authors as Charles G. Fenwick, William Manger, Jorge Castañeda, and L. S. Rowe.

5. We do not include in the present exposition some aspects related to the "subregional" organization of the Americas, as, for example, the Organization of Central American States and efforts, not yet crowned with full success, toward creation of an association of countries in the northern part of South America under the name of Great Colombia.

6. As it is well known, Canada, despite repeated attempts, renewed in 1960 and 1961, to draw it into the Inter-American cooperation orbit, still does not consider it possible to join the OAS in view of her links to the British Commonwealth.

7. Of the remaining enclaves of the former old colonial empires on the territory of continental America only Belize (British Honduras), claimed by Guatemala and in part by Mexico, and the three Guianas in South America remain. We do not mention here numerous islands, with colonial or semicolonial dependent status in the Antilles (part of which, under the name of the West Indies Federation, will change in 1962 to become a new and independent entity within the British Commonwealth), as well as various others, geographically situated to the south of the equator, along the coast of South America.

8. The basic philosophy of Pan-Americanism in the past was linked, first of all, to the ideas formulated by Simón Bolívar (El Libertador) in his famous letters of 1815 and 1818, as well as, indirectly, to the doctrine proclaimed by James Monroe, on the occasion of the opening of the United States Congress, on December 2, 1823.

9. The very concept of regional unity in the Americas is, at times, subject to contradictory interpretations. It is frequently effectively argued that the American states lack homogeneity, given the pronounced discrepancies between the North and South, in regard to

1. their respective economies, with differing degrees of evolution (the "affluent society" and various "diffluent" ones), which do not even have parallels on any other continent, economies whose complementary character diminishes in the face of the processes of industrialization in Latin America;

2. the contrasts between the system of unrestricted free enterprise in the United States and the national and social tendencies in the other countries of this hemisphere; and last, but not least,

3. the attitudes, ever less uniform, that the countries of that region assume in the international political arena in relation to the Soviet bloc and the neutralist groupings (the case of Cuba).

All these and various other differences, although eased by the recent decline of caudillo regimes and tyrannical dictatorships, certainly do not contribute to a position of solidarity for the American countries in the face of the great world problems of 1961. There are some who believe that the absence of such unity would affect the natural base of Pan-Americanism, which should extend to the whole area of this continent.

10. Recently divided into two departments, economic and social.

11. Convention of Montevideo, February 18, 1960, which created the Free Market Association, with the coparticipation of eight countries, and that of San Salvador, January 9, 1960, which created such an association for the Central American area.

12. See the Ad Hoc Committee of OAS-IDB-ECLA Cooperation, Minutes of the First Meeting (March 6–14, 1961), Pan American Union.

13. It should be mentioned that this supervisory organ is at present presided over, for the second time, by the eminent Brazilian diplomat, Ambassador Fernando Lôbo.

14. The Act of Bogotá, Part IV.

15. Selections for this high post do not seem to have been very felicitous with the exception of that of the present President of Colombia mentioned below. They were as follows: between 1920 and 1946, L. A. Rowe (USA); between 1947 and 1954, Alberto Lleras Camargo (Colombia), Carlos Dávila (Chile); and since 1955, José A. Mora (Uruguay).

16. First Annual Report, 1960, IDB, January 1, 1961.

17. See the failure of the second meeting of that particular commission, held in Mexico City, beginning on April 25, 1960.

18. IA ECOSOC, Doc. OAS/Ser. H/VES, No. 49.

19. IA ECOSOC, PAU, Doc. of June 13, 1960.

20. See the third meeting of the interorganizational work group, called by ECLA and held—in accordance with Resolution No. 149 of Session VIII of ECLA in 1959—in Santiago, Chile (Doc. ECLA SMLA [D. 70, 1960]) on May 17–18, 1960.

21. Except for the Argentine Project suggested by Dr. Cecilio Morales, favoring the creation of an autonomous entity, with socioeconomic powers, and divorced from the Pan American Union (see Document CECE/III 29, September 6, 1960), which, for obvious reasons, could not be approved at the Meeting of Bogotá.

Section II

The Foreign Policy of Mexico

Introduction

Of the elements which involve the foreign policy of Latin American countries geography is probably more important to Mexico than to any other nation. The geopolitical problem faced by Mexico was succinctly but clearly put by Porfirio Díaz in the second half of his widely quoted "so far away from God and so near the United States." In view of the power held by Mexico's northern neighbor on the one hand and by its southern neighbors on the other, Mexico finds itself today in a very interesting and unique security position; there is nothing it can do in the first case and nothing it need do in the second. The realistic appraisal of Mexico's security position on the part of its policy makers for the last thirty or forty years helps explain the progressive reduction of the Mexican military establishment, very clearly reflected, as usual, in its share of the national budget.

Faced with one of the two superpowers on the north and with a vacuum on the south, and with neither the desire nor the ability to maintain significant military forces, it is not surprising that Mexico has taken refuge in a legalistic posture and in the process has made some interesting contributions in the areas of international and inter-American law.

The articles by Luis Padilla Nervo and Javier Rondero unequivocably outline this legalistic approach, which in the case of Cuba has made it possible for Mexico to withstand American pressure for a complete break and domestic pressure for a foreign policy which, through an extension of the Estrada doctrine, would not discriminate against a Latin American regime either because it subscribes to the Marxist-Leninist ideology or because it is disliked by the United States. The type of foreign policy followed by Mexico in regard to Cuba, the inter-American defense force, and the role of the United States in the 1965 revolt in the Dominican Republic takes into account the power relationship between the United States and Mexico and the defense of Mexico's national interest as defined by the majority of those Mexicans who participate in the political process.

This foreign policy constitutes more of a compromise than meets the eye. First of all, while it is true that the Mexican government was the only Latin American government that refused to comply with the decision of the January, 1962, Punta del Este conference which suspended the present Cuban regime from membership in the Organization of American States and asked its members to break diplomatic relations with it, the fact is that the relations thus maintained by the Mexican government have been extremely formal. Furthermore, it is a well-known fact that all travelers who utilize the Mexican air route to and from Cuba are carefully identified and that this information is made available to (and, some people say, is actually obtained by) United States security agencies, as well as to the intelligence services of other Latin American countries. It is also known that the Mexican government has gone to great pains to make it quite difficult for Cuban books and propaganda to enter Mexico and that travelers to Cuba who use Mexico as a jumping-off point are subject to significant restrictions as to the time they may spend in Cuba. Thus, it would seem that the legalistic grounds on which Mexico based its decision to continue "normal" diplomatic relations with Cuba were more realistic than many people thought when this policy was first announced. No implicit or explicit criticism of the Mexican position is intended here; on the contrary, it is a recognition of this country's ability, as reflected in this particular episode, to find a common denominator between the interest of the United States and what appears to be the feeling of the majority of the Mexican population. The fact that the makers of foreign policy actually found this common denominator and were able to articulate it in legal terms within the general trend of the country's foreign policy is a remarkable achievement.

There are indications that in the last few years the Mexican Ministry of Foreign Relations has moved in the direction of making its relations with the United States the cornerstone of its foreign policy. At the same time it exhibits its independence in certain matters, such as preference for the universal international organization over its regional counterpart (as discussed by Professors Faust and Stansifer, as well as by Mr. Padilla Nervo). This preference became quite clear in the Dominican Republic episode of 1965. The overall objective would appear to be to force the United States to use Mexico as the "natural intermediary" in the former's relations with the rest of Latin America and to encourage other countries to accept Mexico in that role. All indications are that so far the Mexican Ministry of Foreign Relations has not achieved its objectives, although it is too early to pronounce the attempt a failure.

The relationship between Mexico and the United States is not based exclusively on diplomatic considerations. It has been estimated that 74 percent of all foreign investments made recently in Mexico come from its northern neighbor and that approximately 60 percent of both imports and exports are tied to the American market. Of the four hundred largest corporations operating in Mexico, more than 50 percent are in reality foreign controlled or have a strong foreign participation, regardless of the provisions of Mexican law. The American influence is also felt in newspapers and magazines: between 62 percent and 78 percent of all foreign news published by Mexican newspapers comes from the United States, and three American publications (*Life en Español, Selecciones del Reader's Digest*, and *Visión*) have more circulation in Mexico than all Mexican magazines put together.[1] In these circumstances it is not surprising that Mexican policy makers have decided to abandon their limited isolation in favor of intensified bilateral relations with their neighbor to the north.

The role played by Mexico at the Punta del Este conference of January, 1962, which suspended the present Cuban regime from membership in the Organization of American States (OAS), constitutes perhaps the best illustration of the direction and boundaries of the present Mexican foreign policy. On that occasion Mexico refused to go along with the majority (which subscribed to the American position) by maintaining that there was no provision in the OAS Charter for either expelling or suspending a member, which of course is true. But the Mexican delegation stopped short of following the Argentine and Brazilian position, which in effect maintained that the controversy was between the United States and Cuba, and therefore the OAS and/or its other members were not necessarily involved; furthermore, the two largest South American nations were in fact saying that the course of action being sponsored by the majority was both a mistake and, more importantly, against their national interest, as defined by the Frondizi and Goulart administrations. To what extent this stand cost these two men the presidency of their respective countries is still a relatively open question, but it seems clear that it had something to do with their political demise. It would seem that the prudent opposition of the Mexican government was more acceptable to the American State Department, as was the stand taken in regard to the 1965 revolt and intervention in the Dominican Republic. Another aspect of this prudent foreign policy is the limitation of Mexican criticism to the actions of the United States in the Western Hemisphere, and silence in relation to everything else.

Mexico has maintained relations with the Soviet Union and has encouraged the formation of neutralist blocs, but these formalistic actions should be interpreted more as an expression of its freedom of choice than as an actual objective of its foreign policy. Thus, relations with Communist countries have been cool, and trade has not been significant. The degree of economic penetration by United States investors and the heavy dependency on American tourism and markets may have something to do with this coolness toward Communist regimes, as Professor Padgett somewhat naively points out:

> For a time, 1959–61, the Mexican position in fact became pro-Castro to the point that United States investment sources became harder to tap. This caused a modification of the Mexican posture. Mexican pronouncements on Cuba became more neutral, but there was no substantial shift in the positions of either government.[2]

Mexican legalistic foreign policy has found fertile ground in the area of recognition of governments; this has been and is a complicating factor in Latin American international relations because of the frequent accession to power by other than constitutional means. The Estrada doctrine, formulated by former Foreign Minister Genaro Estrada, applied the Mexican concept of nearly absolute nonintervention in the internal affairs of other nations to the area of recognition. In brief, the doctrine maintains that Mexico will continue or discontinue its relations with other governments in accordance with Mexico's national interest, regardless of the way the other governments have come to power, the ideology to which they subscribe, or their domestic policies.[3] This doctrine is relatively easy to apply as long as there is no strong internal sentiment about another government, but it should be pointed out that the Mexican government has been extremely consistent in applying the Estrada doctrine, thus to divest its relations with new regimes of value connotations.

This overall view leaves the observer with the impression that the Mexican administrations of the last three or four decades have identified national development, particularly in the economic sphere, as the most important objective of the national policy, and have subordinated their foreign policy to it. In spite of the land reform and *ejido* programs, Mexican national development has been defined in terms of industrialization and modernization of the urban areas; this concentration has been reinforced by the growth of political power enjoyed by the industrial upper class and the new middle class, which exercise overwhelming influence over the machinery of the dominant *Partido Revolucionario Institucional* (PRI). Consequently, Mexico's foreign economic policy has been directed toward the development of markets; this has been done by refusing to join the General Agreement on Tariffs and Trade (GATT) in order to retain Mexico's high tariffs, and by participating enthusiastically in the Latin American Free Trade Association (LAFTA) in the hope that it may be able to use this organization to open the less developed countries of Latin America to Mexico's industrial goods. Although the Latin American Free Trade Association has not been too successful so far, the Mexican Ministry of Foreign Relations continues backing it and has, in principle, subscribed to the idea of joining a Latin American common market if and when it becomes a reality.

The subjection of Mexico's foreign policy to the nation's economic development and the downgrading of the armed forces as a political power factor have led the various administrations since the presidency of General Cárdenas to limit military expenditures, which are now at an average level of less than 10 percent of the federal government's budget;[4] these expenditures are substantially below those of other large and middle-sized Latin American countries. Because of this trend, it is not surprising that Mexico has forcefully pursued disarmament agreements with other Latin American countries, a policy which culminated in the recent treaty banning nuclear weapons in the area, not fully accepted by Brazil and Argentina, the two countries with greatest atomic ambitions and capabilities, as well as by Cuba.[5]

Within this framework there have been pressures from the left side of the Mexican political spectrum to become more independent in its foreign policy, not in word but in deed. These pressures have in part been caused or justified by the American unwillingness to settle border issues such as the high salt content of the irrigation water supplied to the Mexican region from the Colorado River and the treatment and status of migratory workers. While the Colorado River dispute seems to have been settled by the agreement signed by the United States and Mexican representatives to the International Boundary and Water Commission on March 22, 1965, other border issues continue to provide arguments to this school of thought.[6] Perhaps the most important move made so far to satisfy these pressures is the loan obtained from the French government in June, 1963, whereby the Mexican authorities borrowed 100 million dollars from French banks and 50 million dollars from the French government under quite favorable conditions; the action seemed to have been intended to obtain a direct relationship with the European Common Market and to play the latter's interest against that of the United States.[7] More stringent curbs on foreign banking, enacted in December, 1965, appeared to have been directed at American financial institutions along the lines suggested by the left-wing critics.[8]

The foreign policy of Mexico will undoubtedly continue to be influenced primarily by the direction of its own political processes (which can be glimpsed in the article by Mr. Castañeda), by United States foreign policy toward Latin America in general and Mexico in particular, and by the changes which may take place in the domestic and foreign policies of the other large members of the inter-American system. The future success of the Latin American Free Trade Area and of the proposed Latin American common market, as well as the revitalization of the Organization of American States along the lines suggested by the Mexican Ministry of Foreign Relations, may cause this country to visualize its national interest in terms of the Western Hemisphere. On the other hand, the failure of these regional organizations, in Mexican terms, may lead Mexico toward both European blocs and the uncommitted "third world," always within the boundaries established by United States flexibility.

NOTES

1. See Pablo González Casanova, *La Democracia en México* (México: Ediciones ERA, S.A., 1965), chapters II and III, and tables XVIII to XXII (pp. 194–202).

2. L. Vincent Padgett, *The Mexican Political System* (Boston: Houghton Mifflin Company, 1966), p. 154 (emphasis added).

3. On the Estrada doctrine see George I. Blanksten, "Foreign Policy of Mexico," in Roy C. Macridis (ed.), *Foreign Policy in World Politics*, second edition (Englewood Cliffs, N.J.: Prentice-Hall, Inc., 1962), pp. 311–33, and Herbert W. Briggs (ed.), *The Law of Nations*, second edition (New York: Appleton-Century-Crofts, Inc., 1952), p. 123.

4. See González Casanova, *op. cit.*, pp. 31–3 and 189–90. On this point see also Edwin Lieuwen, *Arms and Politics in Latin America*, revised edition (New York: Frederick A. Praeger, 1961), chapter 4. The 1 percent figure given by Irving Louis Horowitz, "The Military Elites," in

Seymour Martin Lipset and Aldo Solari, (eds.), *Elites in Latin America* (New York: Oxford University Press, 1967), p. 155, and reproduced by José Nun, "The Middle Class Military Coup," in Claudio Veliz (ed.), *The Politics of Conformity in Latin America* (London: Oxford University Press, 1967), p. 68, is unrealistically low and should be discarded. On the other hand, the figure of 0.72 percent of the Mexican gross national product given by Horowitz (p. 156) is perhaps more significant and illustrative.

5. On the essential points of the proposal for banning nuclear weapons in Latin America, and reactions within and outside the region, see the *New York Times*, Apr. 17, 1966, p. 33, and Oct. 2, 1966, p. 27.

6. For an example of these pressures see *Política* (Mexico City), Nov. 1, 1965, back cover and p. 13; *Siempre* (Mexico City), Nov. 5, 1965, p. 76; and the *New York Times*, Nov. 27, 1965, p. 62. However, the basic foreign policy guidelines proposed by one of these organizations, the *Partido Popular*, do not differ markedly from what has been and is being done; for a text of the proposals see *Política*, Nov. 1, 1965, pp. xii-xiv. On the question of the Colorado River and other border problems see the *New York Times*, June 7, 1964, p. 32; Mar. 23, 1965, p. 18; and May 7, 1967, p. 69.

7. The details were reported in *Comercio Exterior* (Mexico City), 13:475, July, 1963. For an analysis see Rogelio García Lupo, *A que Viene De Gaulle?* second edition (Buenos Aires: Jorge Alvarez Editor, 1964), pp. 98–102.

8. The *New York Times*, December 12, 1965, p. 21.

The Presence of Mexico at the United Nations: The Cuban Case*

Luis Padilla Nervo

The problem which the Political Commission of the United Nations has now under consideration has been and is as much a cause of deep concern to the nations of this continent as to those of other regions of the world. The grave and dangerous tension that exists between the United States and Cuba deeply concerns the Mexican government and public opinion in Mexico. In few countries has this conflict had as great a repercussion and impact, and the reason is easy to understand. The excellent friendly relations that exist between Mexico and the United States are one of the principal mainstays of its foreign relations. On the other hand, the close bonds that have traditionally united Mexico to Cuba are now further strengthened by the natural sympathy that we feel for the aspirations of the people of Cuba and for the efforts that they are making in order to improve their living conditions rapidly.

As the President of Mexico, Adolfo López Mateos, stated publicly last year upon receiving the President of Cuba, "you will find that Mexico, which respects the self-determination of every country, is mindful of Cuba and understands it with fraternal concern, since it knows that whatever takes place there cannot be ignored by us and that the Cubans will know how to find, amidst the intense sacrifices which all changes

* This article was originally published in Spanish as "Presencia de México en las Naciones Unidas. El Caso de Cuba," in *Cuadernos Americanos*, 20(3):72–83, May–June, 1961. Translated and printed by permission.

inevitably bring, the best way to fulfill their genius and national aspirations."

We participate in this debate with the consciousness of fulfilling an obligation not only as members of the United Nations but also as good neighbors of the United States and Cuba, while we are imbued with a sentiment of fraternal amity toward both. We feel that we can perform our obligation fully only by stating our opinion clearly and without reservations and by adopting whatever position we may sincerely consider most constructive. Our position can be summed up in the following points presented, not in order of importance, but in logical sequence:

Concerning the question of competency, I do not think that anyone would now dare question the jurisdiction of the United Nations to hear a complaint or a situation arising between two member states because of the fact that both might at the same time belong to a regional organization. The delegations of Ecuador, Uruguay, and Argentina criticized this theory severely in a plenary session in 1954 when they discussed the deplorable decision that the Security Council took in that year when it refused to register on the agenda a complaint by Guatemala. Argentina rightly maintained that the acceptance of this theory "would result in the absurd situation that a state which besides being a member of the United Nations Organization is also a member of a regional pact would have a lesser standing than those states which, for whatever reason, do not belong to regional organizations." Secretary General Hammarskjöld in his annual report for 1954 states as follows: "any policy that entirely recognizes the role that regional organizations perform can and ought to protect the right that the Charter confers upon the member states to be heard by the organization."

However, there is another aspect of the question that should be clarified. The recognition of the competency of United Nations agencies to deal with situations or controversies, even when the parties thereto are members of regional organizations, has a necessary logical and legal consequence, namely, once a complaint or situation is presented before the United Nations, the agency that takes the situation under advisement can recommend at its discretion the method of peaceful solution that seems most conducive to the solution of the problem according to the peculiar conditions of each case. It is not necessarily obligated to adopt as the sole procedure, or even as the first, the referral of the matter to the regional agency. The theory that the conflict must necessarily be submitted to a regional agency would entail unjust discrimination against the members of a regional agency vis-à-vis the others, since the former could not be advised to use a number of channels under the direct auspices, help, and supervision of the United Nations, while other members could be so advised. In our opinion the Assembly can recommend the proceeding that seems most effective according to all the factors in the case, including, among others, the preference of the parties.

In the case we are considering, we believe that the action of the ad hoc Committee of Good Offices established at the Seventh Meeting of Consultation of Ministers of Foreign Affairs of the American continent held last year in San José, and composed of the presidents of six Latin American countries, would constitute an adequate and impartial method of clarifying the facts and helping the parties to reconcile their differences, subject to prior request by the governments directly involved, as provided in the resolution that established the committee. However, in case one of the parties does not find it convenient to use this procedure, the General Assembly should strive to arrive at a solution of the problem by other means. Because of the seriousness of this matter and the dangers that it may involve for peace, especially in the light of recent events, it is imperative that the Assembly exercise its pacifying action immediately and effectively, thus to avoid further deterioration of the situation.

The principles applicable to this situation are the following: the principle of nonintervention; the right of peoples to establish the political, economic, and social form of government they may desire without foreign intervention; the principle of territorial integrity and political independence of states; and the principle of respecting treaties and the requirement of solving all controversies peacefully.

The inter-American concept and formulation of the principle of nonintervention are particularly stringent. They exclude not only armed intervention, direct or indirect, individual or collective, but also any form of interference threatening the personality of the state, its political, economic, and cultural elements, for any reason whatsoever, as stated in Article 15 of the Charter of the Organization of American States.

Article 16 of the same Charter completes the concept by establishing that "no state may use or encourage the use of coercive measures of an economic or political character in order to force the sovereign will of another state and obtain from it advantages of any kind."

The right of a nation to determine its own economic, social, and political system is a fundamental right of the states of the Western Hemisphere or of any other part of the world. This right must be respected despite any aversion that might be felt toward a particular system of government, despite the foreign interests it might affect, or despite the fact that the course of its foreign policy might seem to others reckless and contrary to the best interests of that country. The effective exercise of representative democracy is one of the principles of the inter-American system, but it is not to be imposed or sanctioned internationally. As the Foreign Minister of Mexico, Don Manuel Tello, has said, the Organization of American States was not formed to create, maintain, or overthrow governments. At the Tenth Inter-American Conference I had the opportunity to state on behalf of the Mexican delegation:

> We reject the idea that has been expressed on various occasions that the mission of guarding the maintenance of our institutions has ceased to be a matter within the exclusive national jurisdiction of our respective governments, and has become an international concern subject to collective action. If we accepted this doctrine we would be encroaching upon the authority reserved to the states, and consequently we would be violating both the Charter of Bogotá and that of San Francisco which prohibit our intervening individually or collectively in matters involving the internal jurisdiction of the states, and we would be converting our organization

into a supranational tribunal commissioned to pass judgment on our institutions and to regulate the democratic zeal of our governments.

The government and public opinion of Mexico are particularly sensitive to this aspect of the problem, that is, to the strict observance of the right of self-determination, among other reasons because of the memory of bitter historical experiences.

Our recognition of the right of self-determination implies, as is natural, the recognition of the right of a nation to rebel against oppression. No principle could be more dear to the Mexican people; our principal historical stages have had their origin in armed rebellions. The political life of Latin America would not have had historical meaning without revolution.

Certainly the Charter of the United Nations does not prohibit internal armed rebellion, and the United Nations has no reason to defend established governments against internal rebellion. To the extent that the matter of Cuba is, as has been said, the business of the Cubans, the United Nations has no reason to intervene. However, we have the right and, I would add, the clear duty of asking that in this respect the obligation of states to observe all pertinent international agreements not be violated.

Revolutions have been so frequent in Latin America and their international projections so dangerous both with respect to their organization and to their consequences that the American states have had to regulate this whole situation internationally through treaties. Our concern that American revolutions be basically internal matters and our desire to avoid indirect foreign intervention have been mirrored in an obligatory instrument signed in Havana in 1928 and ratified by, among other countries, Mexico (1929), the United States of America (1930), and Cuba (1934). The purpose of the Convention on Duties and Rights of States in the Event of Civil Strife is to prohibit the aid of other states to the rebels, thus to avoid illegal foreign interventions. Its stipulations are particularly stringent. Because of their importance, I shall read the main points:

ARTICLE 1. The contracting states bind themselves to observe the following rules with regard to civil strife in another one of them:

First: To use all means at their disposal to prevent the inhabitants of their territory, nationals or aliens, from participating in, gathering elements, crossing the boundary or sailing from their territory for the purpose of starting or promoting civil strife.

Second: To disarm and intern every rebel force crossing their boundaries, the expenses of internment to be borne by the state where public order may have been disturbed. The arms found in the hands of the rebels may be seized and withdrawn by the government of the country granting asylum, to be returned, once the struggle has ended, to the state in civil strife.

Third: To forbid the traffic in arms and war materiel, except when intended for the government, while the belligerency of the rebels has not been recognized, in which latter case the rules of neutrality shall be applied.

Fourth: To prevent that within their jurisdiction there be equipped, armed or adapted for warlike purposes any vessel intended to operate in favor of the rebellion.

ARTICLE 3. The insurgent vessel, whether a warship or a merchantman, equipped by the rebels, which arrives at a foreign country or seeks refuge therein, shall be delivered by the government of the latter to the constituted government of the state in civil strife, and the members of the crew shall be considered as political refugees.

In 1957 a Supplementary Protocol to this Convention was opened for signature, though the Protocol has as yet been scarcely ratified. The primary purpose of that Protocol is to make more complete and precise the provisions of the Convention with reference to vessels and aircraft of whatever type, whether civilian or military.

President Kennedy has declared that "under no conditions would there be intervention in Cuba with American armed forces," and added the following: "this government will do all that is possible, and I believe that it can discharge its responsibilities, to insure that American citizens do not become involved in any action within Cuba."

This is an important element in preserving the domestic character of the Cuban situation. However, this prohibition does not exhaust the obligations of states. The treaty obligations the American republics have assumed are the ones I have stated, and they refer with great precision to practically all forms of indirect aid.

Obviously, this does not mean the internment of refugees and those seeking asylum, nor the prohibition of all forms of political activity. The countries of the Western Hemisphere, and especially the United States and Mexico, like other countries, can be proud of their long tradition of harboring the politically harassed. However, there is a great difference between not interning and silencing the refugees and open incitement to rebellion and public preparations to bring it about. Just to give an idea of the feelings of the American republics on this matter (in spite of their traditional policy of harboring refugees), I will read two measures adopted by the Convention on Territorial Asylum, signed at Caracas in 1954, although this document has not yet been ratified by various states. Nevertheless, it clearly reveals the preoccupation and the desire of the American Republics to avoid to the maximum degree the internationalizing of revolutions. They are as follows:

ARTICLE VII. Freedom of expression of thought, recognized by domestic law for all inhabitants of a state, may not be ground of complaint by a third state on the basis of opinions expressed publicly against it or its government by asylees or refugees, *except when these concepts constitute systematic propaganda through which they incite to the use of force or violence against the government of the complaining states.*

ARTICLE VIII. No state has the right to request that another state restrict for the political asylees or refugees the freedom of assembly or association which the latter state's internal legislation grants to all aliens within its territory, *unless such assembly or association has as its purpose fomenting the use of force or violence against the government of the soliciting state.*

The United Nations itself has already pronounced against international aid to revolutions. Resolution 290(IV), titled "Essential Bases for Peace," states as follows;

The General Assembly,

Invites all nations . . .

3. To abstain from any threat and any acts that, directly or indirectly, tend to impair the liberty, the independence, or the integrity of any state, or to foment civil dissensions or to subvert the will of the people of any state.

It is the opinion of the Mexican delegation that international obligations in this matter are not vague but clear and precise. The states are obliged to employ, not ordinary, but maximum diligence, the circumstances of each case being considered, in order to avoid having individuals carrying out within their territories acts against the political independence and territorial integrity of another state. In the famous case of the Alabama, the Tribunal,* relying on the so-called three rules of Washington that have become customary rules of international law, ruled in that sense. In spite of the fact that in that case there had already been recognition of belligerency—which is obviously a less dangerous situation than when there is only one established government vis-à-vis groups of individuals that do not have any international status—the Tribunal did not accept the argument of Great Britain that its responsibilities were limited to exercising the same diligence that she exercised in domestic affairs, diligentia quam in suis rebus.

The Tribunal said: "The due diligence to which rules 1 and 3 refer must be exercised by neutral governments in exact proportion to the risk to which one or the other of the belligerents might be exposed as a consequence of noncompliance with the obligations of neutrality on the part of said neutral governments."

There is another international aspect of the Cuban problem

*Translator's note: The author refers to the joint United States-Great Britain Claims Arbitration Tribunal of 1872 provided for in the Treaty of Washington signed by the two countries on May 8, 1871.

that preoccupies the Mexican government profoundly. The Western democracies are engaged in a wide-ranging struggle which has been imposed upon them and in which victory will be decided, not on the battlefield, but in the minds of men. Because of the nature of this struggle, the best weapons of the democracies are moral principles, strict observance of treaties, and the principle that difficulties and controversies between countries are to be resolved, not by guns, but by negotiation. On more than one occasion civil wars aided from outside have put international peace in jeopardy, and the West has resisted, and is today resisting in other parts of the world, the attempts to take over countries through the use of destructive dissident factions inspired, financed, and supplied from outside. The democracies must preserve all their moral authority to denounce and fight against other cases of internal revolution instigated and aided from the outside. As Mexico's Minister of Foreign Relations said in another context, referring to the limits that we should impose upon collective intervention, "let's not fling into the air of the future a boomerang that might turn in time against our own peoples."

This case can be a touchstone that will put to the test the policy and the principles invoked in other cases that the General Assembly has considered. The precepts of the Charter should be fulfilled. We are all trying to establish a world order where law rules and treaties are obeyed, because in a chaotic world the revolutionary urgency of destitute peoples will favor extreme ideas.

In the future, what would be the social structure of a world where basic principles like those of nonintervention, of self-determination, and the faithful execution of treaties would be abandoned, and where the largest and strongest states would want to impose upon the weak ones the features which they prefer because they better serve their interests?

I am sure that we all bear in mind the noble concepts recently voiced by the President of the United States, and which seem to us to constitute not only a unilateral postulate but a guideline that should serve as a standard for collective behavior:

"We promise," said President Kennedy in his inaugural address, "to convert our good words into good deeds. . . . Let us remember that civility is not a sign of weakness, and sincerity is always subject to proof. . . . Let us never negotiate out of fear. But let us never fear to negotiate."

The Mexican delegation is convinced that norms such as those I have just cited should inspire us, so that violence will not prevail in the solution of the deplorable situation which is presently being examined by this Political Commission and so that the parties will make sincere efforts to insure that the conflict which faces us can be resolved through negotiation or some other peaceful measures provided for in the United Nations Charter.

A country has the right to resort to arms in order to expel from its territory a foreign armed intervention, or to overthrow a tyrant, or to carry out a social revolution. But no foreign state has the right to intervene, instigate, or foment the downfall of a government that is not to its taste.

In this constantly shrinking world it is impossible to avoid a situation where any country in any part of the world may become the battleground of third powers unless the principles of nonintervention and self-determination are respected. Each intervention contrary to the purposes and principles of the Charter propagates the seeds of world conflict.

We do not want Cuba to be the place, the occasion, or the motive that might start a chain reaction that might bring on a new world explosion.

Cuba is in the Americas, but it is also at the center of today's political worlds, as are Laos, the Congo, Korea, and Germany. In our age no nation is actually far from another; each passing day finds us closer and more united in a common destiny. Sooner or later, all of us will be measured by the standards by which we measure others.

The security of everyone of us will depend increasingly upon our adherence to the principles and goals that we proclaim we defend and upon strict respect for the rights of others.

A few days ago President Kennedy quoted a sentence from Jefferson, who many years ago said, "Liberty is contagious." Let us rejoice that we can bear witness to this great truth, but let us not forget that hatred too is a contagious disease. Our greatest desire is that all of us in this organization may contribute to the propagation of liberty and the struggle against hatred, thus to create the necessary conditions for the maintenance of peace.

In conclusion, Mr. President, I must read the following declaration made by the Ministry of Foreign Relations of Mexico:

> In regard to the situation prevailing in Cuba, the Secretariat of Foreign Relations deems it indispensable to reiterate some of the essential postulates of the international policy of Mexico.
>
> In exercising the right of self-determination of peoples, without which the concepts of sovereignty and independence would be wanting in content, it behooves the Cuban people, without foreign interference, to translate into concrete reality its aspirations for economic and social improvement, aspirations which have found such favorable response in the conscience of the peoples of the Americas.
>
> The government of Mexico reiterates its firm adherence to the principle of nonintervention, according to which no state or group of states may intervene, directly or indirectly for any reason whatsoever, in the internal affairs of other states, since it is convinced that this principle constitutes the best guaranty of peaceful coexistence among nations.
>
> Pacifist by tradition and conviction, Mexico has not resorted to war except in cases of legitimate defense and has invariably condemned foreign aggression against established governments.
>
> Mexico is certain that there are no conflicts, no matter how serious, that cannot be solved by the peaceful means sanctioned by positive law, and publicly and through official communiqués, it has offered its good offices for the solution of situations such as now face our hemisphere. It will not cease to endeavor to do so on any propitious occasion.
>
> The Secretariat of Foreign Relations has given instructions to the Permanent Delegate of Mexico at the United Nations to adjust his conduct to the principles stated herein.
>
> On the other hand, Mexican authorities will exercise strict vigilance to prevent any aid that may favor elements opposed to the Cuban government from leaving Mexican national territory.

Mexican Foreign Policy in the United Nations: The Advocacy of Moderation in an Era of Revolution*

John R. Faust and Charles L. Stansifer

Recent Mexican foreign policy in the United Nations deserves special attention from those concerned with the East-West rivalry, the struggle for self-determination, and the economic development of the poor countries. Mexico's experience with internal growth and stability in the last forty years and Mexico's success in pursuing an independent foreign policy, especially in the postwar bipolar world, have much to offer the newly emerging states.

Mexico's leaders, suspicious of both the United States and the Soviet Union, have consciously sought to avoid commitments to either side. This is well illustrated by Mexico's record in the United Nations. On the important Cold War issues debated in the United Nations—intervention, membership in the United Nations, collective security, disarmament, colonialism, and economic assistance to underdeveloped areas—Mexico has voted independently of the wishes of either East or West. This policy of nonalignment has been growing stronger as the Cold War progresses. Mexico, perhaps still restricted by the basically negative principle of nonintervention, which is the cardinal principle of her foreign policy, has often revealed her independent attitude by abstention from voting. As Luis Padilla Nervo, Mexico's chief delegate to the United Nations and one of Mexico's ablest diplomats, pointed out in 1953, Mexican nonalignment results

* This article was originally published in *Southwestern Social Science Quarterly*, 44(2):121-9, Sept., 1963. Reproduced by permission.

from the feeling that democratic institutions and defense against foreign ideologies are a matter of domestic jurisdiction rather than issues to be settled by international collective action.[1]

An early example of Mexico's approach to East-West issues was the absence of Mexico's delegates during the 1946 roll-call voting on Soviet resolutions seeking international prevention of anti-Communist activity in refugee camps located in Western Germany. Opposed by the United States, the resolutions failed to pass.[2] In the same year Mexico twice abstained on Soviet proposals to allow the left-wing World Federation of Trade Unions a voice in the deliberations of the United Nations Economic and Social Council.[3] On a third vote relating to this question Mexico voted with the Soviet Union.[4]

From 1947 to 1949 Mexico often abstained or was absent on votes relating to charges of Hungarian and Rumanian violations of provisions in the Balkans treaties protecting the rights of individuals and minorities. All other Latin American nations voted with the United States and against the Soviet Union on this issue. Mexico also failed to vote on Soviet resolutions in 1949 condemning Western intervention to aid the royalist regime in Greece.[5]

In the case of Soviet intervention in Hungary several years later, however, Mexico strongly supported the West. As a consistent adherent of the principle of self-determination, Mexico found it easy to vote with the United States on thirty roll-call votes relating to the Soviet violation of Hungarian sovereignty.[6] In this instance Mexico probably demonstrated its greatest solidarity with the West on a Cold War issue.

Mexico has usually supported the principle of universal membership in the United Nations regardless of the political orientation of the state in question. This policy has on occasion caused her to side with the Soviet Union. For example, Mexico supported the admission of Albania, Hungary, Rumania, and Bulgaria to the United Nations in 1955 while the United States abstained.[7] On the other hand, Mexico has generally followed the lead of the United States with regard to Communist China. While Chinese Communists were fighting United Nations forces in Korea, Mexico regularly supported the United States in its refusal to consider the question of seating Communist China. However, with the cessation of hostilities in Korea, Mexico has abstained on this question on a number of occasions.[8] In the 1961 Session of the General Assembly, Mexico, along with all the other Latin American states except Cuba, voted not to seat Communist China in the United Nations.

The case of Spain is another matter. When in 1955 Spain was admitted into the United Nations, Mexico abstained, even though both the United States and the Soviet Union supported the admission of Spain.[9] It may be pointed out that in the case of Spain Mexico violated the principle of according early recognition to new governments regardless of political makeup, even though this principle has been a cornerstone of Mexico foreign policy since 1930.

Mexico has often supported the United States position on East-West issues in Asia. The outbreak of the Korean War in 1950 brought forth strong Mexican denunciations of the North Koreans as aggressors. Luis Padilla Nervo, speaking in response to a question about North Korean aggression, observed that his government "had constantly and without exception opposed all foreign military intervention in the internal affairs of a state," and that his government "had always supported the principle of the right of nations to self-determination, and its policy regarding Korea was promoted by the same principle."[10] In spite of Mexico's formal support for the United Nations action against North Korea and Communist China, she did not see fit to send troops to aid the cause of opposition to aggression.

On the perennial disarmament question, which has aroused almost as much bitter recrimination between East and West as the Korean War, Mexico has sought to avoid taking sides. Mexico has often supported Western resolutions, but only on the basis of their relative merits. While critical of most Soviet disarmament resolutions, Mexico has frequently abstained rather than actively oppose them. It would appear that such abstentions are prompted by a desire not to discourage the Soviet Union from making further, perhaps better, proposals.

In general the Mexican attitude is that disarmament can only be successful through agreement between the major world powers and that Mexico ought not to stand in the way of any such agreement. On some occasions Mexico has taken the lead in attempting to bring the opposing powers closer together. Along with a growing number of United Nations members, Mexico has sought compromise resolutions in the field of disarmament to avoid questions on which the major powers disagreed. For instance, in 1958 Mexico sponsored a resolution avoiding the proposals of both sides and calling for the major powers to work constantly for agreements acceptable to all.[11] These efforts were fruitless, for neither the United States nor the Soviet Union would abandon its own substantive proposals.

On one occasion Mexico voted with the Soviet Union and against the United States on a plenary roll-call vote concerning disarmament. This was in November, 1957, prior to the 1958 Geneva Conference on nuclear testing. On an Indian resolution calling for the banning of nuclear and thermonuclear testing prior to actual arrangements for inspection and control, Mexico and Guatemala were the only two Latin American states to vote with the Soviet Union.[12] The Mexicans apparently thought that such test bans were desirable even without inspection because such first steps could lead to the relaxation of international tensions.

It may be that without disarmament the United Nations can never realize its collective security goal of suppressing breaches of the peace. In the meantime, however, Mexico has consistently supported measures which would strengthen the United Nations in its aim of establishing collective security. In 1946 and 1949, when the Soviet Union introduced resolutions supporting the unanimity principle that each of the five major powers had the right to block collective action through the machinery of the Security Council, Mexico voted with the West and against the Soviet Union.[13] During the Korean crisis Mexico supported United States-sponsored proposals such as the "Uniting for Peace Resolution" for strengthening the General Assembly's role in security matters when the Security Council was unable to act.[14] However, with the passage of time, Mexico has increasingly emphasized the danger of utilizing the United Nations machinery on security questions without the unanimous support of the major powers. For instance, in September, 1953, when hostilities were drawing to a close in Korea, Luis Padilla Nervo commented that "the auxiliary collective security system" which was hastily pieced together to meet the Korean crisis had to give way as soon as possible to an armed force under the jurisdiction of the Security Council. The smaller powers, including Mexico, realize that the veto might give them some advantage. According to Jorge Castañeda of the Mexican Foreign Service, in his authoritative study *Mexico and the United Nations*, "the veto serves as a check against dragging small countries, often against their will, into undertakings which fundamentally serve the interest of the great powers."[15]

On most East-West issues, as has been noted, Mexico has supported either the West or efforts toward mediation. On colonial questions, which also frequently divide the Soviet Union from the United States, Mexico has usually voted with the Soviet Union. Russian intransigence on colonial matters, however, has not won support from Mexico. On those occasions when administering powers have shown a willingness to accept compromise resolutions promoting eventual self-determination, Mexico has voted with these powers and against the uncompromising anticolonial positions of the Communist-bloc members.

An instance of Mexico's milder anticolonialism as compared to the rigid stand of the Soviet Union occurred in the First Session of the General Assembly. In 1946 the Soviet Union introduced a resolution calling on the members to reject the trusteeship agreements submitted by the administering powers because such agreements allegedly aided colonial rule in many areas of the world. Mexico opposed this resolution on the grounds that it was important first to establish the trusteeship agreements as a means of providing a measure of international control over colonial areas. These agreements should be supported, Mexico held, even though many members felt they did not adequately reflect the interests of the indigenous populations.[16] Once the

Trusteeship Council was established, however, Mexico, along with most members from Latin America, the Middle East, Africa, Asia, and Eastern Europe, rather consistently supported resolutions to hasten the independence of trusteeship territories.[17]

Beginning in 1957 the Western powers administering trusteeship territories supported resolutions providing for orderly progress toward independence. Mexico, like most other nonadministering powers, thought that steps toward independence and the orderly transfer of power would be facilitated by close cooperation with the administering powers. For this reason Mexico and nearly all United Nations members except the Communist bloc supported resolutions favoring gradual independence for the French Togoland, the British and French Cameroons, Tanganyika, and Ruanda-Urundi. The Communist members abstained on four such resolutions and voted against Mexico and other non-Communist states on an Indian resolution congratulating France and the indigenous population in French Togoland on their steps toward independence.[18] The subsequent admission of Togoland and the Cameroons into the United Nations may be traced in part to the efforts of states such as Mexico to steer a moderate course between the extreme positions of East and West. Ultimate success in achieving independence for trust territories has depended on close cooperation with the administering powers, an approach which the Communist-bloc members have consistently rejected.

Mexico's most consistent opposition to the Western powers has occurred on roll-call votes on measures to speed up the process toward independence in non-self-governing territories.[19] The Western powers recognized obligations under Chapter XII of the United Nations Charter to prepare trusteeship territories for independence. But it has been their contention that the obligations under Chapter XI, dealing with non-self-governing territories, only require the administering powers to submit information to the United Nations on the progress toward self-determination and measures to promote the welfare of the people. Mexico, like most other states having a tradition of political or economic intervention by Western powers, has not accepted this interpretation of Chapter XI. Such states, in their attempts to extend United Nations influence through a broad interpretation of Chapter XI, have been strongly supported by the Communist-bloc members. However, as on trusteeship questions, the approach of anticolonial states such as Mexico has been different from that of the Communist states. This difference is illustrated by the divergency of reaction to a series of four resolutions introduced by the Fourth Committee in 1948 and supported by the Western powers. The resolutions in essence approved of limited machinery for the transmission of information to the United Nations on conditions in non-self-governing territories.[20] Mexico and most other non-Communist members, while not entirely satisfied with the compromise resolutions, formally supported them. Raul Noriega of Mexico stated his preference for a permanent committee (instead of the temporary committee provided for in the resolution) to receive information on non-self-governing territories. He noted that, in spite of this shortcoming, the resolutions "would benefit the peoples who enjoyed neither political independence nor complete development of their economic potentialities."[21] The Soviet Union agreed with Mexico in her preference for a permanent committee, but rejected the resolutions because they did not require the transmission of specific information concerning the development of organs of self-government or on-the-spot surveys of United Nations personnel.[22]

In 1953 Mexico's anticolonial policy placed her in direct opposition to the United States. The question concerned Puerto Rico, which had gained increasing control over its internal affairs since becoming a possession of the United States after the Spanish-American War. The United States in 1953 sponsored a resolution for the cessation of information from Puerto Rico on the grounds that the island was now self-governing and would therefore be insulted by the requirement of further transmission of such information. A majority of the United Nations members voted with the United States on this resolution, but Mexico joined the Communist-bloc in refusing to recognize the independent status of Puerto Rico.[23] Mexico and Guatemala were the only Latin American nations to vote against the United States.

Mexico's position in the United Nations on economic assistance to underdeveloped areas follows the familiar pattern of avoidance of the more rigid attitudes of the capitalist and Communist nations. In general, Mexico has supported resolutions favoring varying forms of economic assistance to underdeveloped areas. While the Communist-bloc members of the United Nations abstained on resolutions calling for a technical assistance program in 1949 and a special economic development fund in 1952, Mexico supported both. But this does not mean the Mexicans agree entirely with the Western position. Mexican delegates have on occasion exercised great caution in their support of international assistance programs. Like the Soviet Union, Mexico has emphasized the need for states to utilize their own resources for development purposes whenever possible. According to Antonio Carillo Flores, a member of the Mexican delegation to the United Nations, "economic development should be based essentially on the internal resources of the underdeveloped countries and foreign aid should only be considered as a subsidiary source of capital."[24] In the same statement he pointed out that his country was not opposed to international assistance per se and refuted the Soviet contention that there was no need for an international development fund. Although Mexico abstained on the 1952 resolution for a special development fund when it was voted on in the Second Committee, she has supported all proposals for a special United Nations fund for economic development when considered in plenary session.[25]

The United Nations, under constant prodding from the underdeveloped states, has gradually expanded its economic assistance programs, but a fundamental faith in private enterprise in the capitalist countries has led to numerous resolutions calling upon members to encourage private foreign investment where appropriate. The Communist-bloc members have voted against all resolutions to encourage the flow of private capital to underdeveloped areas. Mexico, occupying a middle position, abstained rather than support or oppose such proposals. The Mexican position, rooted in its own experience with foreign capital, was explained by Victor A. Urquidi, who noted "that the promotion of economic development required both public and private investment." He pointed out that "foreign capital had been subject to the same treatment as national capital," and that such matters came under domestic jurisdiction.[26] On a resolution encouraging private foreign investment introduced into the General Assembly in 1958 the Communist-bloc members voted in the negative, while Mexico, Afghanistan, and Yugoslavia abstained, and all the other members supported the resolution.[27]

Mexico, it would seem from the foregoing analysis, is not a willing slave of the United States nor a remote puppet of the Soviet Union. Mexico does not adhere rigidly to either capitalist or Marxist ideology. Nor is she a military partner of either East or West. Instead, Mexico has pursued an independent course on issues arising in the United Nations. Her voting record is a reflection of this independence, and on no issue has she aligned herself consistently with any member of the United Nations. It would appear that the Mexican approach to world problems is to assess the merits of each proposal, from whatever quarter, and to vote according to its merits.

This is not to say that the Mexicans are more virtuous than other people represented in the United Nations. Her adherence to such principles as economic and political self-determination and nonintervention represents a sound assessment of her national interests. In fact these policies have evolved from dealing with past internal and external problems dating back to the nineteenth century. Today Mexico's policies toward both the United States and the Soviet Union are based on past experience and present realities. She does not fear invasion from north of the Rio Grande because, though the United States has intervened militarily in the past, the right to do so has subsequently been given up; she does not fear military intervention from the Soviet Union because such an event would be regarded as harmful to the interests of the United States, which would certainly come to the rescue in case of need. In addition she has no major specific interests outside the American hemisphere to protect and defend before world opinion. From this relatively secure territorial and moral position Mexico can work in a more disinterested way than the great powers for the general aims of the United Nations.

The record of Mexico in the United Nations reflects a stable approach to most of the burning issues of our times. Today many nations are facing economic and political problems similar to those confronting Mexico. In an era marked by instability the Mexican record is indeed refreshing, and her policies of moderation and avoidance of ideological stands on economic and political questions could be an important factor in giving encouragement and stability to the newly emerging nations who now constitute a major portion of the United Nations membership. Mexican achievements, both domestic and foreign, demonstrate the possibility of a peaceful transition to economic and political self-determination while at the same time avoiding entanglements in the ideological and power struggles which presently threaten world peace.

NOTES

1. *United Nations General Assembly Official Records* (hereinafter cited as G.A.O.R.), Eighth Session, 447th Plenary Meeting, Sept. 28, 1953. p. 188; *Hispano americano*, XXXVI (Mar. 20, 1960), pp. 33–6.

2. G.A.O.R., First Part of First Sess., 30th Plen. Mtg., Feb. 14, 1946, pp. 434–9.

3. *Ibid.*, 33rd Plen. Mtg., Feb. 17, 1946, pp. 532–4.

4. *Ibid.*, Second Part of First Sess., 66th Plen. Mtg., Dec. 15, 1946, p. 1414.

5. *Ibid.*, Third Sess., 203rd Plen. Mtg., Apr. 30, 1949, pp. 272–3; Fourth Sess., 246th Plen. Mtg., Nov. 18, 1949, pp. 263–5. See also Jorge Castañeda, *Mexico and the United Nations* (New York: Manhattan Publishing Co., 1958), p. 69.

6. For example see G.A.O.R., Second Emergency Sess., 564th Plen. Mtg., Nov. 4, 1956, p. 20; 571st Plen. Mtg., Nov. 9, 1956, pp. 77–80.

7. *Ibid.*, Tenth Sess., 555th Plen. Mtg., Dec. 14, 1955, pp. 433–4.

8. *Ibid.*, Eleventh Sess., 580th Plen. Mtg., Nov. 16, 1956, p. 83.

9. *Ibid.*, Tenth Sess., 555th Plen. Mtg., Dec. 14, 1955, p. 436.

10. *Ibid.*, Fifth Sess., First Cmtte., 353rd Mtg., Oct. 4, 1950, p. 53.

11. General Assembly Document A/c. 1–L.208. For the Mexican view see Luis Padilla Nervo, G.A.O.R., Thirteenth Sess., First Cmtte., 946th Mtg., Oct. 13, 1958, p. 21.

12. *Ibid.*, Twelfth Sess., 718th Plen. Mtg., Nov. 19, 1957, p. 467.

13. *Ibid.*, First Sess., 61st Plen. Mtg., Dec. 13, 1946, p. 1264; Third Sess., 195th Plen. Mtg., April 14, 1949, p. 130.

14. *Ibid.*, Fifth Sess., 302nd Plen. Mtg., Nov. 3, 1950, p. 347; Sixth Sess., 359th Plen. Mtg., Jan. 12, 1952, p. 326.

15. *Ibid.*, Eighth Sess., 447th Plen. Mtg., Sept. 28, 1953, p. 189; Castañeda, *op. cit.*, pp. 139–40 (Note 11).

16. G.A.O.R., First Sess., 62nd Plen. Mtg., Dec. 13, 1946, p. 1286; First Sess., Part II, Fourth Cmtte., 26th Mtg., Dec. 11, 1946, p. 168.

17. From 1948 through 1955 Mexico voted with the Soviet Union sixteen times on plenary roll-call votes concerning the promotion of independence of trusteeship territories.

18. G.A.O.R., Twelfth Sess., 724th Plen. Mtg., Nov. 29, 1957, p. 557, 729th Plen. Mtg., Dec. 13, 1957, p. 596; Thirteenth Sess., Plen. Mtgs., Mar. 13, 1959.

19. For example, see alignment with the Soviet Union and against states such as the United Kingdom in G.A.O.R., First Sess., 64th Plen. Mtg., Dec. 14, 1946, p. 1369.

20. *Ibid.*, Third Sess., 155th Plen. Mtg., Nov. 3, 1948, pp. 393–4.

21. *Ibid.*, Fourth Cmtte., 57th Mtg., Oct. 14, 1948, p. 57.

22. *Ibid.*, 54th Mtg., Oct. 11, 1948, p. 22.

23. *Ibid.*, Eighth Sess., 459th Plen. Mtg., Nov. 27, 1953, p. 319; Arthur P. Whitaker, "Anticolonialism in Latin America," in Robert Strausz-Hupe and Harry W. Hazard (eds.), *Idea of Colonialism* (New York: Frederick A. Praeger, Inc., 1958), pp. 165–6.

24. G.A.O.R., Sixth Sess., Second Cmtte., 164th Mtg., Dec. 11, 1951, pp. 120–1.

25. See *ibid.*, Sixth Sess., 360th Plen. Mtg., Jan. 1952, p. 338; Thirteenth Sess., 788th Plen. Mtg., Dec. 12, 1958, p. 565.

26. *Ibid.*, Thirteenth Sess., Second Cmtte., 568th Mtg., Nov. 29, 1958, p. 262.

27. *Ibid.*, p. 265; 788th Plen. Mtg., Dec. 12, 1958, p. 565.

Mexico at Punta del Este*

Javier Rondero

Truth is nothing other than the adaptation between our intellect and reality. Therefore, to find the truth, I must give up any subjective inclination, impression, or position in order to consider as objectively as possible what has just taken place at the Eighth Meeting of Consultation of Ministers of Foreign Affairs of the American republics which convened at Punta del Este.

For this purpose I need to use many citations, some of them tedious, from international texts and documents and the opinions of prominent Mexican and other Western Hemisphere statesmen, internationalists, and diplomats, both to base my conclusions and to help me arrive at such an interpretation.

THE LETTER OF CONVOCATION

The meeting which has just taken place was officially known as "The Eighth Meeting of Consultation of the Ministers of Foreign Affairs to Serve as the Organ of Consultation in the Application of the Inter-American Treaty of Reciprocal Assistance." This treaty (known more briefly as the Rio de Janeiro Treaty because it was signed in that city on September 2, 1947) has a double significance: first, it is an agreement to organize and exercise legitimate collective defense, in accordance with Article

* This article was originally published in Spanish as "México en Punta del Este," in Ciencias Políticas y Sociales, 8(27):49–72, Jan.–Mar., 1962. Translated and printed by permission.

51 of the Charter of the United Nations which recognizes the inherent right of lawful defense, individual or collective, in cases of armed attack against a member of the United Nations, without any provision of the Charter impairing this right.

On this matter, Article 3 of the Rio de Janeiro Treaty provides that "The High Contracting Parties agree that an armed attack by any state against an American State shall be considered as an attack against all the American States and, consequently, each one of the said Contracting Parties undertakes to assist in meeting the attack in the exercise of the inherent right of individual or collective self-defense recognized by Article 51 of the Charter of the United Nations." In such an event the Organ of Consultation acts by means of the meetings of the ministers of foreign affairs of the American republics (Article 11) in order to agree on the collective measures which should be adopted, in addition to the immediate measures which have been taken individually, including armed force, the only requirement being that they be immediately communicated to the Security Council of the United Nations (Article 5).

The second aspect of the Treaty of Rio de Janeiro—in addition to that of the organization of legitimate collective defense— is that of a regional agreement or organ whose objective should be to deal with matters related to the maintenance of international peace and security and susceptible to regional action (Article 52 of the Charter of the United Nations); and the Security Council shall utilize the said regional agreements or organizations, if appropriate, in order to apply coercive measures under its authority. But no enforcement action shall be taken under regional arrangements or by regional agencies without the authorization of the Security Council, with the exception of measures against any enemy states (Article 53). Enemy states are understood to be those that fought the 1945 signatories of the United Nations. Here it is appropriate to recall that the permanent members of the Security Council—the United States, England, the Union of Soviet Socialist Republics, France, and China—have the right to veto.

In the second case, that of maintenance of international peace and security, and within this second aspect—that is, as a regional agreement or organ—the Treaty of Rio de Janeiro textually establishes in its Article 6: "If the inviolability or the integrity of the territory or the sovereignty or political independence of any American State should be affected by an aggression which is not an armed attack or by an extracontinental or intracontinental conflict, or by any other fact or situation that might endanger the peace of America, the Organ of Consultation shall meet immediately in order to agree on the measures which must be taken in case of aggression to assist the victim of the aggression or, in any case, the measures which should be taken for the common defense and for the maintenance of the peace and security of the continent"; and "For the purposes of this Treaty, the measures on which the Organ of Consultation may agree will comprise one or more of the following: recall of chiefs of diplomatic missions; breaking of diplomatic relations; breaking of consular relations; partial or complete interruption of economic relations or of rail, sea, air, postal, telegraphic, telephonic, and radiotelephonic or radiotelegraphic communications; and use of armed force" (Article 8). These decisions "shall be binding upon all the Signatory States which have ratified this Treaty, with the sole exception that no state shall be required to use armed force without its consent" (Article 20) and "The Organ of Consultation shall take its decisions by a vote of two-thirds of the Signatory States which have ratified the Treaty" (Article 17).

Bearing the foregoing in mind, that is, what the Rio de Janeiro Treaty prescribes and the manner in which it operates, we should analyze the legal bases of the convocation of the Eighth Meeting of Consultation of Ministers of Foreign Affairs.

This meeting was convened by resolution of the Council of the Organization of American States (OAS), approved on December 4, 1961, to consider the threats to the peace and political independence of the American states and especially to indicate "specific acts which should they occur will justify the application of measures for the maintenance [of peace] and security" in accordance with the Rio de Janeiro Treaty and the OAS Charter and to consider the note presented on November 9, 1961, in which the convocation of such a meeting was requested "in accordance with Article 6 of the Inter-American Treaty of Reciprocal Assistance." This Article 6, which we have already quoted verbatim, refers to acts which, should they have occurred, would have affected the inviolability or integrity of the territory, or the sovereignty or independence of any American state. The convocation of the Council of the OAS refers, not to such acts, but rather to "specific acts which, if they occur in a simple future hypothesis, would call for the application of such measures."

In other words, Article 6 of the Rio de Janeiro Treaty, which was invoked by the Colombian delegation, and which the OAS Council incorporated in its convocation, is completely inapplicable; consequently the convocation of the Eighth Meeting of the Organ of Consultation *lacks any legal basis whatsoever.*

In this connection the Minister of Foreign Relations of Mexico, Manuel Tello, in his speech delivered on January 23 at Punta del Este, said:

> Before expounding the attitude of Mexico, it seems necessary that I refer, though briefly, to the attitude adopted by our representative on November 14 and on December 4 when the OAS Council had before it the proposal of the government of Colombia. In our opinion the convocation lacked a legal basis for three fundamental reasons: first, it did not indicate the element of urgency which must be present for any convocation to apply the Inter-American Treaty of Reciprocal Assistance; second, even though it was based on Article 6, no reference was made to any act clearly connected with the restrictive hypothesis of the same article; and, finally, because the convocation of this meeting for consultation, under the terms it was agreed upon, in view of the background of this convocation and of the draft resolutions which had been suggested to us, led us to suppose that what is intended is to extend the Inter-American Treaty of Reciprocal Assistance (ITRA), a task outside the competency of the Organ of Consultation.

The position of Mexico toward this objective was legally correct and could be neither rebutted nor refuted by anyone at Punta del Este. Mexico was therefore accused through numerous publications of adopting a legalistic policy. Now, international life is based upon and governed by law, or it is based solely on brute force, and all treaties, the charters of the Organization of American States and of the United Nations, are completely superfluous; but if these conventions are invoked, it should be, not to violate or ignore them, but on the contrary to respect them and conform to them.

Strictly speaking, such attacks can be regarded as eulogies for Mexico, since it has based its foreign policy on inter-American and international law. Besides, the juridical rules of international instruments are not empty formalities or mere abstractions, but rather they correspond to facts and to realities of international life, and such juridical rules serve to guarantee the latter in the matter of the sovereignty of states and their juridical equality, from which the absolute principle of nonintervention in the internal or external affairs of other states is derived.

On the other hand and in the same connection, in a discussion on the Punta del Este conference, Mr. Ramón Beteta (former undersecretary of foreign relations and a former Mexican ambassador, a person who has a vast knowledge of the internal and external political affairs of Mexico) stated last February 9:

> However, at Punta del Este no one claimed, and much less concretely proved, an act of aggression by Cuba against another country.
>
> Moreover—and we must say this with complete honesty and frankness—if the question of punishing a country of this continent for attacking another had been presented, the accused would not have been Cuba; the accused would have been the United States and Guatemala, who through the words of their chief executives stand confessed and convicted of having promoted and aided an unsuccessful invasion of Cuba.

President Kennedy with great frankness made a statement to this effect in May, 1961, in assuming responsibility for the invasion at the time the Central Intelligence Agency of the United States was being attacked for a series of blunders in preparing, organizing, and carrying it out.

As for Guatemala, President Miguel Ydígoras, in unprecedented statements made on Guatemalan television (which were fully reproduced in Mexico only by the magazine *Mañana* on January 13, 1962), stated:

This is the first time that my government speaks of the training of armed contingents in Guatemala. We came to an agreement with the Cuban leaders in exile, and they made arrangements with a friendly government which could give them military backing and support for military training and a military campaign.

A secret military encampment was organized for the purpose, and another one in the open. Naturally such zeal would draw upon the members of my government the anger and threats of death of the Castroites and Soviet and Chinese Communists, who are daring and dangerous.

I had to evaluate such a contribution for my government; I did not hesitate, since I had beforehand thought of asking for good offices to convince Great Britain to return Belize, under certain conditions accepted by the majority of the inhabitants of this territory. On the appointed day the Cuban troops were thrown into battle and the so-called Battle of the Bay of Pigs took place.

This was a disaster for those pro-Communists who have infiltrated the press and some governmental positions in the United States; for those who counseled the suspension of the air support which had been offered, it was a defeat; for Castro and his cronies, a victory. Still, taking inventory of the results, we conclude that it was a true victory for us because from that day Castro's warlike activities outside Cuba ceased.

A fear complex overcame him and his cronies when they realized that with a little more organization, courage, and support of the oppressed people, Cuba would have backed the movement.

In spite of the fact that my government kept quiet about such actions the hysteria of the North American press and of the Communist sympathizers produced a state of defeatism and disaster.

Journalists and officials began their recriminations, forgetting the simplest codes of secrecy, chivalry, and good-fellowship. They mentioned Guatemala as a point of training and origin of the invasion.

Never have I seen such impudence. The President of the United States, with the impulse of a great statesman, publicly declared that he took full responsibility for all that had happened.

Now it is up to President Kennedy to direct and assume the responsibility for another point still neither clarified nor fulfilled: the commitment assumed toward Guatemala.

He should also consider that the Bay of Pigs was a victory and not a disaster, and that he who begins like this, under such good auspices, should continue the enormous task of eliminating Communism from this part of the Western Hemisphere.

Guatemala will watch whatever happens at Punta del Este, and there is something else she will be watching. Guatemala has a credit item which is not payable in gold, but in good will. Let us all fulfill our promises.

In view of these admissions why did not Cuba invoke in its favor the Rio de Janeiro Treaty, since it had already suffered invasion, armed attack, an aggression which damaged its inviolability, its territorial integrity, its political sovereignty and independence? Possibly because it knew that the great majority of the Latin American states would not agree on any of the measures which, in case of aggression, would have to be taken to aid the attacked, and would deny the actual existence of such attacks and aggressions, as the present debates of the United Nations General Assembly prove, and that various states would even propose the sanctioning not of the aggressors, but of the attacked state, as actually happened at Punta del Este when the most severe, the maximum sanctions were applied against Cuba, that is, exclusion and expulsion of that country from the OAS. And it can not be said that sanctions are one thing and expulsion is another, since everywhere, whether in a corporation, a club, a school, or an international organization, exclusion is the most serious sanction.

THE MEXICAN VOTE

At the Punta del Este meeting the American states were divided. From the beginning some wanted to sanction Cuba because of the declarations of the Prime Minister, Fidel Castro, that the Cuban Revolution is inspired by the Marxist-Leninist philosophy; others were opposed to these sanctions as incompatible with the principle of nonintervention ratified by Articles 15, 16, and 17 of the Charter of the OAS, binding for all the American states, which read as follows:

Article 15. No state or group of states has the right to intervene, directly or indirectly, for any reason whatever, in the internal or external affairs of any other state. The foregoing principle prohibits not only armed force but also any other form of interference or attempted threat against the personality of the state or against its political, economic, and cultural elements.

Article 16. No state may use or encourage the use of coercive measures of an economic or political character in order to force the sovereign will of another state and obtain from it advantages of any kind.

Article 17. The territory of a state is inviolable; it may not be the object, even temporarily, of military occupation or of other measures of force taken by another state, directly or indirectly, on any grounds whatever. No territorial acquisitions or special advantages obtained either by force or by other means of coercion shall be recognized.

Upon the return to Mexico of the delegation that attended the Ninth Inter-American Conference in Bogotá from March 30 to May 2, 1948, which drew up the Charter of the Organization of American States, Minister of Foreign Relations Jaime Torres Bodet, the chief Mexican delegate, explained to the nation the nature and scope of the approved document and, while doing so (June 1, 1948), declared:

One particularly sensitive area was that of finding a common meeting ground for agreement with regard to the preservation of democracy in the hemisphere. It was necessary to place our solidarity on impregnable democratic bases. And, on the other hand, it was hoped that intervention in the life of the nations of the Western Hemisphere was to be condemned. As Mexico had pointed out from the beginning of the Council's sessions, democracy should not defend itself except through democratic measures. To apply repressive methods or those of ideological censure in order to preserve democracy would have been equivalent to undermining the most respected foundations of our institutions: freedom of thought, freedom of press, and freedom of association.

In addition, the distinguished Mexican diplomat and current Undersecretary of Foreign Relations, Ambassador Pablo Campos Ortiz, also explained the following to our nation:

First, let us see how the principle of nonintervention was stated in the Charter of Bogotá.

In the history of Pan-Americanism this principle is undoubtedly the one that has created the sharpest conflicts. But, it is also true that, perhaps for this very reason, we can also say that there is no American principle that is more firmly established.

As we know, the Convention on the Rights and Duties of the States, which we have repeatedly mentioned, was signed at the 1933 Pan-American Conference. One of its articles, Article 18, affirmed the idea of nonintervention in the following terms:

"No state has the right to intervene in the internal or external affairs of another."

But, even then, when we might say that the new Pan-Americanism, based on mutual respect and confidence, was under way, this still uncertain achievement was not approved without resistance.

Three years later, at the Conference for the Consolidation of Peace which met in Buenos Aires, a multilateral agreement called Additional Protocol of Nonintervention was subscribed, which completed what was stipulated at Montevideo by the text of its key article, which was as follows:

"The High Contracting Parties declare unacceptable the intervention of any of them, directly or indirectly, whatever the motive, in the internal or external affairs of any of the other Parties."

This time the principle was accepted without reservations, and it became, without limitations, a required contractual norm for all the American states.

The text of Buenos Aires was considered very satisfactory. And, in effect, it was. Nonetheless, the Conference of Bogotá notably enlarged and perfected it by adding:

First, that collective intervention is also inadmissible.

Second, that nonintervention excludes not only armed intervention but also any form of involvement, and

Third, that any tendency which threatens the personality of the state is equally excluded.

In a report, Dr. Alberto Lleras Camargo, then secretary-general of the Organization of American States, asked, when speaking of collective interventions:

> What arbitrator can determine when an intervention is just and carried out on the basis of incontestable moral and juridical principles and when it pursues imperialistic purposes? The only judges would necessarily be the interested parties, and every act of intervention efficiently performed by a world power would always find means of justification. . . . The fact that a majority of nations within a given group associate themselves in order to intervene in the internal affairs of a state by no means guarantees the goodness or the uprightness of its purposes. . . .
> This interpretation fixes the authentic scope of Article 15, 16, and 19 of the Charter of the Organization of American States.

During the Tenth Inter-American Conference, which convened in Caracas in 1954, the "Declaration of Solidarity for the Preservation of Political Integrity of the American States against the Intervention of International Communism" was discussed; it was declared:

> Domination or control of the political institutions of any American state by the International Communist movement, which subsequently results in an extension to the American continent of the political system of an extracontinental power, will constitute a threat to the political sovereignty and independence of the American states that would endanger the peace of America and would require a Meeting of Consultation to consider the adoption of the measures which may be in order in accordance with the existing treaties.

When taking part in the debates, the Mexican delegate, Roberto Córdova, now chief justice of the International Court of Justice, left Mexico's point of view on record for posterity by saying very clearly:

> . . . Mexico cannot add an affirmative vote to the United States'

proposal because the way in which it is drawn up could result in any of our nations being subject to interventions that no American state, either isolatedly or collectively, should tolerate. If we were certain, as some delegations seem to be, that the proposal under study does not involve the danger of going backward and returning the hemisphere to the remote times in which we were struggling for the establishment of the principle of nonintervention, our attitude would be different.

We fear that future interpretation of this document may contain elements which might provoke an intervention against a government which might be accused of being Communist, simply because the accusation might come from unavowable vested interests or, rather, because that country might rightly be attempting to acquire its economic independence and to combat capitalist interests in its own territory. We have seen it in the past; it is not a mere hypothesis. Mexico has suffered interventions within its territory, and these interventions have been both extracontinental and by nations of this hemisphere. We know what we are talking about; we know that if we want the unity of America, it is not possible to leave the door open so that at any time intervention may be attempted.

The Good Neighbor Policy strengthened Pan-American solidarity; it was founded, precisely, on the Buenos Aires Declaration and the Protocol of Nonintervention. Subsequently, this doctrine has contributed significantly to international harmony, and we cannot substitute for it another in which each nation sees in its neighbor a possible prosecutor, investigator, or judge of its actions. So interpreted, the doctrine of Buenos Aires will divide the continent into accused states and judge states, into victim governments and executioner governments; it would begin a reign of mutual distrust and fear among us which would irretrievably isolate us.

The proposal being studied mentions that adequate measures will be adopted in accord with the existing treaties. These treaties can be no other than the Charter of Bogotá and the Rio de Janeiro Treaty. It seems that the proposal being debated is inspired by the opinion that what we did in Rio with so much mutual confidence and with a desire for unity in facing a common danger may be interpreted as a measure for coercion in the Western Hemisphere to punish governments, to take away from them any possibility of self-determination and of exercising their sovereign right. Because of this, in the Mexican amendments it is made clear that none of us have the right to intervene in the affairs of others, whatever may be the motive, if we are to accept what we subscribed to beginning with the Buenos Aires Conference. The Rio de Janeiro Treaty is formulated, not for punishing a government which is victim of an extracontinental power, but rather precisely to aid it when it is attacked.

In Mexico the causes giving rise to Communism will be fought with utmost energy. We also will fight against interventionism in any of its forms. . . .

The Mexican delegation officially presented its point of view as one of the normative principles of the inter-American system in the following terms: "The political regime and the economic and social organization of the peoples essentially pertain to the internal jurisdiction of the state, so that they cannot be the object of any direct or indirect, individual or collective, intervention, by either one or more countries or by the Organization of American States."

The Mexican Minister of Foreign Relations, Dr. Luis Padilla Nervo, president of the Mexican delegation to the Tenth Inter-American Conference, explained why Mexico could not accept the declaration of Caracas and, after the corresponding balloting, solemnly declared on behalf of the Mexican state:

The Mexican delegation, being in complete agreement with the necessity and the convenience of condemning the intervention of an extracontinental or continental government, whatever its political ideology, in the internal or external affairs of the American nations, wishes to leave on record that it could not give a vote of approval to the Declaration which appears in the Final Proceedings under number XCIII because, in its opinion, some sections of it imply commitments which are inconsistent with the Constitution of the United States of Mexico, which reflects the freedom-loving spirit of our people, and because it considers that the terms of this declaration may result in the weakening of the Western Hemisphere pacts and the principles of nonintervention in the internal or external affairs of the States, as well as of the other fundamental rights and duties of the States.

Commenting upon the Tenth Inter-American Conference, Mr. Isidro Fabela, considered the master of Mexican diplomacy, in his work *The Caracas Meeting and the Anti-Communist Attitude of Mexico* maintains: "With what a precise sense of timing our Minister of Foreign Relations Padilla Nervo, opposed such a resolution, declaring that '. . . the Delegation of Mexico believes that the adoption of this project may result in the weakening of all Western Hemisphere pacts and all the precepts of international law which affirm the *principle of non-intervention in the internal or external affairs of states.*' "

And not only the weakening, we add, but also the *nullification* of the pacts; because, in effect, the Caracas resolution, which was not approved by Mexico for many reasons, nullifies the Inter-American Treaty of Rio de Janeiro, since this instrument was adopted essentially against an invasion or armed attack.

Fabela continues:

> And now something unforeseen, and very serious and unacceptable, results, and that is that *in accordance with the project already approved, it will be possible to convene the Organ of Consultation* (the Western Hemisphere foreign ministers, or, provisionally, the Council of the Organization of American States), and then an intolerable situation would arise: Mexico, a signatory and ratifier of the 1947 Rio de Janeiro Treaty, would be required to attend such a meeting in spite of having rejected the Caracas resolution. And what is more, and completely absurd, to discuss measures which would violate our basic law and the principle of nonintervention established in the Charter of Bogotá.
>
> But there is more; since the Rio de Janerio Treaty stipulates that the Organ of Consultation will adopt its decisions by a two-thirds vote of the Signatory States which have ratified the Treaty (Article 17); and its decisions will be binding on all the states which have ratified it (Article 20)—and Mexico ratified it—the grave situation may result that Mexico, in spite of having rejected the Caracas resolution, will find itself obligated by it.
>
> In view of that, since it is entirely contradictory that our country

obligate itself to perform duties which it specifically rejects, it would be necessary to find a way of avoiding this wrong interpretation, which would violate our national Constitution, as the Mexican Foreign Secretary has said.

It is clear that the decisive way of avoiding the violation of our fundamental code of laws and also of the Charter of Bogotá would be to *denounce the Rio de Janeiro Treaty*, in accordance with Article 25 of the said instrument, *which would free Mexico from a very heavy burden*, because this denouncement would be the only way of defending nonintervention in view of the fact that the Caracas Resolution gives ipso facto an excessive scope to the Rio de Janerio Treaty and completely nullifies it.

Finally, Mr. Isidro Fabela tells us:

> In conclusion, as a Mexican who has always defended liberty, not only in his fatherland but in our hemisphere, I declare that now that our sister republics are threatened by the same danger that for many years impaired their independence as sovereign states, it is deeply satisfying to contemplate the proud attitude of the President of Mexico, Adolfo Ruiz Cortines, who realizing the danger which threatens Hispanic America because of the new theories of the latest version of Pan-Americanism, has, always relying on the law, calmly resolved to proclaim at the Caracas Meeting that the Mexican state is resolute in maintaining and defending by whatever means may be necessary the dignity and full sovereignty of our country, and opposes every kind of intervention, be it unilateral or collective. . . .

As a result of the foregoing, the Mexican delegation at Punta del Este could not vote for the sixth resolution passed by exactly two-thirds of the member states of the OAS without contradicting the entire history of Mexican diplomacy from the time of the Mexican Revolution. To do so would commit it to something inconsistent with the Constitution of the United States of Mexico, as Mexico solemnly declared at the Tenth Inter-American Conference through the head of our delegation, Mr. Padilla Nervo. Such approval would contradict not only Article 2 of the Charter of the Organization of American States, which provides that *all* the American states are members of the organization, but also Articles 15, 16, and 17, which solemnly ratify the principle of nonintervention in the internal or external affairs of any American state.

The Minister of Foreign Relations of Mexico asked that the following declaration of Mexico be entered in the Final Record of Proceedings of the Eighth Meeting of Consultation held in Punta del Este: "The Mexican delegation wishes to enter in the Final Record of Proceedings of the Eighth Meeting of the Consultation of Ministers of Foreign Affairs that in its opinion the exclusion of a member state is not juridically possible without previous amendment of the Charter of the Organization of American States in accordance with the procedure provided for in Article 3 of the said document."

In this connection Article 3 of the Charter of Bogotá says, "Amendments to the present Charter may be adopted only at an Inter-American Conference convened for that purpose. Amendments shall enter into force in accordance with the terms and the procedure set forth in Article 109."

The procedure in question is defined in Article 109 as follows: "The present Charter shall enter into force among the ratifying states when two-thirds of the signatory states have deposited their ratifications. It shall enter into force with respect to the remaining states in the order in which they deposit their ratifications."

Of course, Mexico could never have accepted an amendment, and much less ratified it internationally, in a case where such an amendment excluded a Western Hemisphere state from the organization because of its form of government for two simple reasons, one peculiar to Mexican constitutional law and the other corresponding to hemispheric international law. The first one is that the Political Constitution of Mexico provides that the people always have the inalienable right to alter or modify the form of their government (Article 39) and the other that the Charter of the OAS provides that "no state or group of states has the right to intervene, directly or indirectly, for any reason whatever, in the internal or external affairs of any other state," and Mexico understands that "the political regime and the economic and social structure of the peoples pertain essentially to the internal jurisdiction of the state, so that they cannot be the object of any intervention, direct or indirect, individual or collective, on the part of one or more countries or by the Organization of American States" as was stated in Caracas in 1954.

INCOMPATIBILITY OF THE SIXTH RESOLUTION OF PUNTA DEL ESTE WITH THE CHARTER OF THE ORGANIZATION OF AMERICAN STATES

In spite of the position adopted by Mexico at Punta del Este, where it was joined by Argentina, Bolivia, Brazil, Chile, and Ecuador, the majority of the American states (the United States of America, Panama, Paraguay, Nicaragua, Honduras, El Salvador, Peru, Colombia, Costa Rica, Venezuela, Haiti, Guatemala, the Dominican Republic, and Uruguay) declared Cuba outside the inter-American system, a situation which requires continuous surveillance on the part of OAS members. They resolved to exclude the present government of Cuba from participation in the inter-American system, and recommended that the Council of the Organization of American States and the other bodies and organizations of the inter-American system adopt without delay the necessary provisions to enforce this resolution.

The exclusion of Cuba from the Inter-American System was decided at Punta del Este, and by the Organ of Consultation of the Rio de Janeiro Treaty Cuba was sanctioned by expulsion, which, I repeat, is the most serious possible sanction.

The adoption by the Council of the Organization of American States of this resolution that completely nullifies the Rio de Janeiro Treaty was a circumstance foreseen from the beginning by the Mexican Minister of Foreign Relations when he declared at Punta del Este "the convocation to a Meeting of Consultation in the terms in which it was agreed upon, the background of this convocation, and the drafts which were outlined to us led us to suppose that what is wanted is to broaden ITRA, a task which is not within the competence of the Organ of Consultation," and when the Council adopts this resolution as its own, it places itself in a situation which is incompatible with the Charter of the Organization of American States, which is thereby flagrantly ignored.

This illegal situation places Mexico in a very difficult political position. Is Mexico going to consent actively or passively, expressly or tacitly, to this attempt against the inter-American international order itself? Can it change its traditional position and for momentary political expediency join those who have destroyed hemispheric solidarity? We do not believe it for a moment.

A few days ago in this very place Dr. Luis Quintanilla . . . warned us in his lecture entitled "Living Together in the Western Hemisphere": "The foreign ministers of the Western Hemisphere now presently gathered in Punta del Este are assuming a singular responsibility in the name of their respective governments. The strengthening or weakening of Pan-Americanism is in their hands—this noble continental movement which the American countries have been struggling so earnestly to build up for over a century." Dr. Quintanilla knew, and told us very clearly, that the final decision that they might adopt could cause "an incurable wound in that Pan-Americanism forged with such devotion by our countries." The lecture by this illustrious Mexican internationalist was of such great interest before Punta del Este, and is even more so today, after the Meeting of Consultation, that it should be given in full.

Faced with the impossibility of doing so here, I want only to repeat his main points: "The only interventions which the Rio de Janeiro Treaty deals with are the interventions *of a state in the affairs of another state*; in no way does it consider the intervention *of an idea or an ideology* in the internal politics of any government. The subjects of international law are, in effect, the states and not the ideas. If it were not so, the OAS would be transformed into a political court of an inquisitorial nature."

Exactly ten years ago Dr. Quintanilla, conscious of the importance of the problem which now confronts America, wrote a work entitled *Democracy and Pan-Americanism*. In the Introduction Dr. Alberto Lleras Camargo, former secretary of the Organization of American States and now president of Colombia, states:

> ". . . Quintanilla, who knows, as few people do, not only the diplomatic instruments which provide the structure for the OAS but also the causes which gave rise to it, objectively describes the dangers of an international organization which might attempt to intervene in affairs which until now have been considered as being within the internal jurisdiction of each state . . . a self-seeking opinion or one which is impatient, or adverse to the organization, is irresponsibly expressed against the OAS because it does not intervene to solve the problem of the creation, survival, and progress of democracy. Ambassador Quintanilla offers unanswerable arguments on the dangers of this type of intervention which, in my opinion, would act as the most rapid solvent of the organization and cause the wreckage of all the hopes justly deposited in it as a tool for social, juridical, and political progress for the hemisphere.

For our part, we regret that the President of Colombia, in changing into the champion of interventionism at the Punta del Este Meeting, which was called at his suggestion, should contribute more than anyone else at present to the "wreckage of these hopes" and ignore the unanswerable arguments which Ambassador Quintanilla set forth ten years ago, and does so again today, regarding the dangers of this type of intervention.

In *Democracy and Pan-Americanism* Dr. Luis Quintanilla maintains:

> Perhaps the most controversial question which confronts contemporary Pan-Americanism is that of reconciling the principle of nonintervention with the equally valid principles of democracy and human rights.
>
> In the case of nonintervention the situation is extremely clear: this principle was formally recognized in the Conference of Buenos Aires (1936) by twenty-one American governments as the cornerstone of continental solidarity. Therefore, nonintervention has long ceased to be a theoretical problem. In the Western Hemis-

phere it has become a multilateral obligation committed to writing in the form of a treaty whose violation is automatically considered an act of aggression which brings on collective sanction. Such a state of affairs, juridically recognized, is the successful result of more than half a century of constant diplomatic struggle. We do not want to change it. . . . On the contrary, we must try to keep it intact.

Within the framework of Pan-Americanism, nonintervention appears as a juridical obligation, specifically regulated, which means that the violation of this principle brings with it immediate international sanctions. With respect to democracy or to human rights we have not gone so far. On this point our governments have simply proclaimed a common belief. They have adopted neither a political constitution nor a moral code applicable to the entire hemisphere. They have not agreed that the violation of certain political norms or human rights will automatically bring about the application of collective measures by the regional organization. Far from it, the hemisphere governments still maintain that the unsurmountable curtain of national sovereignty absolutely protects their domestic affairs against any type of outside interference. The Organization of American States, like the United Nations, has not been conceived as a superstate.

The problem is, without doubt, an intricate one. Where is the country of this or any other region that can sincerely present itself as a model of democracy and as an exemplary guardian of human rights? Moreover, assuming that the very originality of democracy rests precisely in its internal constitutional capacity for constant improvement, could anyone, now or in the future, conceive democracy in an unchanging mold which might exclude any peaceful or even revolutionary possibilities of popular changes? Simply as a supposition, let us imagine that, ignoring nonintervention, we might have decided that the Organization of American States would watch over the effective operation of democracy and the actual enjoyment of human rights throughout the entire Western Hemisphere. What would be the immediate consequences of such a grave decision? How would the Organization of American States perform such a mandate?

It is true that most of our republics boast of "democratic" traditions, constitutions, and laws; but if some day we were to accept the policy of intervention *in favor of* democracy and human rights, only deeds would count. And even though a few of our countries tolerate greater liberty than others, or enjoy higher standards of living, we can with complete honesty face the fact that our continent—at least at present—is far from being a continent of democracy. If such is our reality and the practical situation which we must face, what a tremendous task would the Organization of American States have to carry out, year after year, if some day it were asked by an inter-American conference to watch daily over the actual effective practice of democracy and the preservation of human rights. Also, there are other difficulties to be considered.

Under such circumstances, it would not be completely unreasonable even to fear that intervention or inter-American "action" might be used expressly to the detriment of democracy rather than for its encouragement. I insist on this because a large number of well-meaning minds are ready to accept lightly the somewhat vague, but attractive and noble, arguments offered by the respectable champions of "good" interventionism.

Concerning this failure of the Organization of American States and the difficult position in which Mexico is placed, Mr. Jorge Castañeda, former president of the Juridical Commission of the United Nations and now alternate delegate to the United Nations, asserts in his book *Mexico and the International Order* (1956) that

the situation of our country has not been easy. Mexico is one of the countries which has demonstrated the greatest independence and which has been most vigorously opposed to the recent interventionist tendency of Pan-Americanism and to the desire to project it on a worldwide scale. In view of the political attitude now fashionable in the Western Hemisphere, Mexico has usually ended up clearly in the minority when these questions have been debated, particularly in recent times. The experiences of the last two Pan-American Conferences (Washington, 1951, and Caracas, 1954) were especially significant in this respect.

Since it is likely that these tendencies, considered by Mexico to be opposed to her interests and those of Latin America, will become accentuated in the near future, we should ask whether the moment has not arrived for Mexico to proceed with a revision of its Pan-American policy in view of several factors: first, the possibility of Mexico decisively influencing the solution of grave matters diminishes daily, especially when the question is to adopt directives or general trends which are important to the prosecution of extracontinental objectives of the United States; second, when Mexico has as a matter of principle taken a position in opposition to the adoption of measures which it considers to be contrary to the basic purposes of the OAS, it has unfortunately been impossible to avoid giving the impression that there is a serious political antagonism between Mexico and the United States, an impression generally amplified by the mass media, and whose psychological repercussions certainly do not favor good relations between our peoples; third, the participation of Mexico in the Organization of American States has forced it politically to accept dangerous commitments which it obviously basically does not want. Under these circumstances it would seem advisable that Mexico partially withdraw and adopt a more reserved attitude toward the activities and obligations of the Pan-American system. This attitude should be flexible and adaptable to specific circumstances after weighing in each case the seriousness of the possible commitment and the damage which Mexico might suffer by not accepting or disregarding it. As a concrete example of what Mexico's revised attitude might be in relation to certain serious Pan-American commitments we might mention the following: if, as seems possible at the present time, the Inter-American Treaty of Reciprocal Assistance were used, contrary to its intent, to intervene in the internal affairs of the American states, Mexico should seriously consider the advisability of denouncing the treaty in question, and thus freeing itself from the commitments it implies.

In short, at Punta del Este, Mexico clearly pointed out, through its Minister of Foreign Relations, Mr. Manuel Tello, that the convocation of the Eighth Meeting of Consultation lacked a legal foundation. In deference to international law and the Constitution of Mexico he abstained from voting on the resolution which excluded the government of Cuba from the inter-American system for its adherence to Marxism-Leninism.

In view of these sanctions against Cuba, His Holiness Pope John XXIII, with a breadth of vision worthy of a true statesman, gave a lesson of tolerance and respect for international law to officially Catholic leaders and states of the Western Hemisphere when last February 3 [1962], immediately after the end of the Punta del Este Conference, he received the credentials of the new ambassador of Cuba to the Holy See, Mr. Luis Amado Blanco y Fernández, in spite of the incompatibility which exists between the Marxist-Leninist philosophy, which is materialistic, and Catholic philosophy and dogma, which are, on the contrary, spiritualistic.

Was the Minister of Foreign Relations of Brazil, San Tiago Dantas, not absolutely correct when at Punta del Este he affirmed, "The solution does not lie in intervening in Cuba" and "any intervention is alien to the Western Hemisphere"? And was it not absolutely logical for Mr. Vivaldo Lima, president of the Foreign Relations Committee of the Brazilian Congress, to declare in the statement he made in Brasília, "Either Brazil accepts the decision adopted by the majority at Punta del Este and breaks with Cuba, or it withdraws from the Organization of American States"? Can Mexico, Brazil, Chile, Bolivia, and Ecuador continue in the Organization of American States without accepting the decision of the majority? But can we, and should we, align ourselves with this decision which, although that of the majority, nonetheless violates the Charter of the Organization of American States and, in Mexico's case, is contrary to our constitutional system?

The incompatibility we have pointed out between the Charter of the Organization of American States and the behavior of this organization in expelling the Cuban government, thus imposing the most severe and illegal sanction; the present flagrant perversion of the Inter-American Treaty of Reciprocal Assistance, the violation of the principle of nonintervention, until now the very foundation of the inter-American system; the disregard of the most sacred norms of the constitutive Charter of this organization—all these warrant our asking ourselves this question: Is there any point in having Mexico continue to be a member of the Organization of American States? Faced with the necessity and advisability, on the one hand, of having close and good relations with the United States of America, our neighbor to the North and the most powerful nation on earth to which we certainly owe some of our misfortunes but also some of our advantages, and, on the other, faced with the impossibility of having Mexico deny itself, renounce its sovereignty, deny the highest values of its historical tradition in order to align itself with those who without hesitation violate international law, is it not the most natural and logical step for Mexico to leave the Organization of American States? Would there be any point in continuing alone, or almost alone, to defend the most sacred and important principles of international law in this organization which has just failed to recognize the most fundamental and basic of them? Would it not be more useful for Mexico to be, like Canada, the other neighbor of the United States, outside these disputes which cover us with shame and disgrace? Can we, then, without damaging our dignity, accept the sanctions which the majority of the states of this hemisphere have imposed on Cuba, without any reason or right, by breaking diplomatic relations with it and by imposing the most grave and illegal sanction, which is its expulsion? Must we accept, against our express will, against our constitutional system, against even international law of the hemisphere, the decisions of a majority of the countries? Have we any alternative to abandoning the Organization of American States?

On our part we frankly believe that this would be the most juridically consistent path if we take into account that the solidarity of the nations of this hemisphere has already been broken. At any rate, politically and constitutionally, it devolves upon the Ministry of Foreign Relations of Mexico to judge, after taking into account all the elements and factors involved, the advisability of this decision and the proper time for it. What we are not at all in doubt about is that any diplomacy worthy of the name is nothing but putting the principles and the rules of international law into practice and effect. The President of Mexico, Adolfo López Mateos, a descendant of the true liberals and a worthy spiritual heir of those who struggled with toughness and courage to shape the conscience of our Mexico and to defend it both within and outside, will not permit the diplomatic history of the Mexican Revolution, the pure and gallant international conduct of Mexico which has been uninterruptedly sustained in such a masterly manner since the time of Venustiano Carranza —he will not permit, I repeat, this priceless legacy, which is the very *raison d'être* of the fatherland, to be converted into ashes and dust at the hands of any warped diplomat who confuses the managing of ideas with the managing of functions, or the good manners of the gentleman with the servility of the slave, nor will he allow their pusillanimous opinions, which they sometimes try to convert into a thesis, to prevail in the foreign policy of Mexico.

In conclusion, we are certain that President Adolfo López Mateos will uphold the traditional Mexican position, the same position which was honorably supported by the then Minister of Foreign Relations of Mexico, Mr. Luis Padilla Nervo, now Mexican delegate to the United Nations and president of the World Disarmament Commission, and which the latter set forth as follows: *"The political regime and the economic and social organization of nations belong essentially to the domestic jurisdiction of the state; therefore, it cannot be the object of any intervention, direct or indirect, individual or collective, by one or more countries or by the Organization of American States."*

The same thesis was defined thus by another brilliant Minister of Foreign Relations of Mexico, Jaime Torres Bodet, while explaining the meeting and the Charter of Bogotá:

> One singularly sensitive point was that of finding a common ground for agreement regarding the preservation of democracy in America. The question was to build our solidarity on unshakable democratic foundations. And, on the other hand, it was hoped that any intervention in the life of the Western Hemisphere nations would be condemned. As Mexico pointed out when the conference initiated its sessions, democracy should be defended only through democratic measures. To resort to repressive methods or those of ideological censure to preserve democracy would be equivalent to undermining the most respected foundations of our institutions: the freedom of thought, press, and association.

Our certainty that President López Mateos will continue

Mexico's traditional foreign policy has been confirmed by the events of February 14, 1962.

Yesterday, the Council of the Organization of American States met in Washington; its President, Alberto Zuleta Angel from Colombia, officially reported the resolution of Punta del Este, under which Cuba is excluded from the Organization of American States because of its adherence to Marxism-Leninism.

The Cuban representative to the OAS, Ambassador Carlos M. Lechuga, in spite of being refused the floor, insisted on being heard and exclaimed, "We came here to protest against the illegality of the action. We are not interested in remaining."

The Mexican representative, Ambassador Vicente Sánchez Gavito, following faithfully the instructions of President López Mateos' government, confirmed that the interpretation given by Zuleta Angel to the Punta del Este resolution lacked a juridical basis and pointed out that Mexico did not vote for the exclusion of Cuba, since it was neither legal nor just.

Mexico's position, then, continues to be one of traditional respect for international law and justice, to the satisfaction of all Mexicans worthy of the name.

Together with Mexico, the representatives of Brazil, Bolivia, and Ecuador reiterated the attitude they had assumed at Punta del Este when they opposed the expulsion of Cuba. Chile, although pointing out that "The attitude of Chile was established by our Minister of Foreign Affairs at the conference of the Foreign Ministers at Punta del Este" (Chile also opposed the expulsion of Cuba at Punta del Este), accepted, in this instance, the procedure of Zuleta Angel. Argentina, publicly pressured by the country's military, changed the position which it had adopted at Punta del Este, and its representative declared that, "I now accept the decision of the majority of the countries represented at Punta del Este."

On February 3, the President of Argentina, Arturo Frondizi, had stated that the six countries which abstained at Punta del Este had been criticized, but he added, "this powerful group of nations defended above all the juridical rights of the OAS and the basic principles of self-determination and nonintervention" and "we wanted to defend the whole Western Hemisphere from the danger arising from damaging, even in an isolated case, the permanent principles of international law." He went on:

> These juridical reasons are not mere formalities. The entire juridical tradition of civilized humanity rests on the principle that there is no punishment without law and that no one may be judged except under a law in force prior to the indictment. To depart from this fundamental concept is to become involved in the most flagrant arbitrariness. To renounce this principle is equivalent, in human relations, to adopting the law of the jungle. And in international relations it is equivalent to renouncing sovereignty.
>
> Faced with the intrigues and violence of international Communism which threatens our very existence in the Western Hemisphere, we cannot resort to expedient measures which violate international law, the only armor which protects us. Now, they condemn the governments of the six nations solely because at the recent Punta del Este conference they refused to forget the categorical precepts of the legal statutes of the Organization of American States and the basic principles of self-determination and nonintervention.

And Frondizi added, "I will die in the defense of Argentina's dignity."

For our part, we are sure that if, now as in the past, our fatherland should be the only one left defending the law, Mexico will be proud to stand alone.

Revolution and Foreign Policy: Mexico's Experience*

Jorge Castañeda

This study is not intended to cover the events that took place in Mexico, nor in her international relations, during the Revolution. Some of the salient aspects of those relations have been examined in several monographs and, more exhaustively, in a major recent work.[1] It will be more rewarding, rather, to outline the international aims and principles engendered by the internal postulates of the Revolution, and to gauge if, after fifty years, they are still valid, or if, in the light of the new international situation and the present state of the country, a new evaluation of those aims and a restatement of such principles are required.

The international aims of a country are the result of a complex of forces, some, like geography and history, permanent, others, like the changing international picture, transitory. When the action of the constants is particularly strong, the international attitude of a country presents in the course of history a distinct profile and a marked continuity. Thus, in the case of Mexico, its history preceding the Conquest, the centuries under Spanish domination, its nearness to the United States, the different roads followed by the two countries, the nature and limitations of the country's resources, and the very character of the people and the soil have impressed upon its foreign policy certain characteristic and permanent features. Since independence, Mexico's attitude toward the outside world has been cautious and reserved, and

* Reprinted with permission from the *Political Science Quarterly*, 78(3):391–417, Sept., 1963.

its foreign policy essentially defensive. This explains why a special value has been attached to certain international principles in the course of its history and why some international aims have achieved preeminence over others.

I

Mexico emerged into independent life under difficult conditions. The weak economic structure of the country, its lack of social integration, and the ideological split among the leading classes all hampered its first steps and hindered its advance toward the future, in the manner characteristic of new nations. The country's efforts and resources were not utilized for development, but to survive and to preserve its spiritual and physical integrity. The first international loans were earmarked for subsistence itself, and not for development, which may explain why they were obtained on such disadvantageous terms. The domestic upheavals of the first years weakened the country's resistance to North American expansion, and gave rise to innumerable international claims that would become a scourge to the country. Fifteen years after independence, Mexico suffered its first mutilation, and scarcely ten years later it was reduced to half its territory. The succession of internal revolts and foreign interventions, threats, pressures, and invasions seemed endless. Between each episode, new foreign claims accumulated and served as a pretext for the next. Over this tragic period, Mexico was constrained to sign two agreements with the United States (1838 and 1868) for payment of a spate of claims for damages to American citizens that were always excessive, often unjust, and at times fraudulent.[2] Foreigners settled in Mexico benefited from the lack of competition from local capital; yet their governments intervened to protect them against the risks inherent in the political instability of the country, which is a normal consequence of economic backwardness.

The first fifty years of independent life were in the main a sequence of foreign onslaughts. It is not to be wondered that the country's international stand became hermetic, nationalistic, distrustful, and defensive; the "outside world" meant only a source of nameless troubles for the country.

II

International relations became stabilized during the dictatorship of Porfirio Díaz. The order imposed by Díaz during more than thirty years allowed the international situation to settle down, at least insofar as the causes and pretexts for foreign threats were concerned. The French intervention of the 1860's was the last in the series of armed incursions Mexico had to withstand until 1914. During that period, Mexico's northern and southern borders were determined by treaties with Guatemala, Great Britain, and the United States (with the latter, the frontiers of common rivers were defined). A number of treaties of friendship, trade, and navigation were also agreed upon; those with European and Latin American countries included provisions relieving the parties of responsibility for damages caused by civil strife. Mexico participated in the two important peace conferences at The Hague (1899 and 1907) and in the first three Pan-American Conferences of Washington (1899), Mexico City (1902), and Rio de Janeiro (1906). On more than one occasion during this period, Mexico also took part in Central American politics.

The most salient characteristic of the policy of Porfirio Díaz, however, and one that had international repercussions, was his generosity toward foreigners. Convinced that Mexico's progress required the removal of all obstacles to foreign capital, the dictatorship granted concessions for the exploitation of the natural resources of the country and its public services under quasi-colonial conditions. At the end of Díaz' government, the virtual alienation of the national wealth had reached considerable proportions. By 1910, foreigners owned huge agricultural and cattle-breeding latifundia, as well as practically all the mines; they controlled almost all the oil fields and the financial life of the nation, as well as the railroads and foreign trade. In Lower California, for example, three North American concerns owned 78 percent of the territory; the granting of unoccupied lands, mainly to foreigners, covered more than a third of the country. The Mining Code of 1884, upsetting a long tradition, granted the owner of the soil exclusive property over the oil deposits. This provision allowed the great foreign corporations to obtain concessions from the superficiaries by paying nominal rentals and, taking advantage of the ignorance and misery of the indigenous inhabitants, to acquire vast tracts of land on the Gulf Coast at iniquitous prices. But Díaz was even more prodigal with public lands; in 1906 he granted a fifty-year concession to a British citizen, Pearson, for the exploitation rights over all the subsoil of lands under federal jurisdiction in the states of San Luis Potosí, Tamaulipas, Veracruz, Tabasco, Chiapas, and Campeche, in exchange for 10 percent of the product, exempting him at the same time from all import and export duties.

A policy of aid to foreign capital, carried to such extremes, can only be followed at the expense of the essential attributes of sovereignty. The power to legislate, the administration of justice, and the possibility of an independent international position become an empty abstraction when conditioned by such a policy. Thus, the provisions of the Mining Code of 1884 violated an age-old tradition, since oil and other subsoil resources belonged at first to the Spanish Crown and then to the Mexican state; and the Pearson contracts violated the Constitution of 1857, since only Congress was empowered to set taxes by means of general provisions. As far as the administration of justice is concerned, it is common knowledge that foreigners enjoyed privileged status over Mexicans in the Porfirista courts, always eager to ingratiate themselves with aliens and, if need be, willing to obey the orders of an executive determined to favor them. It is no wonder that international claims ebbed during this period, when a docile administration was prepared to satisfy directly the claims of foreigners without stint, and, failing this, to compensate them with new concessions and privileges. It therefore cannot be surprising that this state of affairs became one of the main causes for the Revolution itself.

The stand taken by the government of Porfirio Díaz regarding certain general international problems presents, however, un-expected features. His foreign ministers were not unaware of certain constants in the international policy of Mexico that should guide its attitude in the relations between states. At the three Pan-American and two peace conferences, Mexico con-fronted the United States—sometimes with heat—in defense of a number of principles that were a function of her condition as an underdeveloped nation. She proposed or supported the prin-ciple of equality of rights between foreigners and nationals; the nonresponsibility of the state for damages suffered by foreigners during civil strife or domestic disturbances; the nonrecognition of the validity of territorial conquest; the peaceful settlement of disputes; and the unlawfulness of armed intervention as a means of obtaining payment of public debts (anticipating thus the Drago doctrine). Vallarta and Mariscal ably and effectively defended the country against international claims brought at the time—mostly for acts predating the dictatorship—that had to be settled and paid according to the 1868 Convention; and Vallarta developed the doctrine of the denial of justice in terms that are hard to surpass.

The often wise and patriotic behavior of Mexican representa-tives at international meetings did not succeed, however, in ban-ishing the impression that the government of Díaz adopted a submissive international policy, both as to its dealings with other countries on specific problems and because of its docility toward foreign investors. The experience of this period certainly did not contribute to eradicating the hostile reaction of the Mexican people toward the outside world.

III

Mexico's international conduct varied during the different phases of the Revolution. In order to discover the implication for foreign policy of the Revolution, that phenomenon has to be viewed in all its historic dimensions, from 1910 to, perhaps, 1938. The same constants that gave a certain continuity to Mexico's international policy were present both in the period running from Independence to the end of Díaz' dictatorship, and in that of the Revolution; but at the same time, the international variants, plus the process of transformation, substitution, and juxtaposition of domestic aims, gradually changed the country's international behavior. Few periods are so conducive to an analysis of how far the international policy of a country is conditioned by its domestic aims, and how far, in turn, the possibility of following such a policy is conditioned by external variants.

Although other formulations are possible, the internal aims of the Revolution can be defined, in respect to their international effects and for the purpose of this study, as follows: first, the renewal of political authority; second, agrarian reform; third, the recovery of the country's natural resources; fourth, the labor movement; fifth, the enhancement of national values, primarily cultural ones. This last, rather than an aim or a task, can be understood as a collective state of mind that sometimes was cause and sometimes effect of the other aims; but to the extent that the country became aware of the phenomenon of nationalism, that it was at times deliberately stimulated or oriented and that it produced concrete manifestations, it can properly be included among the aims of the Revolution.

These aims emerged at different times; the relative importance attached to one or the other varied during each phase of the Revolution as did the efforts made to achieve them. All of them had international repercussions, although only the second and third—agrarian reform and the nationalization of natural resources—gave rise not only to distinct international attitudes, but, as will be stressed in due course, to specific international concepts whose projections are felt even today to an extent unforseeable then.

The achievement of the purely political aims of the Revolution provoked serious international incidents. The overthrow of Díaz, the presidency of Madero and his fall, the usurpation of Huerta, the Constitutionalist Revolution and the strife between rival factions that followed, are all episodes in the painful and at times disjointed efforts made by the country to ensure a periodic and institutional renewal of power. These events gave rise to a number of international incidents, such as the occupation of Veracruz, Pershing's expedition, the effort to bring together in the United States the representatives of the rival factions in order to put an end to the civil war, the withholding of recognition as a means of exercising pressure, and the claims for damages suffered by foreigners during the Revolution.

Regarding Pershing's punitive expedition and also the occupation of Veracruz, Mexico invoked in its own defense such traditional principles as respect for the territorial integrity of states. Despite the fact that both these American armed interventions could have benefited Carranza—whose approval was taken for granted by Washington—and despite the fact that the government of the United States contended that these were not hostile acts toward the Mexican people, Carranza insisted, in both cases, on unconditional withdrawal, thus strengthening the principle that all occupation of foreign soil—even if idealistically motivated—constitutes a hostile invasion and a violation of sovereignty. The firm and uncompromising stand of Carranza was, perhaps, a prelude to the instinctive and determined refusal of the Mexican people to allow the setting up of foreign military bases on Mexican territory, even if such an act served a common cause and had the consent of the Mexican government.

The withdrawal from Veracruz and the matter of good offices in 1915 have a great bearing on the international conduct of Mexico. Carranza revealed an exceptional international awareness when he intuitively anticipated the formulation of an international principle—at least in embryonic form—that would have full meaning and force only with the creation of permanent international organizations.

In both cases, the problem arose of taking part in conferences with Latin American nations and the United States where efforts were—or might be—made to deal with Mexico's domestic situation. In the first question, Argentina, Brazil, and Chile offered to mediate in the conflict that had arisen between the United States and Mexico over the occupation of Veracruz. Huerta sent his delegates to the Niagara Falls Conference, and the United States, a party to the dispute, raised the question of the participation of the Carranza delegates as a way of bringing about an agreement between the two camps. In the second question, the United States and a number of Latin American nations sent a collective invitation to the leaders of the rival factions fighting in Mexico to hold a meeting in the United States in order to pacify the country. The participation of those issuing the invitation was intended to contribute to mediation between the rival factions.

Although the aims of both meetings were unobjectionable, and although the results could have helped Carranza (though his delegates did not attend the second conference, the participating countries recognized his as the *de facto* government of the country), he himself contended that a mere international discussion of the matter would "most profoundly harm the independence of the Republic and set the precedent of foreign interference in the settlement of its domestic affairs." This was more than invoking the principle of nonintervention, that is, that all states are forbidden to interfere illegally in another's affairs. Carranza was ahead of his time when he held that the "domestic affairs" of a country were beyond the jurisdiction of any—even collective—international action, *even if it only consisted in examining these matters and not committing a true intervention,* such as the issuance of a peremptory and dictatorial order accompanied by the threat of force. This principle lies at the root of present-day international organizations, and its defense guided Mexico's position at the Conference of Caracas in 1954 and during the recent Consultative Meetings of Santiago and San José. Naturally, the protection of what the Charter of the United Nations now calls "matters essentially within the domestic jurisdiction of States" against international action could not have been presented as a principle at that time, but the essential idea that underlies it inspired Carranza's stand in both cases.

IV

The two most important international principles of the Revolution were not stated as such, nor even conceived of as principles of worldwide validity to be invoked in defense of Mexico; yet both are clearly implicit in Article 27 of the Constitution and are the international projection of the two main goals of the Revolution; namely, the recovery of the country's natural resources and agrarian reform.

The Mining Code of 1884, breaking, as we have seen, with the country's tradition, granted proprietary rights over oil and other mineral subsoil resources to the owner of the land above them. The 1917 Constitution radically amended this legal rule, stating in Article 27 that "In the Nation is vested the *direct* ownership . . . of mineral deposits . . . petroleum and all solid, liquid and gaseous hydrocarbons . . . etc." "Direct ownership" differs in Mexican constitutional law from "eminent ownership," which is exercised by the nation over all land, waters, and things within its boundaries, including those constituting private property.

In other words, the Constitution reclaimed for the nation some of its most valuable natural resources, which by previous laws had been recognized as private property of individuals, the majority of whom were foreigners. The recovery by the nation of the *resource itself* (as opposed to the installations required for its extraction) does not call for compensation, since it is not an expropriation of things that, according to the Constitution, can be privately owned, but rather the *reclaiming* of resources that, by their very nature, are of the direct domain of the nation, and, as such, are inalienable and imprescriptible. Traditional international law recognized only the right of states to expropriate foreign-owned assets, for reasons of public order and subject to the payment of compensation which, in the view of the industrialized nations, should be prompt, adequate, and effective.

The contention of the Mexican Constitution, perhaps novel in some of its aspects, has, with time, gained ground. The underdeveloped countries, convinced that their economic progress must rest on their own use of their own resources, have struggled to obtain international recognition of the general right of all states to reclaim—not merely to expropriate—domain over their natural resources and exercise permanent sovereignty over them. It is only lately, in the United Nations, that this conception has been strengthened and is beginning to crystallize. Due to the concerted efforts of underdeveloped and socialist countries, the Draft Covenant of Human Rights prepared by the Commission of Human Rights included the following principle: "The right of peoples to self-determination shall also include permanent sovereignty over their natural wealth and resources. In no case may a people be deprived of its own means of subsistence on the grounds of any rights that may be claimed by other States."

The General Assembly of the United Nations has still not pronounced itself on this provision of the Draft Covenant, and the highly industrialized countries with investments in the underdeveloped states are opposed to the adoption of such a provision. But even if the efforts to limit its practical application were to be successful, the mere proclamation of the principle as such would contribute to facilitating and speeding up the process of recovery of natural resources undertaken, or to be initiated, by underdeveloped countries.

By completely *reincorporating* in the nation's heritage the resources of its subsoil, without the intermediate step of expropriating them for reasons of public order and subject to compensation for assets which, according to earlier laws, belonged to private persons, the 1917 Constitution anticipated by many years the statement of this novel international stand.

V

Mexico was one of the first countries to undertake an agrarian reform of such wide-scale proportions as considerably to affect important foreign interests. The international justification of the right of all states to carry out an agrarian reform—based on such principles as the subjection of the foreigner to the laws of the land of his residence, the principle of equality of treatment for foreigners and nationals, and, in the last resort, the right of preservation of the state—is no longer challenged. On the other hand, the different ways in which compensation has been made in practice, the awards of international tribunals on the matter, and the opinions of publicists are far from uniform, varying from the suppression of private rural property without indemnity (decree of the Soviet government of October 26, 1917) to the cash purchase of lands at market prices.

The North American viewpoint is that expropriation is internationally tenable only when accompanied by prompt, adequate, and effective indemnity. The contention advanced by the Mexican Revolution, inherent in Article 27 of the Constitution and its laws, is that expropriation can be carried out subject to compensation, in the amount and within time limits and conditions of payment that will not endanger the economic stability of the country and allow the agrarian reform to proceed rapidly and totally.

The constitutions of a number of countries reflect a similar standpoint, especially since World War I. Lately, due to the Cuban agrarian reform, much discussion has taken place regarding the conditions for the international validity of expropriation of the rural holdings of foreigners, and the Mexican stand is gaining adherents. Probably, when a propitious moment arrives for the international codification of these matters—and the underdeveloped countries must seek that moment—the principle to be established should recognize to every state the right to modify foreign interests when organizing the legal regime of property in the way that best serves the purposes of the country, and *that compensation must be proportionate to the economic capacity of the country to pay and subject to such conditions and terms as do not impair its economic and social development.*

The Mexican agrarian reform preceded these new trends in the development of international law. The Constitution of 1917, naturally, did not formulate an international principle, but the provisions of Article 27 and its laws and regulations clearly highlight the meaning of this principle that is now gaining wide acceptance among underdeveloped countries.

VI

The difficult domestic situation a few years later, added to North American pressure expressed in the nonrecognition of the government of Obregón, forced Mexico to postpone in the early

1920's the achievement of two essential aims of the Revolution: agrarian reform and the reclaiming of the oil deposits by the state.

The establishment of international commissions to settle claims for damages caused to foreigners is not, of course, in itself objectionable. But the principles agreed to in the Bucareli settlements of 1923 (the two conventions and the extraofficial pact), according to which the rights of North Americans and the obligations of the Mexican state were to be determined, not only bespeak a relinquishment of the international tenets of the Revolution (implicit in Article 27 of the Constitution), but also a waiving of the right to apply traditional principles of international law that favored Mexico.

Regarding oil, the Bucareli treaties and the laws that followed made nugatory the constitutional provision reincorporating that resource in the nation's patrimony, since Mexico forbore to apply it to American citizens who had acquired private rights over the oil in accordance with laws predating the promulgation of the Constitution. The principles invoked, those of nonretroactivity and of acquired rights, were not apposite, since this was not a case of affecting preexisting juridical acts or situations created pursuant to previous laws. What was at stake was the right of all states to modify the existing legal situation, that is, to legislate for the future. No state is forced to grant its inhabitants—foreigners or nationals—enjoyment in perpetuity of rights that at a certain time are accorded by its legislation. If the United States had followed during the last century the thesis of the Bucareli treaties, it would not have been empowered to liberate the slaves, since their owners could have invoked the principle of "acquired rights" that they possessed in pursuance to previous legislation. Mexico's acceptance of these provisions was devoid of any juridical basis.

Concerning agrarian reform, Mexico yielded the right to indemnify American citizens on time by issuing bonds—thus giving a privileged position vis-á-vis the Mexicans—except in the single case of lands expropriated in order to convert them into communal lands (*ejidos*) and which were less than 1,755 hectares

(4,260 acres). In all other cases—including especially the expropriation of large latifundia—the compensation was to be in cash. The acceptance of this arrangement meant at the time the partial discontinuance of the agrarian reform movement.

Regarding the criteria for the determination of responsibility in damages suffered by American citizens, the extreme was reached of renouncing the application of well-known and accepted principles of international law. Thus, Mexico first of all accepted the *ex gratia* responsibility for acts committed by revolutionary forces, although the negligence of the state was unproven, because "Mexico feels morally bound" to do so, as Article 2 of the Special Convention states, despite the fact that the international rule in force at the time provided the exact opposite; that is, the nonresponsibility of states for such damages unless negligence is proved.

Secondly, Mexico renounced the application of another clear and well-known international rule, according to which the foreigner must exhaust all domestic remedies before his case can be submitted to an international body. Finally, Mexico went along with the strange institution of "allotment," according to which it admitted responsibility for damages suffered by a moral entity of *Mexican nationality*, in which a juridical interest was held by an American subject, even if only as a creditor of it.

It is difficult to assess how far, at that time, the Bucareli agreements inflicted a wound to the national conscience. Their provisions may well not have seemed as serious then as now, when we can judge them in the light of the historical hindsight of the revolutionary process. But the Bucareli treaties put a complete stop to the Revolution. The fact is that the country gave up its aim to reclaim an essential part of the patrimony of the nation and to achieve a more just distribution of the land. Mexico agreed to exempt American citizens from the most important provisions of the Constitution, and allowed the establishment—in their benefit—of a legal regime of exception and privilege. Above all, however, the Bucareli treaties were another link in the endless and humiliating chain of international claims. To give an idea of the unjust and exorbitant nature of the American claims, suffice it to recall the results. Of the total amount claimed according to the 1868 Convention, Mexico had to pay 0.6 percent (discounting the amount of two fraudulent claims that the American government later returned). According to the global agreement arrived at in 1934, for the settlement of claims for damages to American citizens during the Revolution, Mexico paid 2.64 percent of the total claimed. Despite the slight economic importance that these cases represented for the claimant countries, they served as one of the pretexts for the wars of 1836 and 1847 with the United States; they provoked a war with France in 1837; they gave rise to the lengthy French intervention that began in 1862; and they forced a slowdown in the work of the Revolution. No wonder it has been said that the history of Mexico is the history of these international claims.

VII

A favorable international climate, the Good Neighbor Policy, linked to the strengthening of the domestic situation, and, especially, the establishment of a government enjoying solid popular support and determined to fulfill the revolutionary aims, all united in the 1930's in adding luster to Mexico's international position. For the first time in its history, its foreign policy had effects on the international stage, and the country gained well-earned prestige when it firmly and independently defended all the just causes being debated at international meetings.

Mexico joined the League of Nations in 1931, repudiating again, on that occasion, the Monroe Doctrine, as it was incorporated in Article 21 of the Covenant. At the Conferences of Montevideo (1933) and Buenos Aires (1936), Mexico's efforts were decisive in obtaining inter-American acceptance of the principle of nonintervention. During that period, its agents effectively defended Mexico's traditional position and interests in the Mixed Claims Commission, despite the hamstringing by the Bucareli treaties. Their repeated successes gave rise to the global agreement signed with the United States, which had the favorable results already mentioned. In the League of Nations, Mexico supported China in the Manchukuo case; vigorously upheld Abyssinia at the time of the Italian invasion; protested the Austrian *Anschluss* and the occupation of the Sudetenland; and, in particular, most strongly supported the cause of Spain, bitterly criticising the Nonintervention Committee and contending, in contrast to the Western powers' hesitancy, that the Covenant of the League did not allow for neutrality between victim and aggressor. The generous welcome that the country gave thousands of Spanish refugees also contributed to enhancement of the nation's international reputation.

The oil expropriation in 1938 had important international repercussions. Domestically it implied, at last, the fulfillment of one of the important aims of the Revolution; it reestablished the constitutional order—inoperative, in this aspect, for American citizens—and laid the foundations for the erection of a national industry that was, in time, to become the country's most important.

But with the passage of years the nationalization has also had a salutary and widespread effect on the foreign policy of the country. As the expropriation became consolidated internationally, despite strong external pressures to force the country to return the oil firms, Mexico acquired confidence in her capacity to act internationally and to overcome her suspicion regarding the "outside world." Perhaps for the first time since the fall of the Empire of Maximilian, the country was able to withstand foreign pressure sufficiently to achieve an important national goal that seriously affected the interests of the great powers. The new confidence born of the successful nationalization contributed to forming Mexico's viewpoint of the role of foreign investments, that they are primarily a factor that must be added to the country's own efforts. Doubtless, too, this confidence has strengthened Mexico's stand in many a case of negotiating economic questions with the United States. Not without reason, the oil nationalization is considered in Mexico as a symbol of the economic independence of the country.

VIII

At the end of the war, the world lived through a brief period of hope. Trust was placed in the promises of the Atlantic Charter, and it was believed that the creation of the new United Nations would contribute to disarmament and peace. Mexico did not stand aside from this belief. During the San Francisco Conference that was to draw up the Charter of the new organization, it submitted a document entitled "Views of the Foreign Ministry of Mexico on the Dumbarton Oaks Proposals," which contained a number of well-integrated proposals, stamped by marked internationalism. The powers of the General Assembly were to be expanded, as this would enhance the role of the smaller nations; the veto in the Security Council was virtually to disappear; the protection of human rights would be guaranteed by the Charter; the rights and duties of states would be defined in a binding annex to the Charter; the automatic inclusion of international law in the legislation of member states was provided for. Finally, and as a corollary to these proposals, it was submitted that the Charter should eliminate the principle of domestic jurisdiction as a limitation to the organization's action if any matter—even though internal—could constitute or create "a situation likely to provoke international friction."

However, despite a few contrary signs in the public opinion of the period, the San Francisco Conference saw a powerful recrudescence of nationalism with a concomitant revival of state sovereignty. The principal great powers refused to endow the organization with sufficient power to act without let or hindrance, by failing to renounce certain aspects of their sovereignty, and a number of the Mexican proposals were rejected. Soon enough the reality of the Cold War and the tensions and dangers generated in the American continent forced Mexico to return to its original traditional position. The unconditional application of the sister principles of nonintervention and respect for the domestic jurisdiction of states on the part of international organizations have become the cornerstone of Mexican foreign policy in the postwar period.

IX

Fifty years after the Revolution, what is the international outlook of the country? What are the international principles, aims, tenets, and attitudes most in keeping with the present situation of Mexico?

If we consider the problem from the vantage point of hindsight, we will realize that some of the domestic aims of the Revolution have been duly achieved; the political stability of the country and the periodic and institutional renewal of its government are assured. Some have been partially fulfilled, such as the agrarian reform and the reclaiming of the natural resources of the country. What is still to be done in these fields will not give rise to the same international problems as those raised forty years ago, among other reasons, because of the greater economic capacity of the country and because important international precedents have been set—in some cases, with Mexico's assistance. Nationalism itself, as an end, presents a very different picture in a country that is socially, economically, and politically much more integrated than it was fifty years ago. The consistent firmness of Mexico's international policy since the 1930's is, in itself, a factor that will have its bearing on the future conduct of the country. Mexico has become accustomed to acting with a certain confidence, aplomb, and serenity, which were inconceivable when its immediate past was torn with memories of interventions, submission, and humiliating defeats. That attitude and the international prestige that Mexico has won have resulted in placing its relations, especially with the United States, on a footing of greater respect and equality. Thus, the effect of an earlier stand has become a new premise for the future foreign policy of Mexico.

As is very often the case in such historical phenomena, the very revolutionary process has given rise to new aims and tasks. Industrialization, whose development could not be imagined without the social foundations laid by the Revolution, is today one of the first aspirations of the nation. In order to succeed, Mexico must obtain considerable technical and financial resources, but this, in turn, presupposes a new international viewpoint, in keeping with the circumstances obtaining and with the complex problems of international cooperation.

Finally, the new lineup of power in the world will also exert a decisive influence on future foreign policy. The outstanding characteristic of the postwar period is the bipolarity of world power. Although this trend is becoming even more accentuated in the military field, the almost universal conviction that a new world war can be avoided—since it would be suicidal for mankind—has, paradoxically, allowed the emergence on the political level of relatively independent positions. The imminent danger of war is no longer a valid reason for forcing the small powers into docility. The nuclear balance has indirectly and gradually eroded the borders of the spheres of influence.

Politically—and economically—it would be mistaken to assert that there are only two power blocs. The singleness of purpose of the underdeveloped countries and their overwhelming desire to raise the standard of living of their people at any cost are in themselves factors that have radically redrawn the picture of international affairs. The almost exclusively bilateral nature of the relations of the weak countries with stronger nations is no longer as absolute as it was fifty years ago. The existence of international organizations makes possible the relatively easy marshaling of world public opinion on the side of a weak country. At least in the Western world, the small nation is not totally at the mercy of a powerful protector, as it was in the past. It is interesting to note how many of the conflicts that have been brought before the United Nations, although they reflect the antagonism of the two great blocs, very often arise around the relations between a great power and a small nation of the same "camp."

A country like Mexico has at its disposal today a much wider choice of effective political resources and instruments of defense than at the time of the Revolution. Its traditional concept of the "outside world" as a source of threats and irremediable ills, from which no good could be expected, has had to be brought up to date to meet the new international situation and the new needs of the country.

X

Mexico's accelerated economic and social development requires that she participate actively in all aspects of international life. The industrialization and modernization of agriculture cannot be completed under present circumstances without an advanced technology which the country does not as yet possess. In order to obtain the financial resources that development requires, Mexico will have to diversify and increase the volume of its foreign trade, refine its foreign private investment policies, and, although the reason may not be obvious at first sight, increase its participation in the international political bodies. Postwar experience eloquently confirms the fact that the international standing of a country, the independence of its attitudes, and the consistency of its position do more to attract to it the international financial means it requires, under favorable conditions, than any obsequiousness. It is only through its daily action, its perseverance, that the international prestige of a country can be strengthened. In a word, because of the level it has now reached in its internal evolution, it has become imperative for Mexico to deliberately assume a more active role in the international field.

The postwar attitude of Mexico toward the outside world is still, however, one of mistrust and partial disinterest, and its foreign policy is mostly defensive and anti-interventionist. Until the inception of the present administration, when the international outlook of the country began gradually to change, Mexico's participation in the discussion of world political and economic problems has been, generally speaking, reserved, cautious, and mainly defensive, excepting a few cases like the Conferences of San Francisco (1945) and Bogotá (1948), which gave birth to new international organizations, when Mexico presented important long-range proposals.

In the economic field, the most promising moves, both to increase the flow of public resources for the development of Latin American nations and to create a free trade zone for their economic integration, did not originate in Mexico, but in South

America. Despite an obvious and urgent need, a policy consistent with the expansion and diversification of our foreign trade was not applied for many years. Some facets of our immigration policy are also not suited for a country that needs foreign experts; for a number of years during the 1950's, naturalization proceedings came almost to a standstill, and Mexican nationality was granted in but few cases.

In the political field, Mexico's representatives have often firmly and ably upheld its anti-interventionist stand and the principles that traditionally underlay its foreign policy. But in general international political questions—where the interests of Mexico were not directly affected—Mexico's contribution was rather limited. Aside from a few brilliant initiatives in the United Nations that were more a reflection of its main spokesman's personality than a result of deliberate governmental policy, Mexico placed itself at a cautious distance from world problems. Since 1946, it has not participated in the work of the Security Council of the United Nations; on the other hand, countries like Ecuador, Cuba, Brazil, Argentina, and Colombia have been elected twice and even three times for periods of two years each. This deliberate policy of withdrawal was due to a desire not to become involved in the thorny questions that the Council examines and that do not touch Mexico directly. The need to take decisions on such delicate problems carries with it certain risks and can give rise to domestic and international difficulties; but it is not less true that a country pursuing an independent policy—without overlooking or jeopardizing its clear position within the Western camp—could have done constructive work by sponsoring conciliatory and just proposals. Few places and tasks are as propitious for the establishment or strengthening of the international prestige of a country.

Nor can much be made of Mexican activity in the bilateral field during this period. Until very recently, the successive administrations made no great effort to assert a true political and cultural Mexican presence in Latin America or even in Central America, to say nothing of Mexican neglect in seeking close political collaboration with Latin American countries of similar political ideology and government. Relations with the newly emerged African and Asian states have been very slight, despite their growing importance in the international arena and the fact that—at least in some aspects—their aspirations and problems are similar to those of Mexico and could lead to analogous stands on some political matters and on certain international economic policies. Finally, it is of interest to observe that, barring a few cases of exceptionally important embassies, Mexico's usual diplomatic missions are made up of two—and at the most three—officials. The percentage of the budget earmarked for international relations is less than 1.2 percent, and if we discount contributions to international organizations, Mexico allocates less than 0.9 percent of the budget to the functioning of the Ministry of Foreign Relations and the Foreign Service. This is a low percentage even for a small country.

One of the fields that has been most seriously affected by this dearth of foreign contacts is that of technology, especially in the public sector. It is no rare occurrence that techniques, methods, and formulas known for years in countries no more advanced than Mexico are inexplicably unused in Mexico, or that their application is delayed for a long time. This is very often due not to the ignorance of Mexican scientists or technicians, but to politico-bureaucratic decisions taken by officials who misunderstand nationalism, and, especially, to a tendency to exaggerate the peculiar character of Mexican problems. This lamentable trend is rather general in the administration, particularly in those departments that traditionally maintain few outside contacts.

The development of nuclear energy in Mexico illustrates the degree to which the lack of international aid can slow down the achievement of an important domestic program. Because of the high cost of scientific and technological investigation and the considerable progress made by other countries in this field, it is almost inconceivable for a country like Mexico to undertake a serious program of nuclear development without vast international cooperation. To do otherwise would be to condemn the country to greater backwardness and to the squandering of great resources. Yet Mexico has not even begun to set afoot the formulation of a plan to obtain considerable international assistance in this field. The damage was quickly seen. While Argentina, Brazil, and Venezuela have experimental reactors in operation, Mexico has limited itself to extracting uranium-bearing minerals and sending a few—very few—scholarship-winners abroad. It has not even begun the drawing up of a national inventory of minerals with nuclear applicability. The use of radioisotopes in Mexican industry and agriculture is hardly in its infancy, although these techniques have been in use in other countries for years. It is not difficult to come to the conclusion that excessive caution in the use of international assistance—politically as well as scientifically—has had negative effects in the development of these most promising activities. Although in the past the assistance available could be only of a bilateral nature and was accompanied by difficult—though not insurmountable—political problems, the creation of the International Atomic Energy Agency has made it easier to obtain technical resources under acceptable conditions.

XI

The present administration has intensified the country's international activity. The visits of President Lopez Mateos to the United States and Canada, as well as to a number of Latin American countries, point to a new awareness of the importance of international relations in the life of Mexico. The visits to the Latin American countries—the first in history by a Mexican President—give proof, to a certain extent, of the existence of a new aim in foreign policy, the strengthening of political and economic ties with Latin America. The recent visits to Europe and Asia of parliamentary missions also highlight the new importance that the country attributes to international affairs. The now frequent trade missions to many countries show at last a serious effort to achieve diversification of foreign trade. The new and basic aim of Mexican international policy—to speed up the economic development of the country by the use of vast international assistance—is also beginning to take shape. Financial and technical cooperation of European countries in the diversification and expansion of the petroleum industry and in the construction of the large Infiernillo Dam, for instance, is a promising sign of these new tendencies.

The achievement of this end, which daily becomes more important due to the present level of industrial development, does not call for a revision of the basic aims of Mexican foreign policy, but for the introduction of new modalities and the intensification of some activities. Thus, it might be desirable to draw up a national program to send great numbers of trainees in selected fields to foreign countries, perhaps even assuming all the cost. Mexico must increase its participation both in the Expanded Program of Technical Assistance of the United Nations and in the Organization's Special Fund. It must strengthen its efforts—jointly with other states having similar interests—in order to increase the availability of resources from international credit institutions and to liberalize their conditions. In exceptional circumstances, it may even have to overcome its natural dislike for all forms of international interference and surveillance. Thus, for example, without its being necessarily considered as a form of interference, the Statute of the International Atomic Energy Agency—to which Mexico subscribed—contemplates international safeguards for the Agency to supply certain types of assistance.

Another basic objective of present foreign policy is to establish closer political, economic, and cultural ties with Latin America. Generally speaking, Mexico's Latin American policy has developed within the official framework of Pan-Americanism, although Latin America is Mexico's true and natural sphere. Pan-Americanism has contributed to facilitating relations between the countries of Latin America and the United States, and between Latin America as a whole and that country, at least insofar as those relations have become institutionalized and the unilateral action of the United States has been toned down. But Pan-Americanism has not proved to be the best institutional framework for the creation of the indispensable political and economic integration of the countries of Latin America themselves. As a politico-juridical instrument, it does not reflect the community of problems, needs, and aspirations of Latin American peoples on the political, economic, and cultural levels. Latin America's common interests, primarily its economic ones, are very often at variance with those of the United States, although the economy of Latin America and that of the United States may be complementary.

Reality is beginning to impose itself on a somewhat inapt and, to a certain extent, artificial structure. The Latin American Free Trade Association, set up in 1960 outside the Organization of American States, reflects the existence of economic interests common to and exclusive of the countries of Latin America. In time it may become the first step toward a Latin American economic community. For the time being, the obstacles in the way of greater political integration of Latin American countries are very great; but there is at least a glimpse of a trend to examine, purely within the context of Latin America, certain common problems, such as, for example, disarmament. As President Lopez Mateos stressed in his speech to the Peruvian Congress—before him, Presidents Alessandri of Chile and Prado of Peru made the same point—this problem takes on certain peculiarities in Latin America, different from its universal features, which warrant specific Latin American treatment. The smaller percentage of votes that these countries command in the United Nations at present (it was almost 40 percent of the membership in 1946, as compared with 20 percent at the end of the General Assembly Session of 1960), may perhaps in time encourage closer political collaboration among Latin American nations in order to increase their capacity to influence the decisions of the organization.

The practical measures that Mexico could adopt at present to contribute to Latin American unity are few, but not devoid of importance. It should vigorously support the work and development of the free trade zone now in operation, even if the immediate benefits are not apparent. It should also take full advantage of any opportunity to examine common political problems from the Latin American standpoint, within or without the international organizations. Furthermore, Mexico should increase its diplomatic activities in each of the Latin American countries, make greater efforts to widen cultural exchanges with them, and seek the coordination of its policies, or even, when appropriate, a closer political collaboration with the liberal, democratic, and like-minded countries in the region.

XII

Another factor that may have a decisive bearing on Mexican foreign policy is the future conduct of the United States, not only concerning Mexico, but also toward all the other countries of Latin America. Lately, bilateral relations with the United States have been good, and it is to be hoped and presumed that they will continue to improve. But anything that may occur between the United States and the other countries of Latin America cannot, in the future, be alien to us. Latin American problems have inevitably become essential elements in Mexican foreign affairs.

Recent events in Cuba point to the fact that the day is not far distant when profound social transformations will take place in various countries of the hemisphere, and they will, naturally, considerably affect North American interests. The United States' position vis-à-vis those revolutions will decisively color Mexican relations with that country. To a certain extent, these are problems outside Mexican control; the attitude of the United States will depend to a certain extent on the world situation and on domestic factors in the country itself. However, the constructive influence that can be wielded by a country like Mexico, that went through similar experiences in the past, might have a certain bearing on the solutions.

It is difficult to forecast what United States policy will be toward Latin America. Since the days of President Truman and until the inception of the present administration, its Latin American policy has been markedly negative and conservative. Its sole aims seemed to be to protect North American investments and obtain the submissive alignment of the countries in the anti-Communist camp. In order to insure both ends, the United States did not hesitate to support hated dictatorships. What was worse, the United States, to all intents and purposes, supported precisely those extremely retrograde Latin American groups that opposed any change in societies that were often badly in need of it. The United States showed for a long time, for example, an utter lack of understanding of the question of economic development, repeating *ad nauseam* that the magic formula was to "offer a propitious climate" to North American private investment. One wondered at times if the United States were not more eagerly seeking the servile obedience of their natural allies than their strength and prosperity.

Lately, the United States has withdrawn support from Latin American dictators. This highly desirable and oft-expected measure does not, however, get to the root of the problem. The basic problem today is the United States' stand regarding the need both to build the economy on solid national foundations and radically to modify the social structure of many Latin American countries. An important, if not the only decisive, factor for this end is the granting of intergovernmental loans on favorable terms, and, concurrently, acceptance of the inevitable and essential role of state intervention in the economic life of Latin American countries. Private investments also will play an important part, but new formulas will have to be devised in order to avoid the creation of an exaggerated dependence on these investments; this was the case in Cuba, where the economy was unbalanced, vitiating the social life of the country and inflaming anti-American feelings. But most important is the tolerance and sympathy —in a word, the true support—that the United States is prepared to give the nationalistic social revolutions that will probably take place in Latin America, as they did in 1910 in Mexico and in the initial phase of Cuba's revolution in 1959.

Recently the Alliance for Progress has been launched. This important and far-reaching program will no doubt have a great impact in the economic development of Latin America through the capital assistance that will be made available. But, potentially, the political and social effects of the Alliance for Progress could be even more important.

As is well known, the preconditions envisaged for assistance under the program are tax and agrarian reform; and rightly so, if the help is to be effective. But the social groups and classes which exert political power in Latin America, and which benefit from a frequently archaic and quasi-feudal structure of society, will not by themselves perform the radical changes which are needed, for these would mean the end of their privileged position. A significant degree of social justice cannot be promoted rapidly in Latin America, under present circumstances, without drastic changes in the distribution of wealth and, therefore, also of political power; and these changes will not be achieved without a struggle, because they will be at the expense of the vested interests of a privileged and powerful minority.

That is why revolutionary ferment is, or will soon be, the strongest force in Latin America. To succeed in the long run, the Alliance for Progress should not be conceived as a substitute for, but rather as a complement to, revolution, using this word in its broadest sense, to mean either violent or peaceful, but in any case, swift and radical, change where present conditions are intolerable.

Of course, the main stimulus to achieve the required far-reaching changes will have to be provided by the Latin American peoples themselves, with their own means, through normal political action, where possible, or through revolutionary action. But the reaction of the United States to these efforts could be decisive. Within the frame of the Alliance for Progress or through parallel action, the United States could contribute greatly, without actual intervention, to the success of these revolutionary trends, which, at least initially, will probably seek only purely national goals.

Among other things, the United States should not oppose, but should rather encourage, significant agrarian reform, whether or not it affects the interests of its citizens, even so far as to contribute to its financing. It should tolerate the nationalization of certain basic natural resources and public services at present owned by its nationals, agreeing to compensation under terms and conditions that will not disjoint the economic life of the country. It should undertake a program of vast public loans that will allow governments to exploit natural resources, provide adequately for essential public services, and strengthen their economies, even if this departs somewhat from the American conception of free enterprise and means much more governmental intervention in the economies of these countries than the United States is willing to tolerate at home. It should encourage and assist the economic integration of Latin America. It should neither hinder nor corrupt workers' movements; and, above all, it should cease to give moral and material aid to reactionary forces, causes, and political parties. Instead, it should establish closer and meaningful contacts with the intellectual circles of these countries, which generally represent leftist tendencies, as well as with other progressive groups. To sum up, the United States should envisage and encourage in Latin America what the Italians graphically call, though in a different context, an *apertura a sinistra*.

It may be argued that such a program for the United States would be paradoxical, and its Latin American policy of the last fifteen years would bear out such an assertion. More than once, however, the United States has given proof of its ability to adapt to changed circumstances. The reversal of its policy toward India, the United Arab Republic, and other countries—a policy which had been based on the idea that neutrality was immoral and that a neutral state was necessarily a member of the "other camp"—and the improvement which has been noted in the relations with those countries since that attitude was discarded are a good example of that power of adaptation. The change of attitude vis-à-vis Latin America will have to be no less significant if serious dangers are to be avoided.

A North American policy that lacks understanding of Latin America would have grave domestic and international consequences for Mexico and influence its foreign policy in a manner which is now difficult to foresee. As I have said earlier, these developments are outside Mexican control, though Mexico's position could have some importance in future relations between the United States and Latin America. The Mexican Revolution, seen as an international experience, places Mexico in an ideal situation to understand, explain, and bring together differing views. But the mediating function naturally presupposes a high moral authority in the one fulfilling it; and the best, if not the only, way of maintaining Mexico's international prestige and authority is to defend firmly and perseveringly the basic principles underlying her foreign policy, placing them above circumstantial considerations of temporary value.

NOTES

1. Isidro Fabela, *La Historia Diplomática de la Revolución Mexicana,* 2 vols. (Mexico, 1958–1959).
2. Fabela, 19.

Section III

The Foreign Policy of Brazil

Introduction

Any discussion of the foreign policy of Brazil has to begin with some reference to the nation's geographic rank in the world. Brazil is by far the largest country in Latin America, both in terms of territory and population. With an area of 3,287,204 square miles (larger than the continental United States), an estimated population of more than 85 million heavily concentrated in the coastal area, and a highly industrialized sector in the southern part of the country, Brazil possesses many of the elements necessary for playing an important role in international politics. But the country also has significant drawbacks which may help to explain why it has not played such a role: a relatively low level of living, illustrated by a per capita income variously estimated to be between 220 and 340 dollars per year, which is compounded by a highly uneven distribution of wealth within the social structure and the country. The contrast between the relatively wealthy, industrialized, and more highly integrated south and the poverty-stricken Northeast is even more striking than regional statistics proclaim. A relatively low level of participation in politics and a lack of legitimacy further detract from the effectiveness of Brazil's foreign policy.

Because of the natural endowments of the country, Brazilian intellectuals have shown a greater inclination to study and discuss their country's role in the world than their Hispanic-American counterparts. Evidence of this is the greater variety of materials available on this subject, as demonstrated by the selections included in this section. The historical background has been ably discussed by Professors Burns and Rodrigues, and very little can be added here, but perhaps it could be pointed out that the traditional foreign policy of Brazil as structured by Rio Branco, by emphasizing a close relationship with the United States and a total dedication to the inter-American system, put

169

this country on a natural conflictive course with Argentina (see Section IV). It must be said, however, that Brazilian policy makers and political leaders do not appear to have been or to be now as obsessed with matching every Argentine foreign policy move as are many Argentines in regard to Brazil. This characteristic of Brazil's foreign policy is brought out in the article written by Professor Bastian Pinto.

The traditional foreign policy of commitment to the United States and the inter-American system was violently broken during the administrations of Presidents Quadros and Goulart. The former put into practice a foreign policy of the "independent" variety, which had been outlined and sponsored for some years by the nationalist intellectuals known as O Grupo Itatiaia,[1] which under the leadership of the distinguished political scientist Helio Jaguaribe created in 1955 the Instituto Superior de Estudos Brasileiros.[2] This independent foreign policy, outlined in the article written by President Quadros, was articulated and carried out by Foreign Ministers San Tiago Dantas and Arinos de Melo Franco. According to the former, this foreign policy has as its main objectives (1) economic independence and development through Brazilian control of the national economy and (2) the control of external factors so as to make it possible to reconcile a representative democracy with the social reforms intended to eliminate the unequal distribution of rewards between classes and groups. Specific steps were to include reestablishment of diplomatic relations with the Soviet Union, opposition to the isolation of the Castro regime, a noncommitted role at the Geneva disarmament talks, an anticolonial position at the United Nations, broadening of foreign markets in Latin America and the Socialist bloc, and total Brazilian control over development plans and foreign assistance.[3] It was emphasized that the new Brazilian position was neither neutralism nor an imitation of Perón's "third position." Its sponsors made clear that Brazil did not belong to any bloc, not even to the neutralist bloc.

The source of this nationalist reaction to Brazil's traditional foreign policy may be traced back to the results of the country's policy during World War II. Brazil did not hesitate to follow the leadership of the United States in declaring war on the Axis powers and even contributed a full division of ground troops which distinguished themselves in the Italian campaign. It also granted air and naval bases to the Allied forces located primarily in the northeastern part of the country. In exchange for its contribution, Brazil received some weapons under the Lend-Lease program and vague promises to share in the benefits of eventual victory. Argentina, on the other hand, refused to join the Allies until the last minute, made no contribution to their war effort, and continued its international trading activities as long as it was feasible to do so. When the war came to an end, Brazil did not receive the sizable assistance many of its leaders had expected; in fact, its position vis-à-vis Argentina deteriorated significantly because the latter had accumulated a favorable balance in its trade with the Allies and particularly with Great Britain. This surplus made it possible for Argentina to purchase many of the items that Brazil had expected but did not receive. Those Brazilian intellectuals engaged in the analysis of foreign affairs could not ignore the heavy purchases of military equipment made by the Perón regime, mainly in Great Britain after the end of the war, utilizing the favorable balances accumulated during the conflict. These purchases, which included tanks and jet planes, more than compensated for the matériel received by Brazil under the Lend-Lease program; in reality, Argentine purchases upset in its favor the military equilibrium between the two countries. The United States, occupied with Europe, was unwilling or unable to do anything about this development; these nationalist intellectuals could not avoid coming to the conclusion that Brazil's traditional foreign policy had failed.

The executors of this independent foreign policy made some bold moves, both within Brazil and on the international scene. Quadros opened the ranks of the Brazilian foreign service (perhaps the most professional one in Latin America) to Negroes and assigned them almost exclusively to the African states. Brazilian representatives before the United Nations joined the anticolonial majority and even voted against Portugal, thereby to modify a relationship which had existed for more than 140 years;

they also favored the admission of Communist China to the United Nations, at the same time that Brazilian diplomats made contacts with the Chinese and trade missions were exchanged (the rationale for these moves is outlined in Mendes Viana's article). In the Latin American area the Uruguayana agreement between Quadros and Frondizi clearly was directed at the creation of a Latin American bloc intended to counterbalance United States leadership; it is interesting to note that this move had been recommended by Jaguaribe and reiterated by Dantas.[4] One observer wrote that in 1961

> The departures in policy won wide acceptance almost at once, confirming the broad appeal in Brazil of a line strongly affirmative of national sovereignty. These moves met with general approval even before it became clear that they would not jeopardize the country's chances for much needed help from abroad. Apparently, as nationalist thinkers had been saying all along, the firmer and more independent Brazil's position on international issues, the greater the disposition of creditor nations to accommodate new demands.[5]

The resignation of Jânio Quadros from the presidency a few months after he had taken power and the process whereby Vice-President Goulart succeeded him appeared to have damaged the effectiveness of the independent foreign policy. Evidently, Goulart was suspected by a number of influential power elites, and the conduct of foreign relations became a victim of the powerful opposition which ended his term as president by the 1964 coup d'etat. Whatever the direct role of external factors may have been in this episode, it is apparent that the United States was highly satisfied with the event, as evidenced by the letter addressed by President Johnson to the coup leaders and by the numerous pronouncements of the American Ambassador to Brazil, Lincoln Gordon. As Professor Skidmore put it,

> The Brazilian government began, after April 1, 1964, to enjoy much fuller cooperation from the United States in receiving economic and financial assistance. At the same time, *the Castelo Branco government adopted an unequivocally pro-American policy.* Brazil became an enthusiastic supporter of the intervention in the

Dominican Republic in April, 1965, and contributed a military force to the OAS peace-keeping operation there. . . . The total effect of the Brazilian change in foreign policy was to repudiate the "independent" foreign policy of the Quadros-Goulart period and to implement instead a "pro-Western" philosophy that had been spelled out in the courses and lectures of the Higher War College.[6]

The foreign policy of the military regime which followed Goulart in 1964 has been, in reality, a return to the essential principles of Brazil's traditional policy, adjusted to satisfy new requirements such as the creation of a permanent inter-American military force which the military strongly supported. The articles by Professors Dubnic and Bóer outline and explain the essential aspects of this course of action which, with a few minor modifications, has been taken up by the present administration of General Costa e Silva. Once more Brazil's apparent hope is that the United States will recognize it as the great power of South America and will act through it in dealing with the countries of the region. Such a scheme would in fact create a "subsphere of influence" assigned to Brazil within the Inter-American system and would be reflected in substantial economic assistance and privileged trade arrangements.[7]

It may be too early to pronounce this return to Brazil's traditional foreign policy a failure, although it is quite clear that so far it has not produced the results publicly predicted by the military government. Nevertheless, it should be remembered that a policy, almost any policy, usually benefits some groups and damages others. The independent foreign policy appeared to have widespread popular support, at least during the Quadros administration. Some people suspected that it was in fact a smokescreen to cover up unpalatable domestic measures which Quadros felt he had to undertake.[8] It is possible, however, that if positive results do not bring about greater support for the present course, as well as for the government, those now in power may be forced to veer in the direction of the Quadros-Goulart period and to go even beyond the limits recognized by the articulators of the independent foreign policy.

NOTES

1. Literally, "the Itatiaia Group"; the name refers to Itatiaia Park, where the members used to meet. See Frank Bonilla, "A National Ideology for Development: Brazil," in Kalman H. Silvert (ed.), *Expectant Peoples; Nationalism and Development* (New York: Random House, 1963), pp. 232–64.

2. Literally, "Institute of Higher Brazilian Studies." It became a research center within the Federal Ministry of Education. The Institute published some of the most important expressions of nationalist opinion, such as Helio Jaguaribe, *O Nacionalismo na Atualidade Brasileira* (Rio de Janeiro: Instituto Superior de Estudos Brasileiros, 1958).

3. These views are presented in San Tiago Dantas, *Política Externa Independente* (Rio de Janeiro: Editora Civilização Brasileira S.A., 1962), *passim*.

4. Jaguaribe, *op. cit.*, p. 279; Dantas, *op. cit.*, p. 21.

5. Bonilla, *op. cit.*, pp. 250–1.

6. Thomas E. Skidmore, *Politics in Brazil, 1930–1964: An Experiment in Democracy* (New York: Oxford University Press, 1967), p. 329.

7. This objective is recognized in Jayme Azevedo Rodrigues, "A Diplomacia Brasileira e a 'Crise' do Sistema Interamericano," *Política Externa Independente*, 1:157–64 (May, 1965).

8. Data indicating broad popular support for the independent foreign policy in 1960–1961 can be found in Lloyd A. Free, *Some Implications of the Political Psychology of Brazilians* (Princeton: Institute for International Social Research, 1961), *passim*. The idea of the independent policy as a cover is presented by Skidmore, *op. cit.*, pp. 199–200.

Tradition and Variation in Brazilian Foreign Policy*

E. Bradford Burns

I

Mounting anxieties, frustrations, and fears in Brazil effected a change of government by military force at the end of March of 1964. President João Goulart fled to an Uruguayan exile. Congress, urged by the military, conferred supreme executive power on Marshal Humberto Castelo Branco. Many other sweeping changes followed. None was more complete than the about-face taken in foreign policy.

Castelo Branco spoke out early and unequivocally in his regime in favor of a return to more traditional policies. The graduation exercise of the foreign service school, the Instituto Rio-Branco, on July 31, 1964, provided the propitious place and moment for him to outline the foreign policy goals of his government.[1] He paid homage to the ideals consecrated by tradition: world peace, disarmament, self-determination, nonintervention, and anticolonialism. Moving into the more pragmatic realm of national interests, the president emphasized that his government's foreign policy aimed to increase national power through social and economic development. A practical way to realize that goal would be through trade. Brazil was ready to trade with anyone, even with the East so long as such commerce "did not serve as the vehicle for unacceptable influences." In another part

* Reprinted by special permission from the *Journal of Inter-American Studies*, 9:195–212, Apr., 1967. Copyright © by the University of Miami Press.

of his address, the President let it be known in unmistakably clear terms that Brazil identified with the Western world in its struggle to protect its values threatened by the Soviet sphere. He committed Brazil to closer Pan-American relations and especially to a firmer friendship with the United States. Thus, this policy, at least according to its author, was a return to more established patterns of international behavior. For that reason, Castelo Branco concluded for the young diplomats present that the nation's exterior policy followed the dictums enunciated by the founder of its modern foreign policy, the Baron of Rio-Branco. He advised, "In order to worthily represent Brazil abroad, you need to have nothing more before you than the teachings of Rio-Branco."

II

Brazilians of the twentieth century have regarded those teachings as sacrosanct. The influence of Rio-Branco on diplomacy has been profound. In fact, to understand the diplomacy of the largest Latin American nation during this century it is essential to know that statesman and to understand his work. The Baron of Rio-Branco assumed the portfolio of foreign relations in 1902 and held it for a Latin American record of ten years, during the administrations of four different presidents, until his death in 1912 at the age of sixty-seven. In every respect his long administration was a period of transition, the pivotal point upon which modern foreign policy turned.

His first accomplishment was to settle the four-hundred-year-old boundary disputes between Spanish-speaking and Portuguese-speaking South America by definitively delineating the frontiers. Since remote colonial times, the vague and extensive frontiers had preoccupied Brazil. In the years between discovery, 1500, and the foundation of Belém at the mouth of the Amazon River, 1616, the Luso-Brazilians had conquered the long coastline between the equator and 26° south latitude. In so doing, they expelled foreign interlopers from those domains. With the coast secured, the missionaries, cattlemen, Indian slave hunters, and mining prospectors fanned out into the interior, eventually reaching the foothills of the Andes. Their rapid and deep penetration into the heartland of South America is the most epic chapter of Brazilian history. The Spaniards, more stationary in their mining centers high in the Andes, realized too late that they had forfeited half of the continent to the more restless Luso-Brazilians. In a rare moment of fraternal Iberian sentiment, they agreed in the Treaty of Madrid, 1750, to the principle of *uti possidetis*, thereby conceding to Brazil a frontier similar in its broad outlines to the modern one. The years after 1750 were spent trying to work out the details as to precisely where the boundaries should fall. The newly emergent states of South America inherited that search.

The able diplomats of the Empire (1822–1889) devoted most of their energy to those boundary problems. Their work was facilitated by a strong continuity of policy, a characteristic noticeably absent in the neighboring Spanish American republics. They slowly prepared the necessary groundwork upon which future agreements were to be made, always insisting on the principle of *uti possidetis*, which, needless to say, favored the Empire's claims. Rio-Branco continued in the best traditions of the Empire to attempt to come to boundary agreements with the neighbors. Thanks to his intimate knowledge of South American history and geography and to considerable patience and skill, he won a series of brilliant victories beginning with the arbitration award of the Missions territory made by President Grover Cleveland in 1895 and ending with the agreement with Peru in 1909. The "Golden Chancellor" delineated nearly nine thousand miles of frontier and bloodlessly won for his country approximately 342,000 square miles of territory, an area larger than France. In that way, he brought to a successful and peaceful conclusion more than four centuries of expansion and consolidation, as well as concern with just and legal recognition of that expansion and consolidation. An era in diplomatic history ended.

The Baron's second accomplishment during his long tenure was to set the course for a new foreign policy. Under his direction, Brazil lifted its eyes from the more limited horizons of the

frontiers to the world beyond. At peace with its neighbors, enjoying unprecedented prosperity at home thanks to increasing
coffee sales abroad, Brazil was ready to play a new role on a larger
international stage. Rio-Branco's new foreign policy for the
nation consisted of four related goals.

First, he sought to increase national prestige abroad. The newly
renovated and augmented navy called at more foreign ports to
show the flag. The number of diplomats in Rio de Janeiro and
the number of Brazilian diplomats abroad increased. The government invited distinguished foreigners, such as Elihu Root,
Georges Clemenceau, and Julio Roca, to visit Brazil. Brazilian
representatives made their debut at world congresses. Indeed,
nothing revealed the new international interests better than
the attitude toward the two Hague peace conferences. Brazil
declined an invitation to attend the first one, claiming that no
questions of national interest would be discussed. Eight years
later, clearly under the influence of Rio-Branco, Brazil not only
eagerly accepted an invitation to the second conference but sent
one of the largest delegations (larger than that of the United
States for example) under the leadership of an outstanding jurist,
Ruy Barbosa, who played an active role in the discussions and
held the position of *president d'honneur* of the commission
responsible for arbitration.

Second, he wanted Brazil to exercise a leadership role in Latin
America in general, but in South America in particular. Diplomatic missions were established in those capitals which hitherto
had lacked Brazilian representation. Rio-Branco coordinated the
Argentine, Brazilian, and Mexican recognition of Panama. Ruy
Barbosa spoke with the support of all of Latin America when he
demanded the equality of nations on the arbitration court
debated at The Hague. The foreign office helped to mediate the
conflict between Peru and Ecuador, found a solution for the
impasse over the Alsop claims threatening Chilean-United States
relations, and urged the United States to send a permanent
diplomatic representative to Paraguay.

Third, the Baron placed a new emphasis on Pan-Americanism.
Brazil, set apart from the rest of the hemisphere for nearly a

century because of its unique monarchical institutions, joined
the fraternity of republics in 1889, the same year in which the
modern Pan-American movement got under way. The amicable
settlement of the frontier problems put to rest the major potential source of conflict between Brazil and its neighbors, so that
inter-American friendship could become a reality. Whatever the
personal feelings of the Brazilians toward their sister republics,
all responsible leaders understood the importance of friendly
relations with them. On Pan-Americanism, Rio-Branco wrote,
"I express the deep hope which we have that the spirit of cooperation and good will manifested in the American conferences
will produce the practical results we all ought to desire to see
realized in America."[2] He organized the highly successful third
Pan-American conference in Rio de Janeiro in 1906, which consolidated and gave permanence to the Pan-American movement.

Fourth, he closely aligned his country with the United States,
thereby shifting Brazil's diplomatic axis from London to Washington. Throughout the nineteenth century Great Britain enjoyed a commercial and financial monopoly over Brazil, and the
English government served as the unofficial model for the Second Empire. In contrast, the republican constitution of 1891 was
based heavily upon that of the United States, the new political
mentor. Also, by the last decades of the century, the North
American market was by far the prime purchaser of Brazil's
exports. And furthermore, the elite had been prepared to accept
such a shift because of the convincing arguments put forth
throughout the nineteenth century by such precursors of the
idea of approximation as the Marquis of Aracati in 1827, Sérgio
Teixeira Macedo in 1848, Tavares Bastos in 1862, and Salvador
de Mendonça in 1891.

There existed then a political, economic, and psychological
gravitation of Brazil toward the United States. Rio-Branco foresaw that the newly emergent world power, if properly cultivated,
could serve well Brazilian interests. He classified Washington
as the "number one" post of importance for Brazilian diplomacy and counseled his diplomats there to maintain the closest
contact with the State Department.[3] In its turn, Washington

seemed delighted with the overt friendship of the largest Latin
American republic. The two nations exchanged ambassadors in
1905; Washington thereby received the first Brazilian ambassador, the distinguished and pro-American Joaquim Nabuco, and
Rio de Janeiro welcomed the only United States ambassador
accredited to South America. The visit of Elihu Root to Rio de
Janeiro in 1906—the first visit of a secretary of state abroad—
climaxed the growing *entente* between the two giant republics
and served notice to the rest of the hemisphere of the special
relationship existing between them.

Close relations with the United States, Pan-Americanism,
Latin American leadership, and international prestige were the
four major points of the new foreign policy. Those goals were
being implemented at the same time that Itamaraty, as the Ministry of Foreign Relations is known, was bringing frontier diplomacy to a successful conclusion. That foreign policy constituted
the legacy of the Baron of Rio-Branco.

III

In the five decades following the Baron's death, his policies
became traditional and his successors proudly carried them out.
His exalted position in diplomatic history, or, for that matter, in
national history, placed him beyond the pale of criticism. To
question the wisdom of his policies would have been—perhaps
still is—tantamount to treason.

So it was, then, that Brazil took an active part in the increasingly frequent Pan-American conferences, more often than not
expressing ideas harmonious with those of the United States.
There were ample opportunities to demonstrate leadership of
the Latin American community: in the peace conferences following both world wars, at the League of Nations, in the Leticia
affair, and in the settlement of the Chaco War. International
prestige continued to be a desired if somewhat nebulous goal.
The Brazilians left the League of Nations because they received
no permanent seat on the council; decades later Brazil was
elected for the fifth time to the Security Council of the United

Nations, a vote of confidence pleasing to its quest for international recognition.

The single most important question which arose over the proper interpretation and execution of the Rio-Branco policy concerned the degree of cooperation Brazil should give to the United States. That question was settled soon after the Baron's death. Domício da Gama, whom Rio-Branco appointed ambassador to Washington in 1911, grew increasingly suspicious of "dollar diplomacy," and there is reason to believe that the chancellor himself developed a distaste for it just before his death.[4] Distraught at the unfavorable attitude of the United States government toward the valorization scheme his government had adopted to save the falling price of coffee and at the impending antitrust suit against the storage of coffee in the United States, Ambassador da Gama chose the usually cordial dinner of the Pan-American Society in New York City to criticize, in the presence of the Secretary of State, American policy:

> My hopes for a new era in our commercial relations received a heavy blow with the endorsement by the government of the United States of the somewhat arbitrary and quite revolutionary doctrine of paying for other people's merchandise not the price they ask for it, but the price the United States, I mean the American merchants, want to pay for it. It is a brand-new doctrine, and the United States seemed disposed to enforce it even to the sacrifice of long-standing international friendship. In their eagerness to establish their right to meddle with the property of a foreign state certain officials of this government went as far as to proclaim before an American court of justice the forfeiture of the sovereignty of that foreign state and this with an unthoughtfulness of the consideration due to a friendly government, which borders on international discourtesy. So you see, Mr. Chairman, we, the South Americans, have still much to learn of the new American ways in dealing with foreign countries, as well as Americans have still to learn the way to our hearts.[5]

Da Gama had reached the conclusion that cooperation with the United States was good policy only so long as it demonstrated advantages. Otherwise he favored friendship "without any

dependency" and recommended a more independent course for
Brazilian foreign policy.[6]

The new Minister of Foreign Relations, Lauro Muller, thought
his ambassador's gratuitous remarks prejudicial to Brazil's ultimate goals. He reprimanded him.[7] Here was the essence of the
struggle over the interpretation of Rio-Branco's intentions. Ambassador da Gama was pro-American but felt that friendship and
cooperation with the United States should extend only to the
point where national interests were clearly benefited. Minister
Muller was willing to give unrestricted cooperation and friendship, feeling that in the end the benefits would outweigh any
transitory inconveniences. Muller's interpretation triumphed.
Da Gama later left his Washington post for the court of St.
James.

Not even the usual historical dividing line, the Revolution of
1930, which diminished the power of the coffee interests and
put Getulio Vargas in the presidential palace, marked a change
in foreign policy. Diplomacy took a slightly greater interest in
commerce after 1930, but that was the only modification in the
established pattern. Proof of the continuity is evident in Jayme
de Barros's book, *A Política Exterior do Brasil*, a summary of the
diplomatic history of the first decade of the Vargas rule. The
author devoted 304 pages to hemispheric relations and only six
to "relations with the countries of Europe and other continents." Clearly Brazilian interests continued to be with the Pan-
American community, in particular with the United States.
Foreign Minister Oswaldo Aranha stated the government's position tersely in Washington in 1939: "Your policies are the same
as ours."[8]

The Vargas government may not have been revolutionary in
its international orientation but it did introduce a new ingredient which, in time, when added to that mixture producing foreign policy, would precipitate changes. The new ingredient was
nationalism.

Foreign policy had been the domain of the elite, unchallenged
by any public opinion. It is not surprising to find that until the
fall of the monarchy in 1889, a majority of the foreign ministers

and certainly a considerable number of diplomats came from the sugar-producing provinces of the Northeast, an area which dominated the politics of both empires. During the Old Republic (1889–1930), when political power shifted to the south-central, coffee-producing states, a majority of the foreign ministers came from that area. The elite of both areas had much in common, such as a concern with national unity and the frontiers. They had differences as well. The sugar barons eyed England fondly. The new coffee class sold most of its product to the United States and was eager to please—at any rate not to alienate—its best customer. The shift of the diplomatic axis from London to Washington came significantly at the same time that internal power shifted from the sugar to the coffee interests. In general, however, it can be concluded that the governing groups representative of the elite were more in harmony than in conflict over foreign policy matters. Few and mild were the debates which beset the makers of foreign policy until the 1950's.

It was in that decade that the seeds of nationalism cultivated by Vargas began to bear fruit. Until the Vargas regime, the intellectuals had monopolized whatever nationalist sentiment there had been. They gave a tremendous impetus to its growth during the Modern Art Week in 1922 when they sought to define the indigenous elements of national culture. Increasing industrialization, seriously underway since World War I, and the resultant urban growth provided the fertile ground upon which nationalism grew. The working and middle classes in the burgeoning metropolises were increasingly exposed to the nationalistic ideas of the intellectuals through the expanding networks of press and radio. Vargas saw the advantages of combining and utilizing the political potential of the rapidly increasing working class and the growing popularity of nationalist doctrines. He gave the workers their first voice in government and infused in them a pride in being Brazilian. Nationalism for the first time had a broad base. The intellectuals could speak for someone besides themselves.

Like their counterparts everywhere, the Brazilian nationalists emphasized the fatherland's welfare—their own definition of it, of course. They became suspicious of foreigners, particularly of foreign interests in Brazil. To be truly independent politically, they affirmed, it would be necessary to declare their economic independence. Brazil must control its own resources, produce its own power, manufacture its own steel and automobiles. Symbolically of greatest importance, it must exploit its own oil reserves. The nationalists sought to remake their country along grander lines, which meant in practical terms economic development. In the process of agitating for that goal, they questioned traditional concepts which they felt were retarding Brazil.

One such concept which came under sharp criticism was the by then traditional foreign policy. The nationalists condemned it as not serving Brazil's best interests. They accused it of sterility. One prolific nationalist writer, José Honório Rodrigues, remarked, "The classic diplomacy was a kind of pasteurized product, very pure, very white, but hardly national."[9] The nationalists formulated another. They not only had the opportunity to express their ideas, but in January of 1961, with the inauguration of Jânio Quadros as the new president, they were given the opportunity to put their plans into action.

IV

The foreign policy of the nationalists paid homage to a number of ideals which served as guiding principles. Reduced to their briefest, those ideals consisted of five major points. First, the nationalists pleaded for the preservation of peace. Second, they put great hope in the United Nations as an instrument of peace as well as a balance to regional organizations such as the Organization of American States, which they felt to be too much under the influence of the United States. Third, they urged a program of worldwide disarmament with the use of some of the resources thus freed for the development of the less favored countries. Fourth, they supported the traditional principles of self-determination and nonintervention. And finally, they pledged support to those colonies which sought independence.[10]

On a more practical level, the foreign policy of the nationalists pursued two basic interests: increased development—both economic and social—and greater diplomatic independence. Pursuit of those interests coupled with allegiance to the above-mentioned ideals promised, among other rewards, increased prestige and leadership. Both Presidents Jânio Quadros and João Goulart accepted those goals and in varying degrees contributed to the realization of them. They were aided by two able foreign ministers, the first by Afonso Arinos de Melo Franco and the second by Francisco Clementino de San Tiago Dantas.

To carry out this new foreign policy, the government thought it necessary to disengage Brazil from the Cold War. It had been, of course, firmly committed to the Western bloc. Rigid adherence to that bloc and subservience to the leadership of the United States the nationalists believed inhibited Brazil's scope of action. The doctrines of neither the West nor the East served Brazil's best interests. Expanded trade was one of the primary means of reaching the desired goal of development, and trade knew no ideology. Although traditional markets must be maintained, it was imperative to open new ones as well. The nationalists envisioned eager markets awaiting not only Brazil's agricultural products—coffee, sugar, cocoa, and tobacco—but also the increasing array of its industrial products. President Quadros sent a trade mission to Red China with the hope of interesting that potential consumer. It was from that mission that Vice-President Goulart was summoned to assume the presidency in 1961. Goulart continued the foreign policy of his predecessor by welcoming a Chinese trade mission to Rio de Janeiro and by establishing diplomatic relations with Moscow, suspended since 1947, and with other Eastern countries. Trade was obviously only one of the purposes of this recognition. The desire to exert independence of action was a compelling psychological motive. Augmented prestige through increased diplomatic representation both abroad and in Rio de Janeiro cannot be overlooked as a motive either.

The disengagement from the Cold War not only brought Brazil at least formally closer to the East but, of at least equal significance, it put Brazil into close contact with the countries of Asia and Africa. Many of the countries of those two continents likewise felt that development should take precedence over alliances which caused the bipolarization of the world into two war camps. Brazil shared much in common with those countries. They suffered from similar social and economic problems. They sought a better life. United in their common concern for development, they could demand what they considered a fair price from the industrialized nations for their raw products and could regulate capital investment more to their own advantage. Of course, Brazil also saw for itself a unique opportunity for leadership among the underdeveloped nations which it could not hope to enjoy in the more traditional alliance with the Western world. Such a leadership role appealed mightily to nationalist pride.

In particular, Quadros saw an opportunity to exert Brazilian leadership among the newly emergent African states.[11] Geography and history provide a convincing rationale for his hopes. The Brazilian subcontinent juts out into the South Atlantic providing the closest point of physical contact between the Western Hemisphere and Africa. Furthermore, during the three centuries in which the slave trade flourished between the two areas, Africa supplied a large percentage of Brazil's population. The African presence is very much a part of contemporary Brazil. Whoever reads Gilberto Freyre's brilliant study, *The Masters and the Slaves,* understands fully the African contributions to the new tropical civilization. Based on these considerations, President Quadros saw Africa as a new dimension in his foreign policy. He believed his country could serve as a link between the newly independent Africa and the Western world because Brazil was closely connected to both. Accordingly, he recognized the new states, exchanged ambassadors with them, dispatched trade missions, offered fellowships to African students, established the Afro-Asian Institute, and denounced Portuguese colonial policies. The program was broad and audacious. The Brazilian Negro community welcomed and approved the new attitude toward the African states.[12] At least one African leader, Joseph Medupe Johnson, Minister of Labor of Nigeria, stated that Brazil became known in his country only after the election of Quadros.[13]

Quadros and Goulart widened Brazil's diplomatic vision to its maximum. The whole world fell within its scope as Brazilian diplomatic missions sprang up in such unlikely places as Albania, Algeria, Ceylon, and Thailand. Brazil was not only disengaging itself from the Cold War, it was forming a part of the "third force," the growing alliance of neutralist nations.

There was much that was old as well as much that was new in the nationalists' foreign policy. It supported the traditional policies of peaceful solution of international disputes, nonintervention, self-determination, international order, and so forth. What was strikingly new was the determination to exercise leadership and to gain recognition on a much broader plane than ever before. If Rio-Branco had weakened Brazil's ties with Europe in favor of closer friendship with the United States, the nationalists were prepared to de-emphasize those connections in favor of a new Southern Hemispheric alliance among the underdeveloped nations of Latin America, Africa, and Asia. Brazil would be seeking its traditional goals of leadership and prestige, but within a new context which seemingly, to the nationalists at any rate, offered more rewards.

V

Acceptance of the nationalists' foreign policy was by no means unanimous. Persuasive voices of criticism spoke out. Many questioned whether Brazil's primary interests would best be served by closer association with Yugoslavia, Egypt, and India.[14] The critics argued that Brazil needed greater capital investments and despaired of seeing any forthcoming from either the Eastern or neutralist countries. They agreed that new markets were also desirable but pointed out with irrefutable statistics that most of the nations of the Southern Hemisphere exported the same or similar raw products. In truth, as the world's economy was structured in the mid-twentieth century, the underdeveloped countries were more competitors of Brazil than potential customers. Decrying the unrealistic attitudes of the Quadros-Goulart policies and fearful of the damage they might inflict, the critics urged a return to more traditional patterns. Close Pan-American relations and solidarity with the United States were the columns of support for the foreign policy they sought to reconstruct.

The coup d'etat of April 1, 1964, provided the opportunity to reinstitute that policy. First, President Castelo Branco repudiated many of the concepts and certainly the emphasis of the nationalists. He repeatedly reprimanded the supporters of the Quadros-Goulart policy for being "false nationalists," out of contact with reality and out of harmony with the well-being of their own country.[15] Then, evoking the spirit of Rio-Branco to demonstrate the continuity of his policy with that of the great statesman at the opening of the twentieth century, he extended a warm abraço to the sister republics of the hemisphere in general and to the United States in particular. His foreign ministers acted accordingly. Vasco Leitão da Cunha stated that the objectives of the external policy were:

> To defend the traditional policy of the good neighbor in America and the security of the continent against aggression and subversion, whether external or internal; to strengthen all the ties with the United States, our great neighbor and friend of the north; to broaden our relations with Western Europe and with the Western community of nations.[16]

Significantly he employed the phrase "the traditional policy." Nor was it surprising that, during his tenure, Itamaraty* paid less attention to Africa, Asia, and the Eastern bloc.

His successor, Juracy Magalhães, formerly ambassador to the United States, in a major foreign policy speech on November 21, 1966, reiterated those guidelines.[17] Most of that speech concerned relations with the nations of the Western Hemisphere. He acknowledged the United States as the "unquestionable leader of the Free World" and the "principal guardian of the fundamental values of our civilization." As an "ally for over 140 years," the United States was Brazil's best customer, largest investor, and foremost source of technical knowledge. Therefore,

---

* Itamaraty Palace, offices of Brazilian Foreign Office [Editor's note].

the relationship with the northern neighbor must be especially intimate and cooperative. The Foreign Minister regarded this hemisphere as the natural international stage of action for Brazil. Emphasis on fraternal relations with the other American republics was emphatic. Three Pan-American themes received stress: (1) hemispheric unity, (2) collective security, and (3) economic solidarity. He mentioned only *en passant* relations with the non-Western world, a marked contrast to foreign policy statements during the 1961–1964 interlude.

One of the most notable characteristics of this foreign policy as it is being implemented is the obsession with security. The military leaders who carried out the coup of 1964 and then assumed the reins of government brought with them a nervous fear of Communism. It would be difficult to exaggerate their concern with that doctrine. In their minds, Goulart was not only permitting Communism to flourish in Brazil but he was encouraging it for demagogic purposes of his own. They felt that the government was being taken over at an increasingly accelerated rate by local Communists, their allies, or their sympathizers. To avoid the Cubanization of Brazil, the military felt that there was no alternative but to overthrow Goulart. Once in control of the government, the officers set out to eliminate Communist influence wherever they felt it existed. They instituted a great purge, the vestiges of which are still very evident. The reaction, then, to what the military hierarchy considered a Communist threat was this unflagging concern with national security. Since Communism was an international movement, the defense of the nation from Communist subversion required appropriate external as well as internal policies.

In shaping their foreign policy, the new leaders viewed the international scene as a gigantic struggle between East and West. There could be no neutral position. Brazil must choose sides. Without hesitation, the leaders chose the West and acknowledged the United States as the leader of that bloc. It is for that reason that the recent policies of Brasília often reflect decisions made in Washington. Brazil promptly broke diplomatic relations with Cuba, although only a few years before

Quadros had bestowed Brazil's highest order on Ché Guevara and Goulart had tried to serve as mediator between Havana and Washington. The Brazilian delegation voted against the seating of Red China in the United Nations, although Quadros had once ordered his delegation to do just the opposite. President Castelo Branco expressed his government's solidarity with the United States' position in Vietnam, another complete about-face in policy. Brazilian troops took part in the intervention in the Dominican Republic. The Brazilian government was as convinced as the North American government that a Communist take-over of the Dominican Republic was imminent. The influential officers saw in the Caribbean an opportunity to play an active role in the East-West struggle and accepted it with alacrity. As one *coronel* expressed it:

> The Armed Forces brilliantly stopped Communism from taking over Brazil. Another brilliant example is their participation in the Dominican Republic in the operation initiated by the American Marines where they also stopped Communism from taking over that country.[18]

Active participation in the fight against international Communism pleased certain groups within the military as well as the government which sought to expand that participation or to institutionalize it.

Itamaraty emerged as the most enthusiastic supporter of a permanent inter-American peace force. Washington first suggested such a force but then discreetly dropped the idea for lack of sufficient support. Brazil did not feel the same inhibitions as did the United States, universally suspected of imperialistic motives in Latin America. Foreign Minister Magalhães visited seven South American capitals to urge support for a peace force. The success of those missions has been negligible, but those reverses have only strengthened the dedication of Itamaraty.

The idea of collective security is certainly not a new one in Brazil, although the peace force must be considered as a different approach. The Treaty of Rio de Janeiro signed by the nations of the hemisphere in 1947 considers any armed attack on one of the

American states as an attack on all. Two well-known foreign ministers of the post World War II era, João Neves da Fontoura and Raúl Fernandes, called the nation's attention to the inevitable decline of sovereignty and the growth of interdependence in the modern world.[19] It is only natural that a nation with extensive, underpopulated frontiers bordering ten different states or colonies must think realistically of cooperation. It must also think in terms of possible defense of those frontiers. Should one of the ten neighbors adopt Communism or fall under Communistic control, the present government would feel itself threatened. Therefore, there exists in the highest echelons of the government and military a climate of opinion favorable to the creation of an international police force which would diminish the threat (and here one must reemphasize the intensity with which that threat is felt) of Communist expansion in Latin America. Such a force would provide a measure of the security the present government desires.

A foreign policy dominated by a fear of Communism and overly dependent on the United States has not been without its critics either. As could be expected, the nationalists attack it as unrealistic and subservient. The press in general is hostile to it. In particular of late, the newspapers have singled out the inter-American peace force for criticism.[20] In response to a questionnaire recently distributed by the *Revista Civilização Brasileira*, one state governor, one general, one bishop, and five federal deputies answered disparagingly about the present foreign policy.[21] They lamented the overdependence of Brazil on the United States and the consequent loss of diplomatic independence. They emphasized that public opinion did not support the present foreign policy. It is significant to note that the magazine received no replies favorable to the present policy and that none of the leaders questioned, some of whom were high in the ranks of the government, felt obliged to come to the defense of the foreign policy.

The significant innovation in the history of Brazilian diplomacy is that now for the first time there are two quite different foreign policies being advocated. On certain levels, they seem to

192 BURNS   Tradition and Variation in

offer much in common but that superficial similarity is highly deceptive. Both pay at least lip service to the Baron of Rio-Branco by claiming to be the modern interpreter of his ideas. The present government points out that it was Rio-Branco who intensified friendship with the United States, a policy which in that tradition receives current emphasis. The nationalists, on the other hand, believe that Rio-Branco's cordiality toward the United States was based upon the benefits Brazil could and did extract from it. They plead that the Baron always placed national interests above every other consideration and was never subservient to the United States. Rio-Branco, they assert, wanted to increase Brazilian leadership and prestige and was willing and able to use the United States as a means to obtain those ends. They accuse the present government of making friendship with the United States an end in itself.

Both foreign policies favor self-determination and nonintervention. The nationalists condemned participation in the occupation of the Dominican Republic on that basis. Just the opposite, the military argued that it participated in the inter-American peace force to prevent extracontinental intervention and to guarantee the self-determination of the Dominican people. Both advocate the traditional policy of peace, essential for the mutually desired economic and social development. The present government would bring about that development through cooperation with foreign capital, always under the suspicion and condemnation of the nationalists. Both deplore colonialism. The nationalists denounced Portuguese policies in Africa, voted against the former motherland in the United Nations, and supported the independence movement in Angola. The present government has been extremely cordial to Portugal. That cordiality coupled with a silence on Portuguese Africa has been interpreted as at least tacit support of Portugal in Africa.[22] On these and other points there is an exterior verbiage common to the two foreign policies. Beneath the surface, as the examples above indicate, lies a wide variance in the interpretation of terms. Certainly then on the practical level of implementation, if not always on the subtler level of semantics, the different foreign policy philosophies of the nationalists and the present government are easily discernible.

A clash between the two foreign policies is nowhere more evident than in the international area of action each selects for itself. In effect, the present government would limit Brazil's role in international affairs to the Western Hemisphere or at most to the Western world. This government is enthusiastically pro-American. The nationalists see the whole world as their stage and covet a role of leadership in Africa and among the under-developed nations. They tend to be anti-American.

During this decade, Brazilian foreign policy is in an unprecedented period of fluctuation. Gone is the stability characteristic of a century and a half of diplomatic history. Missing too is much of the continuity long a trademark of Brazilian diplomacy. Never before have there been such well defined and divergent alternatives from which to choose. The principal reason for this new state of uncertainty is the infusion of nationalist ideology into the formulation of foreign policy, an innovation encouraged by Jânio Quadros. For the time being, the nationalists have fallen from power and, at least officially, their foreign policy has been disapproved. The new president, Marshal Artur da Costa e Silva, was handpicked by Castelo Branco, and the recently promulgated constitution was written for him. He seems disposed to follow the foreign policy of his predecessor. Consequently it is unlikely that there will be any major policy changes in the near future. But nationalism is far too strong a force to remain in the background for long. The nationalists continue to challenge the traditional ideas. The outcome of the clash of the forces of tradition and change will decide the new direction of policy. For the moment, Brazilian foreign policy is clearly in a period of transition.

NOTES

1. Humberto de Alencar Castelo Branco, A *Diplomacia da Revolução Brasileira* (Rio de Janeiro: Ministério das Relações Exteriores, 1964).

2. Rio-Branco to Domício da Gama, Sept. 28, 1911, Arquivo Histórico do Itamaraty (hereafter cited as AHI), Despachos 235/2/8.

3. Rio-Branco's statements to this effect were frequent. As examples see: Rio-Branco to Brazilian Minister, Washington, Jan. 5, 1903, AHI, Teleg. Exp. 235/3/15; or Rio-Branco to American Legation, Feb. 20, 1903, AHI, Rep. Americanas, Notas, EUA, 208/3/15.

4. Rio-Branco to Brazilian Embassy, Washington, Nov. 22, 1909, AHI, Teleg. Exp. 235/4/1; Da Gama to Rio-Branco, Jan. 31, 1912, AHI, Ofícios 234/1/3.

5. Da Gama to Lauro Muller, Anexo 1, May 30, 1912, AHI, Ofícios 234/1/13. The speech given on May 27, 1912, was widely reported and commented on in the American press.

6. The context in which the quoted phrase appeared was as follows: "We do not need a hypothetical protection, but we do want a friendship without any dependency. . . . In such a way we would soon reach the stage where we could deal with the Americans as equals." Da Gama to Lauro Muller, Jan. 18, 1913, AHI, Ofícios 234/2/1. On March 3, 1912, Da Gama sent a long letter to Foreign Minister Muller recommending an independent foreign policy "which will allow us to appear before the world as a self-made nation . . . conscious of our responsibility and zealous of our sovereignty." AHI, Ofícios 234/1/13. Two Brazilian scholars have commented on the implications of this course of action suggested by Da Gama: Renato de Mendonça, *Fronteira em Marcha. Ensaio de Geopolítica Brasileira* (Rio de Janeiro: Companhia Editôra Americana, 1956), p. 262; and José Honório Rodrigues, *Interêsse Nacional e Política Externa* (Rio de Janeiro: Civilização Brasileira, 1966), pp. 31–32.

7. Da Gama to Lauro Muller, May 30, 1912, AHI, Ofícios 234/1/13.

8. *Correio da Manhã* (Rio de Janeiro), Feb. 11, 1939, p. 3.

9. *Interêsse Nacional*, p. 91.

10. An excellent outline of their ideas is contained in "Apresentação," *Política Externa Independente*, No. 1 (May, 1965), p. 7.

11. Jânio Quadros, "Brazil's New Foreign Policy," *Foreign Affairs*, Vol. 40, No. 1 (Oct., 1961), p. 24.

12. Clóvis Scarpino and Jorge Aguiar, "Brasil A Escalada do Negro," *Manchete* (Dec. 3, 1966), p. 75.

13. Rodrigues, *Interêsse Nacional*, p. 176.

14. In this particular case, it was Assis Chateaubriand, head of a vast journalistic empire, who spoke out in an article whose content is sum-

marized adequately in the title: "O nosso reino não é o dêste mundo indú-árabe," *O Jornal* (Rio de Janeiro), Feb. 12, 1961, p. 3. In part he said, "For the benefit of Brazil we cannot and we ought not to expect anything from the United Arab Republic, India, or Yugoslavia. The trips planned by the heads of government of those nations will be purely touristic excursions, devoid of any practical ends."

15. President Castelo Branco frequently hurled the charge of "false nationalists" against his opponents. As examples see the *Brazil Herald* (Rio de Janeiro), June 14, 1965, p. 13; and *Jornal do Brasil* (Rio de Janeiro), Dec. 4, 1966, p. 22.

16. Interview on national network of radio and television, July 6, 1964.

17. The speech was distributed in mimeographed form by the Ministério das Relações Exteriores.

18. Quoted in Mário Afonso Carneiro, "Opinião Militar," *Cadernos Brasileiros*, No. 38 (Nov.-Dec., 1966), p. 25.

19. Delgado de Carvalho, *História Diplomática do Brasil* (São Paulo: Companhia Editôria Nacional, 1959), pp. 273, 276–7.

20. For an example see the editorial in the *Jornal do Commercio* (Rio de Janeiro), Nov. 22, 1966, p. 4. It emphasizes that military force is a poor method of fighting Communism in Latin America and that only economic development will insure the establishment and prosperity of democracy in this hemisphere.

21. "Questionário proposto pela Revista Civilização Brasileira a Personalidades da Vida Pública Nacional," *Revista Civilização Brasileira*, No. 7 (May, 1966), pp. 15–73.

22. Recently there has been an adverse reaction to Brazilian policies from some African states. The diplomatic representatives of Algeria, Ghana, Senegal, and the United Arab Republic publicly asked for some clarification from the Brazilian government on (1) the declarations made in Lisbon by Marshal Artur Costa e Silva with respect to the Portuguese colonies in Africa; (2) the projected visit of Brazilian naval vessels to ports of Angola; and (3) the possible political implications of the increased Brazilian economic interest in Angola and Moçambique. *Correio da Manhã* (Rio do Janeiro), Jan. 7, 1967, p. 2.

The Foundations of Brazil's Foreign Policy*

José Honório Rodrigues

Brazil adopted a foreign policy even before the proclamation of independence on September 7, 1822. The Prince Regent, D. Pedro, soon after the return of his father, D. João VI, to Portugal in 1821, fought the *Côrtes* (the Assembly of Estates) of Portugal, which tried to restrict his powers and to reduce Brazil to her former condition of colony after she had been for some years a kingdom and the seat of the monarchy. D. Pedro denounced the *Côrtes* to the principal nations of the world and asked them to recognize the government of Brazil as the only legitimate organ of the monarchy, sending, for this purpose, four emissaries to Europe (to Great Britain, France, Vienna, and the Holy See), and others to Washington and Argentina. After September 7 these emissaries worked for the recognition of independence.

The negotiations were protracted and arduous, for the question was now that of a revolutionary movement comparable to those of the other South American colonies, and the powers of the Holy Alliance wanted to reestablish the principle of the legitimacy of royal power which the French Revolution and Napoleon had denied. Recognition was all the more difficult to obtain because D. Pedro had proclaimed himself Emperor "by the unanimous acclamation of the people," ascribing the legitimacy of power not to hereditary law but to popular suffrage, thus violating the principles of the Holy Alliance. The title of Em-

* This article was originally published in *International Affairs*, 38(3): 324–338, July, 1962. Reproduced by permission.

196

peror was an additional impediment in the negotiations with Portugal for independence, says Sir Charles Webster, for in it was implied the idea of superiority.[1]

What D. Pedro really wanted was the future reunion of the Portuguese Empire, when he would be called to Portugal to reign as D. Pedro IV. The United States was the first country to recognize Brazil's independence, on May 16, 1824, but the fate of Brazil was linked to that of Europe, and chiefly to that of Great Britain. The European powers imposed, as a condition for their recognition, recognition by the Lisbon court, which was achieved only through British intervention. The price of recognition included the sum of two million pounds sterling paid to Portugal and the renewal of the most favoured nation privileges given to Great Britain, as well as various special concessions that virtually made Brazil a British protectorate until 1844, when she refused to renew the agreements. For her part Brazil did not put an end to the slave trade, as she had agreed to do, postponing this step until 1850.

The statesmen of the Empire (1822–1889) were soon aware of the difficulties created by independence, especially the fact that Brazil's enormous territorial area was not being put to use and that her natural and economic resources were not being developed. With a population of almost four million people and a territorial area of 8,511,965 square kilometers, there were more than two for each person. Compared with the small Spanish states, Brazil, occupying half of South America, was a unit singularly *sui generis*.

As a consequence of all these circumstances, the following principles guided Brazilian foreign policy, which was very troubled in the first nine years and very timid until 1844.

1. As a country potentially subject to attack on account of her small population and her rich but unexploited resources, Brazil adopted, vis-à-vis Europe and the United States, a pacifist ideology, favouring international arbitration. Brazilian foreign policy has always preferred juridical to political solutions. Of Brazil's 167 foreign ministers, 145 graduated in law, although two of the greatest distinguished themselves not by their legal knowledge

but by their political *savoir faire* and their historical and geographical learning.

2. In her relations with neighbouring countries, most notably over frontier problems inherited from the colonial era, the general principle has always been to aim at a peaceful and legal solution. In the preservation of her frontiers against the territorial pretensions of some neighbouring countries, Brazil, firmly supported by historical rights and by *uti possidetis*, has always sought a juridical compromise.

3. In the defence of her territorial integrity, threatened by the possible re-creation of the Viceroyalty of the River Plate, Brazil's foreign policy was orientated not by legal but by political and military considerations. In her so-called interventionist policy, Brazil used the same methods that Europe and the United States applied in their differences with her. The policies of power and influence, of coercion and persuasion, of intervention and nonintervention, were variously applied in accordance with circumstances, aided by the political sagacity and the tactical skill of her statesmen.

RELATIONS WITH EUROPEAN POWERS

Vis-à-vis the European powers, especially Great Britain and France, and also in her relations with the United States, which used persuasion and force, Brazil's entire defence consisted in peaceful resistance and in eventual concessions. She always tried to keep intact her territorial patrimony and her national unity, two indispensable conditions of her future claim to respect and prestige in international life. She was forced to sign ignominious treaties from 1825 onwards, especially with Great Britain and France—for which the statesmen of the Empire who directed her foreign policy or discussed it in the Chamber of Deputies or in the Senate always expressed the greatest repugnance—paying exorbitant prices and granting special economic and legal privileges that were really equivalent to extraterritorial rights. Violence, insults, threats, pressures fill the pages of her diplomatic history of that time.

In the first twenty-eight years of Brazil's independent existence Great Britain was the focus of her international life, domi-
nating her, harming her interests, threatening her, obtaining
concessions and privileges that would be inconceivable today,
but it was also on Great Britain that her independence and her
sovereignty depended. The British demand that she abolish the
slave trade, for instance—a consequence of the policy of Cas-
tlereagh and Canning—which would have resulted in the ruin of
her agricultural economy, damage to commerce and navigation,
reduction of the income of the state, and an end to the importa-
tion of the slave labour she was not in a position to dispense
with, could not be obeyed until 1850, when she began to prepare
for the substitution of free for slave labour. The nonfulfilment
of this obligation was the greatest obstacle to the recognition of
de facto independence. It was thus necessary to find a compromise solution that would satisfy Brazil's aspirations to independence and sovereignty and at the same time not harm her agricultural interests, particularly the coffee and sugar plantations,
which depended on slave labour. Torn between two quintessen-
tial interests, one permanent, the other of primary concern to
the ruling classes, Brazil accepted the legal obligation of abolition without implementing it immediately.

Brazil's relations with Portuguese Africa were a keypoint in
her diplomatic policy. These relations resulted in constant
conflict with Great Britain, on account of Brazil's failure
to fulfil her obligation to free the slaves, which she had assumed
in a convention and which Britain sought to enforce by considerable pressure and threats. "There are two things," Lord Aberdeen told Guizot, "on which my country is not tractable . . .
the abolition of the slave trade and Protestant propagandism";
and when Guizot asked him what might be the strength in the
House of Commons of the abolitionist group called the Saints,
he replied, "They are all Saints on such questions."[2] While
the British demand may have been inspired by humanitarian
motives or coloured by economic interests and the desire to expand in Africa[3] and while Brazil's policy may have been to protect the needs of the landed class which ruled the country, the

fact remains that Brazil never betrayed her interests except on paper. While resigning herself to stoic toleration of all forms of European coercion, she nevertheless continued the slave traffic and her commercial relations with Africa, especially with Angola, which was practically a Brazilian colony and depended on these relations.

The struggle for freedom from British tutelage went on until 1844, when Brazil declared that the Treaty of 1827 had lapsed.[4] The Aberdeen Bill of 1845 and the assaults on Brazilian ships, the Christie question in 1862 with the reprisals of the British navy at the entrance to the harbour of Rio de Janeiro, the breaking of relations in 1864, all show the decisive role played by Great Britain in Brazil's international life, leading perhaps to the point of forcing her out of Africa.[5] The Aberdeen Bill was one of the greatest insults which a strong people ever offered to a weak one.[6]

Brazil's foreign policy was orientated not toward the American continent but seaward. The River Plate was not at first, as some have written, the dominant preoccupation of her Secretary of Foreign Affairs, and, influenced by the British, she readily agreed to the creation of Uruguay in 1828. Only after 1843 did events in Argentina demand greater attention. Although the Secretary of Foreign Affairs declared in 1831 that he intended to eliminate some European missions in order to establish others in America, by about 1833 Brazil had ten diplomatic missions in Europe and only four in America; in 1859 these were increased to thirteen and seven respectively; there were 157 consuls in Europe and only 37 in America.

The Treaty of 1827 between Brazil and France gave the latter such extraordinary privileges, aggravated by the clause of perpetuity, that on several occasions Great Britain complained of not being the most favoured nation, especially in questions of succession to property and intestacies. The articles of perpetuity that benefited France only were a source of conflict and bitter humiliation,[7] forcing Brazil to conclude several very disadvantageous consular agreements. But nothing would satisfy the ambitions of the great powers, which demanded the exclusive jurisdiction of their consuls in all matters of succession, including those of Brazilian children of foreign parents, in flagrant contravention of Article 6 of the Imperial Constitution of 1824. The consuls, especially the French, considered that they had the right to conduct hearings, to appoint guardians, to open wills, and to apply the law of their own countries in Brazil.

The worst evils came, however, from the clause of perpetuity, with its pernicious effect on Brazilian interests. Every pretext was used by the British and French to make complaints and exert pressure, accompanied by threats of force, even in the simplest cases, as when Brazil used her sovereign right to increase tariffs on products imported from Britain and France.

Animosity against Europe and against the treaties, which inspired Brazil's statesmen and representatives in the first years of her independent life, was only natural. In 1847, after severely criticizing the obligations she had contracted in treaties greatly to the detriment of her development, the Barão de Cairu declared that such treaties were not the best way of strengthening ties between countries and that the Empire should proceed cautiously, agreeing to nothing that had not received the consent of all, and regulating everything else in accordance with the needs of the time and the economic and social interests of Brazil. In the Senate the conservative Bernardo Pereira de Vasconcelos, after declaring himself against the Holy Alliance and an admirer of Great Britain, confessed his indignation at the treaty with France and expressed the opinion that such treaties were hostile and hateful acts against Brazil.

The Empire did not renew the treaty with Great Britain which had lapsed in 1844, and in 1887 it refused a proposal to negotiate a treaty of commerce and navigation. This proposal, wrote the Secretary of State, the Barão de Cotegipe, was contrary to the policy long followed by the Imperial government of signing treaties of commerce and navigation only with neighbouring countries. And he added that experience had shown that special agreements were not necessary to protect British interests. "In fact, the Treaty of Friendship, Commerce, and Navigation of August 17, 1827, between Brazil and Great Britain lapsed in

1844, and since then, or for more than forty years, in spite of the nonexistence of another similar treaty, British maritime and commercial interests have constantly and progressively shown great improvement."

Brazilian foreign policy, therefore, without contracting obligations for unforeseen contingencies, or rather without negotiating agreements on bases proposed by other nations, did not create difficulties in the expansion of commercial relations with the European powers or reduce British investments in Brazil. But the clause of perpetuity contained in the treaty with France remained and was not definitively denounced until 1907.

RELATIONS WITH AMERICAN STATES

After 1843 Brazil's relations with the Republics of the River Plate (Argentina and Uruguay) became more complicated, but it was only in the period 1848–1850 that they began to feature more prominently in her foreign policy. Even so this policy did not become regionalized or continentalized. Brazil endeavoured to guarantee the territorial status quo and the balance of power, based on the principle of maintaining the independence of Uruguay and Paraguay, in order to avoid the dream of the Argentine dictator, Rosas, of re-creating the Viceroyalty of the Plate, which had dissolved during the struggle for independence. The maintenance of the status quo implied keeping these independent states divided and preventing their unification into a new group.

The policy of cautious neutrality pursued by Brazil in 1844 changed when the re-creation of the Viceroyalty, up to this time only a threat, appeared imminent. Before the Brazilian-Argentinian agreement, Domingo Sarmiento once asked if there was any impediment to the union of the republics of Paraguay and Uruguay and the Argentine Confederation in a confederation under the name of the United States of South America. Certainly Brazilian policy was opposed to it, for her statesmen saw in the efforts of General Rosas and his ally Oribe an attempt to separate the Rio Grande do Sul from Brazil and to renew the boundary Treaty of 1777 in order to recover the territory of the

Missions. Furthermore, the *caudilhismo* that reigned there—in contrast to the Brazilian representative parliamentary system, however defective—was the source of continual incidents, violence, and extortions against Brazilian individuals and properties.

As a result Brazil and the Argentine Confederation were involved in several disputes. Argentina, once free from the last Anglo-French intervention (1849–1850), increased her activity in Uruguay, in an effort to absorb the territory, and in 1849 decided to reincorporate Paraguay. Thanks to the skill of her statesmen Brazil concluded a defensive alliance with Paraguay, and shortly after that with the provinces of Entre Rios and Corrientes; the war between Brazil and the Rosas dictatorship thus lost the character of a national struggle between Brazil and Argentina, thereby putting an end to the prejudices that had been generated during the colonial era.

The victory of Monte Caseros (February 3, 1852) marked the beginning of Brazilian-Argentinian understanding and reestablished a strict neutrality which was maintained during the struggles between Mitre's forces in Buenos Aires and those of General Urquiza, ending in the victory of the former in Pavón (September 17, 1861). From then on friendly political and commercial relations between Brazil and Argentina were gradually consolidated, especially during the Paraguayan War (1864–1870), which was, after the defeat of the Uruguayan intervention in 1864, the last step taken by Brazil to maintain the balance of power in the River Plate. In Uruguay and Paraguay, the resentments, hostilities, rivalries, and frustrations resulting from these military actions have still not disappeared altogether; indeed, certain groups still manifest a "victim complex" with respect to Brazil. In Argentina, Mitre, Sáenz Peña, and Julio Roca were instrumental in dispelling feelings of hostility. Minority groups, however, are still unfriendly to Brazil. In the Brazilian military interventions in Uruguay, as well as in the Paraguayan War, the status quo with regard to the possessions of the two states was kept unchanged, based on the principle of *uti possidetis* and in violation of the boundary Treaty of 1777 between Spain and Portugal.

The policy of intervention was complementary to the policy

of balance of power in the River Plate. It aimed at putting an end to the regime of *caudilhismo*, which threatened Brazil's frontiers, and at preventing the setting up of unstable governments. Brazil's statesmen at that time justified intervention by saying it was necessary to preserve her frontiers and the lives and properties of Brazilians. Ramón Cárcano, one of Argentina's Ambassadors to Brazil and one of the best authorities on the subject of Argentinian-Brazilian relations, wrote that the Empire, by helping itself, also helped its neighbours.[8] The foreign policy of the Brazilian Empire vis-à-vis her neighbours was an interventionist one, especially between 1851 and 1870, as was also that of Rosas, who tried to intervene in 1838 in the revolution of the Rio Grande do Sul.

Another aim of Brazilian diplomacy in the American continent has been the defence of the frontiers of the vast area that had been won and occupied by the Luso-Brazilians, their treaty definition, and boundary demarcation. More than 16,000 square kilometers were incorporated in Brazilian territory, without the loss of a single drop of blood, without a shot, based only on historical documents and maps and on the right of possession (*uti possidetis*). Here, as in her relations with Europe, Brazil's policy was dominated by peaceful methods and the principle of appeal to arbitration, precisely because the legal position served her national aspirations—the security and defence of her territory. Whether by direct negotiations or by arbitration, Brazil's frontier policy had only one aim: to defend the land she now possessed. Such was Brazil's integrity that after her victory in the Paraguayan War she agreed to the same frontier which she had previously demanded on the basis of *uti possidetis*, and when her claims on the frontier with British Guiana were not recognized by the arbiter she did not question the decision.

The definition of boundaries is practically completed today. Only a few doubts remain as to the sources of some rivers and the demarcation and definition of certain territorial limits. This task was not achieved by Rio-Branco alone, though between 1893 and 1912 he successfully negotiated the most difficult frontier disputes, thereby incorporating in Brazilian territory about

430,621 square kilometers, and purchased the Acre Territory (403,000 square kilometers). Rio-Branco would not have achieved these victories without the preparatory studies of his predecessors, men such as his father, the Visccnde do Rio-Branco, Joaquim Caetano da Silva, and Paulino Soares de Sousa. Nor was this the achievement of a single regime or any single political party. It was the work of a whole nation, of foreign ministers, diplomats, historians, geographers, and pioneers.

With the establishment of the principle of the maintenance of the status quo, the fixing of frontiers, and the assurance that the balance of power would be maintained, continental harmony has been a permanent aim of Brazilian foreign policy since 1870. "With our neighbours, above all, we must be generous and avoid everything that may force us out of neutrality in all matters, without the sacrifice, however, of our national honour," D. Pedro II wrote in his political advice to Princess Isabel in 1871.[9] From then on it became usual for the Emperor to declare in his speeches to the Assembly that he was doing his utmost to maintain peace and cultivate cordial relations with all nations.

RELATIONS WITH THE UNITED STATES

Whether Brazil's foreign policy tended to broaden or narrow her relations with other countries, she has always sought to keep her contacts with the United States cordial, and thereby to maintain an equilibrium among the eighteen Spanish American republics. Another great country with which Brazil has always cultivated close relations is Chile, whose friendship contributed to an equilibrium in the South and Spanish American world. Brazil's relations with the United States began with the United States' recognition of her independence in 1824, and were strengthened by the Treaty of Friendship, Commerce, and Navigation of 1828. In 1846 Brazil's Foreign Minister observed that relations with the United States were growing more important every day, primarily because of the development of commercial interests between the two countries.

There was, of course, some friction with the United States,

and Brazil was subjected to affronts, threats, intimidations, protests, and discourteous language, such as she had experienced from Great Britain, but she never harboured the feelings of resentment experienced by other Spanish American states which had also suffered in the same way. The usefulness of the United States alliance has always been recognized as one of the foundations of Brazilian foreign policy, and her statesmen have maintained it in order that she should not remain isolated in the inter-American world, or, rather, in order that she should remain a stabilizing factor in the American continent.

As the biggest buyer of Brazilian coffee, especially since 1865, the United States recognized in Brazil an important market, for which she had been competing with Great Britain since the lapse of the Anglo-Brazilian Treaty of 1844, when equal tariffs and privileges were accorded to both countries. In 1870, when the United States was already importing more than half the coffee exported from Rio de Janeiro, Minister Henry P. Blow offered some suggestions for the development of commercial relations and proposed to provide, in exchange for a reduction in the taxes on coffee and sugar, several other articles and manufactured goods at cheaper prices. These goods had until then been chiefly provided by Great Britain, which continued to be the principal exporter of products and capital to Brazil. He affirmed then, as Secretary Abel P. Upshur had previously done in 1843, that the Brazilian Empire had a future that must be looked upon with the utmost interest by the older nations of the world, but that none of them could be so completely sympathetic to her progress as his own nation.[10]

The frequent incidents between Brazil and the United States, especially as a result of Brazil's neutrality during the American Civil War and of United States' demands for the opening of the Amazon to foreign navigation—demands made from 1850 onwards and supported by Tavares Bastos, a Brazilian deputy and writer and a great admirer of the Anglo-Saxon world—did not affect the peaceful development of commercial and economic relations in general. Political relations between the two countries were greatly improved when the Barão do Rio-Branco was Foreign Minister (1902–1912). The greatest opponent of the United States shortly after the proclamation of the Republic (1889) was Eduardo Prado, who wrote a pamphlet entitled *The American Illusion*.[11]

From this epoch dates the tendency on the part of Brazil to draw away from her former European ties and to align herself as far as possible with United States' policies in the American hemisphere. It is certain, as we have said, that during the Empire Brazil had always recognized the advantages of this friendship and the disadvantages of any stand with the Spanish American states against the United States. Teixeira Macedo once wrote to the Marquês de Olinda, Foreign Minister: "We must be extremely careful to prevent the United States from thinking that because of our close relations with the Spanish Americans this means that we are in a league against her. We must not sacrifice the friendship of an important power, whose commercial relations are advantageous to us, to gamble our welfare on future alliances of problematical importance."[12] The same thought was repeated by Rio-Branco: "The so-called League of the Spanish American Republics to oppose the United States is impossible because of the lack of agreement among these states, and it is even ridiculous in view of the well-known weakness and poverty of resources of most of them. It is not with a policy of pinpricks and making nuisances of ourselves to the United States that we will be able to stalemate our opponents."[13]

It is also clear that this policy had been affirmed even before Rio-Branco became Foreign Minister. An official Report of 1896 stated: "Without wanting to assume one iota of responsibility in international situations created and solved by the United States, Brazil is aware of and cannot escape the influence that the United States exerts in the destinies of South America."[14] Ever since she became independent, Brazil had always wanted to devote more attention to regional problems, but only at the end of the century was she able to attain this objective, although the two essentials of productivity, capital and labour, were still of European origin. As her commercial relations with the United States increased, her foreign ministers, and especially

Rio-Branco, sought to achieve that aim. The Americanism of Rio-Branco signified a de-Europeanization of Brazilian foreign policy.

The two pillars of Rio-Branco's foreign policy were friendship with the United States and with Chile; he had, however, inherited the colonial complexes of Spanish-Portuguese hostility and often felt the rivalries of Brazil's neighbours more than their friendships. He had also inherited many remnants of the Imperial interventionist policy in the River Plate. Not only Rio-Branco but also his rivals, such as Estanislão Zeballos, proceeded along the same lines. It was for this reason that Rio-Branco sought to cooperate with the United States and to create in Spanish America a friendlier and more understanding atmosphere for Washington. It is this policy of bringing the three Americas together around the axis of Brazil-United States friendship which Brazil has followed ever since, both on her own and in inter-American congresses.

Since the time of Rio-Branco, Brazilian-American amity has been one of the principal aims of Brazil's foreign policy, even to the point of exaggeration, as in the case of Brazil's indifference toward the doctrine of nonintervention, when a man like John Barrett, Director of the Pan American Union, warned his compatriots in the United States that it was time "to stop this careless talk of interference with the affairs of our neighbours" (*New York Herald*, February 18, 1912).

Although the (Theodore) Roosevelt Corollary of 1904 and American intervention in Nicaragua in 1911 had to a certain extent been counter-balanced by nonintervention in Mexico in 1913 (despite great United States pressure against her), the incidents of Tampico and Vera Cruz in 1914, which called for the mediation of the ABC countries (Argentina, Brazil, and Chile), the complex question of the Mexican boundaries in 1916, and the perpetuation of the Taft–Knox policy of 1916, known as "dollar diplomacy," spread the first seeds of Latin American revolt against the foreign policy of the United States. As a result, in spite of their general sympathy toward the Allies, only eight of the Latin American republics declared war on

Germany and only five of them broke off diplomatic relations with her.

Brazil, however, maintained her friendly relations with the United States. In 1917 the then Foreign Minister, Nilo Peçanha, quoted the opinion expressed by a former Brazilian ambassador to France, namely, that "Brazil's natural allies will always be the Americans from the north and from the south. It is in the United States and in Buenos Aires that Your Majesty must have ambassadors or ministers distinguished for their ability and their honour."[15] This suggestion has not always been followed, but from the time of Rio-Branco up to the end of World War II, Brazil's international policy was directed more than ever to keeping the help and friendship of the United States.

The economic depression of the 1930's and the increased responsibilities of the United States, due to the war and to her growing world power, softened her old interventionist policy, and as a result coercion gave way to persuasion and domination to cooperation. The policy of nonintervention has never triumphed completely because great economic interests, as they become more and more powerful, do their utmost to influence the making of public policy and public opinion. Since the administrations of President Hoover and especially of President Franklin D. Roosevelt, the Good Neighbour policy has become dominant in the American continent.

After World War II, when the Latin American States became conscious of their underdevelopment and expressed their hopes for rapid growth, Pan-Americanism was put to the test. The animosities in the Central American and some South American republics, the lack of United States' help to Latin America while help was given to Europe, the commercial loans offered as proofs of generosity, the fear of the sinister role that United States capitalists might play in internal affairs, the alarm caused by economic groups which manipulate colossal advertising sums to win over or intimidate public opinion, have all jeopardized the leadership of the United States and weakened the general loyalty to the Western community. The Latin American countries which the United States has tried to maintain in her political orbit, eager for progress, irritated by Western indifference to their problems, and fully aware that there are today some European countries more under United States influence than they, are promoting among themselves a unity hitherto inconceivable, and are broadening relations and alliances of which the United States in particular and the West in general are suspicious, and which may indeed come to constitute a threat to democracy in Latin America.

President Juscelino Kubitschek's Operation Pan America (OPA), which burgeoned into the Alliance for Progress of President John F. Kennedy, has sought to meet this challenge, and Brazil's foreign policy since then has been inspired by his consciousness of her being an underdeveloped country, or, to be more optimistic, of being a country in process of development. Operation Pan America's aim is to utilize Brazil's resources to the full and to make this process as short as possible. As a policy of intensive development it seeks voluntary international cooperation where it can find it. With Operation Pan America this cooperation has become regionalized and has moved in the direction of a Latin American common market, without other alliances and within the regional framework. However effective this policy may prove in the promotion of American or Latin American unity, the individual countries are separate cultural entities, with differing historical backgrounds, and have, besides their common future, an individual future which will call for individual action in their international relations. The common economic interests of the Latin American nations do not transcend their historical and cultural divisions and thus the limits imposed by political geography remain a pressing reality.

Brazil, for instance, because of her links and her geographical and ethnic similarity with Africa, and because of her practice of racial nondiscrimination, has been and is conscious of the importance of the African continent in her future foreign policy. Brazil is also a continental nation which is beginning to think intercontinentally, not only in her relations with America but in her relations with the whole world.

RELATIONS WITH PORTUGAL

With particular regard to relations between Brazil and Portugal, it must be stressed that in spite of the community of feeling that has for so long united the two countries, their national objectives do not coincide in the international field. The two form a sentimental, linguistic community, with an economic basis which exists today in name rather than in fact. The colonialism of Salazar has alienated Brazil still further, and if she is united to Portugal by blood the same is true in relation to Africa, which gave her 11 percent of her total population and a large proportion of her mestizo population (26 percent of the total). On the other hand, the number of Portuguese immigrants in Brazil has been diminishing (the Portuguese formed 0.92 percent of the total population in 1940 and 0.65 percent in 1950, with a very low index of naturalizations) while the number of immigrants from other countries has been rising. No country, with the exception of the United States, has received more Japanese than Brazil; no country has received so many Germans; very few have admitted so many Italians (the majority came between 1884 and 1930); and Brazil, with the exception of Mexico and Argentina, has the greatest number of Spanish immigrants, not to mention many other nationalities.

In a population of 70,700,000 inhabitants, only 3 percent are foreigners (the percentage in 1920 was 5.11 percent, in 1940 3.41 percent, and in 1950 2.34 percent). For this reason foreign colonies do not exert an important influence on Brazilian policy and do not weaken the Luso-Brazilian cultural majority. It must be noted that only recently, for the first time in her political history, have Brazilians of the first and second generations of non-Portuguese descent won political leadership. The rate of growth of the Brazilian population, having increased from 2.5 percent per annum in the 1950 census to 3.09 percent according to the 1960 census, implies a demand for greater economic development, and thus makes more urgent the broadening of her foreign relations.

PRESENT-DAY FOREIGN POLICY

For all the above reasons Brazil is essentially pacifist, but she is now more concerned with her own rights, opportunities, and interests. She recognizes that real independence signifies above all a foreign policy free from pressures and threats from other countries but subject to the fulfilment of international obligations, voluntarily agreed in treaties and conventions. Back in 1862 D. Pedro II spoke of the necessity of adopting a policy that was really appropriate for Brazil. This is what President Jânio Quadros sought to do when he defended an independent policy, a policy which, taking into account regional hemispheric interests, did not neglect intercontinental objectives, endeavoured to broaden Brazilian commercial and political relations, refused exclusive commitments, and stood for peace and the defence of representative government.

The making of foreign policy has always been a function of the executive power, sometimes debated in Congress, depending on the times and the issues. International problems have never been given a prominent place in the platform of Brazil's political parties. During the Empire the only aspiration was for peace. In 1870 the Republican party accused the monarchy of keeping Brazil apart from America and the world. After the proclamation of the Republic and until fairly recently, party programmes have expressed in a general way their concern for international cooperation, obedience to the principles adopted by the United Nations, and Brazilian integration in the inter-American community. The Brazilian Labour party, going a step ahead, clearly champions the principle of nonintervention, which was upheld at Punta del Este by a Labour Minister. It was only after World War II that Brazilian political parties began to pay greater attention to international problems and to think of Brazil as an inseparable part of the world. Motions of approval or censure of the Foreign Minister have become more frequent as well as the demand that he explain his policy in the Chamber of Deputies.

Brazilian foreign policy is neither a party policy nor does it represent the interests of a class; but since the country was formerly ruled by an oligarchy which represented landed interests, it has reflected this oligarchy's opinion and aspirations rather than those of the people, who were until a short time ago politically non-existent. The middle and working classes were not organized as a political force. The government of Getulio Vargas, in spite of restricting the ruling power to a very limited circle including the armed forces, promoted national feeling and brought the working classes into the political arena. From 1930 on, new groups of the middle and working classes with their own demands have become more influential in Brazilian politics without, however, affecting the policies and attitudes of the Ministry of Foreign Relations.

This Ministry has undergone several changes in order to keep pace with its growth. Until a few years ago the recruitment of its personnel was dominated by the system of patronage. Public examinations for admittance, as well as the creation of the Rio-Branco Institute for the professional training of diplomats, are recent innovations. The Ministry of Foreign Relations is a closed institution, where all the departmental heads in all fields must be career diplomats. Up to now it has not sought for, or, if it has done so, only to a very limited degree, the advice and counsel of specialists in national or international affairs who could furnish information to policy makers.

Economic groups in former times, such as the slave traders or the coffee planters, knew how to promote their interests in the making of foreign policy; today the new industrial and commercial groups compete with the agricultural classes for influence and advantage. Pressure groups such as the Catholic Church, the Military Club, and powerful economic interests also strive to exert influence, whether or not their interests coincide with the national interest. Regional and sectional influences, which are very important in domestic affairs, have little effect on foreign policy. The only exceptions are Rio Grande do Sul, which has always been sensitive to the problems of foreign policy due to its situation as a border state with consequent involvement in the international conflicts of the Empire, and the Northeast, where the Dutch occupation in the colonial era has left a significant mark.

Just as it is to Rio de Janeiro that, from the earliest days of her independence, Brazil owes her national unity, so it is Rio de Janeiro which has dominated Brazilian thinking in international matters. More than any others the newspapers of Rio de Janeiro, and, subsequently, the press of São Paulo—although they reflected the dominant interests of the great oligarchs, the landowners, and the coffee growers, as well as the prejudices of the middle and upper classes—have always felt a great responsibility in the analysis of Brazil's foreign policy. The reactions and behaviour of the people of Brazil are superior to those of their leaders, and their instincts are more perceptive than the sophistries of the latter; there is no doubt, therefore, that their late but inevitable entrance into the arena of policy decision will mean progress, and will make of their optimism, which is a Brazilian characteristic, a philosophy of her historic hope for development.

NOTES

1. *Britain and the Independence of Latin America, 1812–1830* (London: Oxford University Press, 1938), Vol. 1, p. 57.

2. Sir Charles Webster, *The Art and Practice of Diplomacy* (London: Chatto & Windus, 1961), p. 43.

3. See José Honório Rodrigues, *Brasil e Africa. Outro Horizonte* (Rio de Janeiro: Civilizacão Brasileira, 1961).

4. See Alan K. Manchester, *British Pre-eminence in Brazil* (Chapel Hill: The University of North Carolina Press, 1933).

5. In the recognition of Independence D. Pedro accepted the clause prohibiting the adherence of the Portuguese colonies of Africa to Brazil, which seems to have been a British condition. See José Honório Rodrigues, *ibid.*, pp. 142–4.

6. R. Burton, *The Highlands of Brazil* (London, 1869), Vol. 1, p. 5.

7. See Antonio Pereira Pinto, *Apontamentos para o Direito Internacional* (Rio de Janeiro, 1865), Vol. 2, p. 15 and following.

8. See *Guerra del Paraguay. Origines y Causas* (Buenos Aires: Domingo Viau, 1939), pp. 168, 169, 172, 190.

9. See Manuscript in the Archive of Palacio Grão Pará, residence of Prince D. Pedro, presumptive heir of the Crown. There is a limited (100 copies) facsimile edition.

10. See W. R. Manning, *Diplomatic Correspondence of the United States* (Washington: Carnegie Endowment for International Peace, 1932), Vol. 2, pp. 122–6.

11. See A *Illusão Americana* (São Paulo, 1893). This edition was confiscated and destroyed by order of the Brazilian government. Several editions were published later.

12. See Sergio Teixeira Macedo to the Marquês de Olinda, Minister of Foreign Affairs. Washington, April 26, 1849. Arquivo Histórico do Ministério das Relações Exteriores, Oficios Recebidos Reservado n. 5.

13. See Dispatch of January, 1905, to the Brazilian Legation in Washington. Arquivo Histórico do Ministério das Relações Exteriores.

14. See *Relatorio do Ministério das Relações Exteriores* (Rio de Janeiro, 1896), pp. 5–6.

15. See *Relatorio do Ministério das Relações Exteriores* (Rio de Janeiro, 1920), Anexo A, pp. 5–6.

The Afro-Asian World:
Its Significance for Brazil*

A. Mendes Viana

Asia has an enormous area of 48 million square kilometers, with close to a billion and a half inhabitants; Africa, a fifth of the land of the globe, has approximately 30 million square kilometers and a population of about 210 million. Peoples of almost every color of skin live on these two continents. There are sovereign and subject states; dozens of religions, many different political ideologies; fertile lands and tremendous deserts, torrid and frigid zones; in short, these continents comprise the largest combination of social, political, economic, and moral problems to be studied and resolved.

The world is emerging little by little from that terrible period that was known as the colonial era (begun by the voyage of Vasco da Gama to India 1498), the direct control of which Europe is only now losing, but still attempts to prolong by means other than that of its historic function. The ferment caused by the desire of these oppressed peoples for independence was among the many factors that produced international tension, and is so still. Current revolutionary ideas arose largely from these demands. This period of a little over two centuries of man's intensive parasitic exploitation was to a great extent aggravated by another monstrous social inequality, that is, preju-

* This article was originally published in Portuguese as "O Mundo Afro-Asiatico: Sua Signifição para o Brasil," in Revista Brasileira de Política Internacional, 2(8):5–23, Dec., 1959. Translated and printed by permission.

dice against the so-called colored races. None of the great civilizations of antiquity, whether Eastern or Western, had ever invented the prejudice which bases superiority among men on difference in skin color. The revolt of the East against Western culture uses this prejudice, and it constitutes one of the irritants to Afro-Asian nationalism. It aggravates international tensions still more and is one of the factors in worldwide ideological conflicts.

But then did colonialism produce nothing useful? Yes, it did. It was largely responsible for stirring up these Asian peoples, this mass of immobilized humanity. Their "cursed lash," in the words of an Arab writer, made them feel the need to move forward. And it was the Westerners who in the field of knowledge unearthed the old civilizations and their remains, deciphering their language, showing mankind their political and cultural origins, the roots of the history of those ancestral civilizations. Placing colonialism on another plane than that of moral judgment, it undoubtedly marks a stage of historical progress, restoring those ancient cultures, bringing them into the realms of scientific civilization. Freeing them from their primitive structure, the Westerners integrated these Afro-Asiatic peoples into modern life, into its social, economic, and political problems, which became universal. Colonialism was a stage in the evolution of humanity. It is urgent that colonizers and colonized free themselves of the complexes left by the colonial era, that both cleanse their consciousness of the so-called "imperial-colonial culture."

We must point out still other aspects of colonialism. What is the present condition of these Afro-Asian states recently released from the colonial yoke? First, in almost all there is great poverty despite the fact that many of them possess immense wealth in explored and unexplored resources, particularly in the subsoil. In Africa none among the negroid peoples had a politically organized civilization. Under this circumstance the Portuguese-Spanish and the English-Dutch-French varieties of colonialism established themselves in the Americas by transferring their nationals as colonists, just to occupy the regions discovered with their European way of life and their religions, enslaving the natives as an inferior race and later transferring other enslaved colored races from Africa to the new continent.

But let us look at the results of colonialism: undernourished peoples exploited for the metropolis; lingering endemic diseases which have not been combated; low economic productivity; societies almost without a native elite (we refer to those colonial people who already had a civilization of their own) and without administrative personnel save for small groups of merchants, as in India. Lacking administrative personnel, the new Afro-Asian states have to tackle terribly difficult problems, unlikely to be solved. On the other hand, each retreat of a colonial power was accompanied either by the destruction of the scanty industrial plant through internal fighting for liberation, as in Indochina or Indonesia, or by the ebb of metropolitan capital which migrated directly or by underground processes to other regions, weakening the incipient national economies. It was because of this that the economic structures of the old colonies emerged weak and inefficient. Many of these states are not yet fifteen years old. In Malaysia, Indochina, India, Pakistan, and Ceylon the capital now circulating is more or less the same as that of the colonial era. In Iraq and the Near East in general the capital is mixed, being English, Dutch, French, North American, or Swiss. Western European and North American capitalists employing hidden investments have the advantage in the struggle against scarce national capital in the new states. In this way colonialism lives on, disguised as econo-financial influence, and it is very difficult to say when a new international mentality will develop which will be willing to help the growth of these new states freely, without pressures.

The use of the term "colonialism" in a pejorative sense is very recent, and indeed it does not appear with this meaning in the Larousse Dictionary until the 1929 edition, where it is defined as follows: "name by which the socialists designate and condemn colonial expansion which they consider a form of imperialism derived from capitalist organization." The condemnation of colonialism thus serves to explain the various problems arising not only from the relations between whites and nonwhites but also from those of Western Europe and the continents over which she has in a general way exercised her domination for more than two centuries. The circumstances, however, under which triumphant anticolonialism arose and has developed gave colonialism another special meaning for Europe, a pejorative one also, so that "anticolonialism" has come to mean a special social and political phenomenon strictly opposed to European capitalism. However, we all know that the elimination of European colonialism is far from simultaneously eliminating the exploitation of peoples or even of nations by other nations more progressive or powerful than they. We remember the pseudofederalism of the nations which make up the Union of Soviet Socialist Republics, a state constructed on the basis of a union freely consented to with members equal in rights. The revolts and their repression in Georgia, that of the Tatars of the Crimea, of the Yugoslavs and Czechs, all bear witness to this "free consent" to a union. Moreover, Soviet expansion in Europe, the Baltic, and the states under her protection (the so-called Iron-Curtain or satellite countries) can be compared to the creation of the old colonial empires. The workers' revolts in East Germany and Poland and the Hungarian Revolution were also marked by terrible repressions.

The chief delegate of Ceylon to the Bandung Conference pointed out and denounced this new form of colonialism to the Afro-Asian peoples. It is true that on that same occasion the Indian Nehru recalled that in free America the United States had used or was using, in cases such as that of Guatemala, a process of disguised colonial intervention along the lines of those denounced by the Ceylon delegate, Sir John Kotelawal. In his book *Conversations with Nehru*, Tibor Mende, a political writer, also classifies as neoimperialism or Latin-Americanization the econo-financial penetration of economically weak nations by the strong through economic ideologies. Such "satellization" and Latino-Americanization, says Mende, are equivalent. We quote this to show how far opinions go with regard to colonialism and its imperialist significance.

II

The theme of nationalism is closely linked to the movements against colonialism, though it does not yet possess a definite ideological configuration. It is the force of the dialectic of some ideology or other that delimits nationalism: it is nothing more than an exaggerated form of retaliatory patriotism, a resultant of the emancipation of these Asian and African states, aggravated by the necessity of creating a force of containment against any new domination, be it political, economic, or spiritual. Since the majority of states are underdeveloped nations or economically backward countries, this sentiment of nationalism was propagated with intensity and violence. During the centuries of Western military and commercial penetration of the immense East, a nationalist sentiment bordering on xenophobia developed, especially in China, which prided itself on its ancient civilization. Hatred of foreigners became an obsession of the governments in China. The Opium War, the insurrection of the Black Flags, that of the Boxers, and finally the nationalist revolutions of Sun Yat-sen and Mao Tse-tung were initially of a nationalistic nature. Japan, when forced to accept coexistence with the West by the opening of her ports by Commodore Perry, adapted herself to Western technology. For this reason she was the only Asian country that rose in status in the eyes of the West and which took part in the system of military alliances and even accepted the colonial method of wars of conquest on the Asian continent. Today China exults in her nationalism. In India it is a cohesive force. In all these Asian and African states ideologies are based on nationalism. And I refer specifically to that vindicating spiritual force which seeks to assert itself as a nation-state.

But these new Afro-Asian states cannot move forward at a normal pace of development. That difference in tempo is what sets them apart. It is not only by the evolution of European technology that they will be able to solve their problems of growth, of fitting into the modern world economy. They are attracted by North American technology and scientific outlook only, within the capitalist system, or by the development techniques of the USSR, but applied at a much faster pace. Such methods as these can adequately accelerate the industrial progress that will raise them to the category of developed states. Also it will be necessary to rush through stages, to skip those considered unnecessary. Within this new rhythm of development the underdeveloped states will be able to advance materially and to give their inhabitants a standard of living compatible with modern material well-being, civil rights, and power. On the other hand, the lifting up of these states through technology, through the very science that formerly debased them (because they had not been able to discover or use this technology and, above all, apply inventions to war industries), will permit them to cleanse their subconscious of their inferiority complex. The course of world history would possibly have been different had the Chinese known how to utilize powder in cannons rather than for fireworks.

Having established a false premise in considering the difference in the way of life between Orientals and Westerners as an obstacle between the East and West, the European, for his part, underestimated the greatness of the ancient civilizations. He had no desire to capture the spirit of those ancient cultures, to complement the pragmatic civilization of Europe, its technical spirit mixed with remnants of humanism, by study of an Oriental world abounding in more spiritual riches than in the wealth that motivated the ambition of the West. We do not believe that the West is capable of realizing or renouncing all that . subtle web of superstition and misunderstanding of the East in the interest of an international coexistence based on moral and legal equality.

Actually all these misunderstandings between the West and the East came about in this way: while the East maintained a refined, spiritual, more static civilization, the West followed the opposite dynamic way, guided by technology and science on the road to material progress and comfort, which it believed, and still seems to believe, to be man's highest objective and the exclusive and lasting heritage of the West. Europe forgot that civilizations had evolved which, since they were not concerned about creating a special technology to achieve wealth and power, could perhaps be considered different and exotic, but were founded on concepts of esthetics, philosophy, and religious meditation, having in that sense attained a high degree of spirituality. Scientific frenzy had dominated the spirit of the industrial European, and it was not possible for the Westerner to appreciate the static way of life of Orientals, which he considered anachronistic.

However, let us see what a rapid industrialization of the Orient and of Africa might hold for the Western world. Communism is victorious in China. The industrio-economic development of the immense Chinese state is proceeding rapidly at a quickened tempo. For this the USSR has served as a model, and Peking receives its greatest aid in economic means and technical assistance from Russia. The other states of Asia are inclined to follow this rapid method, but they protect themselves from Communist infiltration, supported either by their own nationalism or by discreet help from the West, especially from the United States. In almost all the Afro-Asian countries there is no strong working class, and the difficulties of implanting or propagating Marxist doctrines in them result from the lack of this class. An effort to create this class within the briefest possible time would be ideal, but this would necessitate building up an important industrial plant. In any case, the creation of such a plant would require a certain amount of time, especially since it would also be necessary to raise the technical level of the workers and create a specialized labor force.

While this program of industrialization and technoscientific development is being worked out pursuant to the desires of these underdeveloped states, Moscow has also prepared a program for joining local Communist elements to the present efforts of the various nations, to strengthen the concept of nationalism in the struggle against the so-called imperialist powers. The aims are economic infiltration and so-called military alliances; to create in the public mind a distrust for Western capitalism and, increasingly, to alienate Americans and the new nations from each other; to present economic aid as corrupting

and useless because of its insignificance compared to the enormous general needs; to hold up the example of the Soviet Union
as a national pattern, a model of a great power which by its own
efforts passed from a semifeudal regime to the status of an
accomplished industrialized economy.

And China is held up as another model for its aid to North
Korea, for stopping the best-equipped military forces in the
world. Thus, for the moment a highly stressed concept of violent
nationalism replaces that of the class struggle. The Communists
stimulate and aggravate this Afro-Asian nationalism and preach
perfect internal unity, without distinction of ideologies, among
the so-called bourgeois elements, the conservatives, and between
these elites and the revolutionary left, for the sake of the greatness of the country. The alliance of all nationalists, both of the
right and of the left, is the objective of this propaganda. This
policy was initiated in 1930 with the so-called national fronts in
Europe. It was thus possible to create an attitude which permitted declaring at the Seventh Congress of the Comintern
which met in 1935 that the principal task of the Communists
was setting up anti-imperialist national fronts in colonial and
semicolonial countries.

The alliance of the USSR with the Western powers during
World War II interrupted this policy. The Communists were
then able to increase their propaganda campaign by utilizing
psychological and emotional factors. The old ones of the material class struggle were abandoned. The most outstanding aspect
of the psychological propaganda was that it emphasized the
economic dependence of the nations recently liberated from
capitalist colonialism.

In truth there are two phases in the process of passing from a
colony to a sovereign nation. First, the country acquires political
liberty; it is only later that it begins its economic emancipation
when by great effort and by adapting means to ends it organizes
its administrative personnel and its domestic and foreign affairs.
It is this intermediate period between political and economic
emancipation that is the most dangerous phase in the existence
of a new state. This time lag almost always upsets national life.

The political parties, instead of serving the institutions as groups which advise and encourage them and thus creating conditions favorable to the solution of the great economic problems, indulge in mutual recriminations.

In this way, apparently unexplainable vacuums are created which are accounted for by insidious foreign propagandists for the imperialists or the Marxists in ways always favorable to their material and ideological interests. If the new state ventures into the struggle to create heavy industry, the inflationary difficulties resulting from this effort are later explained as an error in the planning of economic policy, since it has upset the normal rhythm and destroyed public finances instead of strengthening them.

However, it is well known that between the moment of conception and development of a heavy and medium industry effort and the moment in which it begins to produce wealth, objective results, and immense benefits for the country, there is an intermediate phase in which capital is consumed and public finances are disjointed. However, it is this moment that is seized upon by false prophets and Communist agents in their desire to weaken the country, reduce its strength, and ruin the nation, to draw over to their side the great mass of unthinking people. This is what has happened and will continue to happen in the Afro-Asian world and in other parts of the world where traces of other forms of colonialism exist. Some affirm that it would have been better to maintain a small basic industry which would be developed systematically at the same time as agriculture. The agriculture is generally colonial, infected by monoculture, and export prices for its tropical products are highly vulnerable. Others think a medium industry which would develop pari passu with systematic mechanization of labor would be better. Others even assert that the ideal would be to expand agriculture, improve and diversify it, while keeping industry within strict limits and buying abroad the excellent foreign manufactured goods available.

We might say that Marxists and imperialists become allies to prevent the development of certain underdeveloped states. This is because the imperialist defends his sales areas and wants to buy agricultural products at low prices in order to obtain greater profits from his manufacture. So-called colonial products such as cotton, sugar, fibers, fats, cacao, and coffee are worth little compared to manufactured products. Statistics prove this. Without industry, mineral products go out, and so do solid and liquid fuels. This is the problem of the Arab countries and of other exporters of oil. Living standards remain low, development is slow, and patriots declaim on national aspirations. Will there be sufficient political sophistication in such countries to enable them to discern such subtle propaganda? This is what gives rise to that atmosphere of constant frustration which we find in the so-called underdeveloped countries; these frustrations cause them to turn to the Communist methods for sensational rapid material accomplishments as the only solution to overcome precisely that critical stage which lies between political and economic emancipation. We cannot deny that the promise is most attractive to those who do not possess a true democratic spirit, particularly when we analyze the mistakes of the opposite camp, that is, of the capitalist states who delay in coming to the aid of the weakly organized economies of the underdeveloped countries, and thus seem to justify the claims of their opponents.

But we must remember that some vigorous elites nevertheless join discredited groups. In general, vigorous Western elites ally themselves in the Afro-Asian countries with discredited conservative groups and oppose the others who are anxious to conduct programs useful to the states. What happens then is that the latter also seek strange alliances in order to create conditions favorable to their victory. But both groups are separated by a static body, the masses. At all times the success of an idea, the triumph of an ideology, the attainment of a program, depend on setting that apparently inert body in motion. Without that body, without that immense energy, no country will be able to develop power. And that mass is tremendous in Asia and relatively large in Africa. Who will be the first to obtain its cooperation?

III

We believe that it will not be possible to govern the world with a modern science which places humanity in the atomic age while with a medieval conscience it attempts to maintain the structure of society. In April, 1955, the first Afro-Asian conference took place in the city of Bandung in Indonesia. Bandung was a symptom of a profound revolution in the political organization of the world. Without resulting in any immediate accomplishment, the conference acted as a catalytic agent for the forces of the world which until then had not been conscious of unity. At Bandung a powerful spiritual current was born, that of neutralism. The general idea of nonviolence preached by Ghandi— his message—was adopted by the twenty-nine countries which took part in that meeting. Neutralism arose as the political expression of nonviolence; it was an answer to the so-called peripheric strategy, an answer still barely articulated. It was specifically moral in tone, an Eastern form of Afro-Asian unity directed against the West: nonviolence against power. The principles which guided the Bandung Conference were inspired by the *Pancha Sila*, the five Indian bases, principles which may be summarized as the rejection of aggression and even of ideological intervention in other states.

The countries which met in Bandung were very diverse. It will be enough to mention them by groups: the Arab countries, the African countries, Red China, those of Southeast Asia, Indonesia—representing almost 1,300 million inhabitants. Nehru, the great Indian political leader, defined Bandung as Afro-Asian opposition to Western domination, because, as he said, it was a point on which all Afro-Asian countries were in agreement. The achievement of Bandung was that it was an international conference where there was no disagreement among the states represented. The patient and the impatient in the social sense met on the same level for the same purposes. The conference bred a feeling of solidarity among these Afro-Asian peoples.

The peace problem was examined in Bandung as a position not necessarily arising from a policy of force. What these underdeveloped countries intended was to profit from the lessons of human experience in the political realm to benefit world harmony, a juridical coexistence of states. The policies of force of all the groups were condemned. At Bandung the Afro-Asian states sought to create a peace zone. Before Bandung relations between the Afro-Asian peoples and the two blocs were conditioned by a world situation dominated by the reality of the Cold War. Consequently, there was no alternative for those peoples other than to accept the dilemma: to be in favor of Communism or of capitalism. Washington and Moscow polarized the situation. The third position, that third possibility for the Afro-Asian countries, was created at Bandung—a position which has validity for all the world.

Asian neutrality, or, rather, the so-called third position, arose from the principles debated at the Bandung Conference. It is a way of noninvolvement in a war on the part of various states of certain areas or of given regions or zones of the earth. It means maintenance of a peace zone between, or on the boundaries of, the belligerents. The division of the world into two opposing blocs, and the fear of the weak states of finding themselves involved in a general international war, is what seems to justify this neutralist third position. Neutralism will be stronger, that is, more positive, the greater the number of countries that consider themselves neutral between the two sides. In this way they will also establish the possibility of peace being maintained by that negative neutral attitude.

To reject neutralism is to accept the idea of the inevitability of war. The neutralists preach conciliation and they trust, or are more or less convinced of, the willingness of the Soviets to accept peaceful coexistence among the opposing groups. The French neutralists tend to credit the "honest" intentions of the Soviet Union. The Soviet Union is interested in upholding the neutralist thesis not only to avoid the rapid rearmament of Germany but also to delay that of other powers or to weaken military alliances. The neutralism of the small powers will have little influence on the balance of power of the two opposing groups, but the neutralism of many nations, whether strong or weak, associated for that purpose might perhaps modify the conduct of international politics.

The neutralization of Western Europe and of North Africa and the neutralism of India and of other Asian states might create a chain of states anxious to maintain peace, an armed neutrality like that of Sweden, which might come to constitute a considerable element of containment against any armed conflict between the two opposing blocs. In the meantime, a neutralism which would begin by disarming states, a neutralism without military power, or many neutralist states without that power, would be more of an incentive to war than a means of maintaining peace. Yugoslav neutrality is intended to keep that country free of obligations to either of the two opposing sides. On the American continent Argentina has been showing itself favorable to neutralism. Its position up to now is clearly one of neutralism. In both World Wars it abstained from taking a position on the side of any belligerent group. It was not a neutrality inspired by the classic type or by the ideological one of nonviolence. The third position Argentina chose for itself was, to put it this way, one of opposition to the United States, an anti-American position, particularly throughout the last war when during the Perón regime, after the peace, and after the beginning of the Cold War, Argentina went as far as an economic rapprochement with the opponents of the United States, which led to the recognition of the USSR and to establishing diplomatic relations with Moscow. Argentine neutralism, therefore, does not allow Argentina to participate fully in the doctrine of collective defense of the Americas on which are based the juridical obligations of the Organization of the American States.

IV

The war in Algeria is another polarizing point of that Cold War which has been disturbing the world for years. Suez also brought a threat of war to the world. The formation of the new Arab states, the uniting of Egypt with Syria and Yemen, that of Jordan with Iraq, are part of the Pan-Arab movement exploited by Moscow against the West. In general, Pan-Arabism is directed against the West. Nasser was spectacularly successful in his policy of supporting the USSR. The United Arab Republic of Nasser has great appeal for the populations of the other Arab states, including Jordan. The danger of such an outstanding triumph is that of a loss of contact with reality and with the real material strength which those states command. This might lead them to an expansionist program against the interests of the Western powers in the Middle East. The problem between Arabs and Jews is another serious point of friction which is always present. The USSR is aware that the great problems of Asia are not political in nature, but rather economical, and that only time will solve them. In the meantime, economic difficulties are so great in Asia and in Africa that they seem unsolvable. Those great Asian leaders, Nehru and Mao Tse-tung, do not conceal these difficulties from their countrymen, and even less do they hide the fact that the future appears even more difficult. Austerity compaigns are launched and advice is given to that effect. Nor was Vietnam, an anti-Communist country, spared by the crisis. Burma, which adopted socialism, and Indonesia, which is a guided democracy, are also struggling with immense economic obstacles.

North America and the Soviet Union, already highly industrialized nations, still devote high percentages of their capital and of their economies to the improvement and development of their industrial establishments according to their economic systems. Now, in the underdeveloped countries or in the economically backward ones of Asia and of Africa, which have limited investment capital and deficient economies, such a percentage is far from meeting their basic development needs. The situation is no better in the Arab countries with their highly productive subsoil, rich in oil. It is useless to give examples because it is obvious. Foreign companies are the ones who exploit this oil, and the part which the countries receive is still very small compared with the immense profit to those who exploit such wealth. Events have proved that Nasser is a leader, whether we wish to accept him as one or not. The Arab world, more than any other group of countries, is inspired not only by the force of nationalism, but by another, equal and more spiritual, which is a burning faith. The Holy War of old now reappears reinvigorated by the politico-social meaning. The only thing which Nasser now lacks is for the Egyptian leader also to obtain the title of Commander of the Faithful. Those two forces being joined—the political power and the religious, spiritual power—the unity of the Arab world would create a powerful community within the Afro-Asian world.

V

During the last days of 1957 and the first of 1958 another Afro-Asian conference, considered by many experts the complement of the one at Bandung, met in Cairo. Called the Conference of Afro-Asian Solidarity, its agenda was prepared by the Preparatory Commission which also met in Cairo at Nasser's invitation in October, 1957. But the idea for that conference arose from an organization called the Committee of Afro-Asian Solidarity, which had for its objective the tightening of the bonds between the nations of Asia and of Africa. Since, as we have already said, those Afro-Asian areas do not possess a strong labor force, Communist propaganda relies on certain entities apparently lacking political or ideological coloring, on intransigent nationalist, anti-Western, and anti-American groups devoted to weakening relations between the West and Afro-Asians. The Cairo meeting did not have the juridico-international character of a meeting of states, as did the Bandung one, and did not go beyond the social sphere. At Bandung, Red China was not allowed to submit questions pertaining to Communism. On the other hand, it would have been difficult for Moscow or Peking to convene an international meeting on the government level toward the end of 1957. The choice of Cairo resulted from the importance Egypt has recently acquired within the political camps. Egypt's position on the side of the Communist sympathizers greatly aided that choice. The Committee of Afro-Asian Solidarity has similar organizations in almost all Afro-Asian countries and receives strong material and political support from Moscow. The so-called Peace Congresses are similar organizations.

Twenty-three Afro-Asian states were represented at the Cairo conference. At the time of the conference, Egypt created the Egyptian Afro-Asian Solidarity Committee, whose president is the editor of the pro-Soviet journal *El Gumhuriya* and also president of Egypt's only political party. The most important points on the agenda were three: consideration of the international situation and its effect on the Afro-Asians; opposition to imperialism and the right of peoples to self-determination and sovereignty; prohibition of the use of atomic weapons and cessation of nuclear bomb tests. As secondary points we might mention the Algerian war and support of technical, economic, and cultural cooperation among Afro-Asians. Among the objectives sought by the Communists at the meeting the following stand out: influencing the delegations not controlled by Communist elements; having the USSR accepted as an Asian state also, which would give it the right to intervene and take part in meetings of the Afro-Asian states; aggravating the tension between the conference participants and the West. To grant the USSR legal status as an Asian state would allow Russia ostensibly to become the leader of the Asians, with even more direct participation in national liberation movements, especially in uniting the Arab world. This would also allow the USSR to cooperate more closely with those states economically. Finally, it is obvious that the status of Asian state would give the Soviet Union direct participation in Asian problems, with access to key positions in the Indian Ocean, and the Red and Mediterranean seas.

The meeting adopted a long series of recommendations making clear Russia's position as champion of peace and the condemnation of military pacts. Colonialism and imperialism were condemned within the spirit of the Bandung Conference. Action in favor of the independence of Kenya, Cameroons, Uganda, Madagascar, and Somaliland was also recommended, as well as the cessation of aggression against Oman and the return of Irian (Western New Guinea) to Indonesia, of Goa to

India, and of Okinawa to Japan. The reunification of Vietnam and of Cambodia was also recommended, and support for the Arab struggle for unity and independence was expressed. The Baghdad Pact and the so-called Eisenhower Doctrine were denounced as outrages against Arab sovereignty. Racial discrimination, especially in South Africa, was likewise condemned. The policy of "atrocities" committed by French imperialism in Algeria was also condemned, and immediate recognition of the independence of that African country was recommended. The aggressive policy of Israel was condemned, and the repatriation of Arab refugees was recommended. Finally, the conference recommended the admission of Red China and of Mongolia to the United Nations and adopted a declaration of ten points which recapitulated the principles of Bandung as the basis of all international policy. We want to emphasize that the USSR was accepted as an Asian country with equality with the other countries participating in the meeting, which goes to show the success of Communist activity in the debate.

VI

We knew or cared little about that Afro-Asian world until the beginning of World War I. We maintained minimum diplomatic relations with Japan and with China at the beginning of the century. Later on relations widened, but (except with Japan, with whom we had greater commercial ties) still with the other countries they were more of a political than of an economic nature. Brazil, until then, had not thought to widen its field of economic action in the East and in Africa. At present our diplomacy takes on a new aspect, adapts to the needs of the moment, to domestic economic conditions, and turns abroad as our economic policy includes those important areas of the world within its sphere of interest. A new examination which will allow us to compete in those Afro-Asian markets is urgent. Meanwhile, great effort will be required, both in the domestic and foreign spheres, in order to attain a place for us among the countries competing for the Afro-Asian markets. On the other hand, the emergence of Africa as a colonial production zone, in competition with the agricultural production of Latin America, as an area to which the international capital from the former colonial areas of Asia has migrated, and the direct or indirect investments by the United States in the Black Continent—all confront Brazilian diplomacy and economic policy with a serious problem which must be studied and solved.

At the United Nations Brazil and Latin America in general have maintained close contact with certain Afro-Asian countries, especially with those known as the Arab World. But lately, in view of certain events, such as acceptance of the protection of Portuguese interests in India, this position has suffered a slight modification. Our attitude with relation to the countries of North Africa during their struggle for independence was not always consistent. By this I do not mean, nor do I wish, to criticize the conduct of the Brazilian Foreign Office, but Brazil has never considered only the practical aspects; it was never opportunistic, and its policies were always guided by a juridical spirit. If it sometimes departed from these norms, it was guided by a policy of tolerance, of understanding, and by a degree of humanism. It was this that allowed us such wise generosity toward Italy after the last war.

If we still do not give the Afro-Asians complete support in certain juridico-political questions, on the other hand, we are almost always with them on essentially economic problems, such as that of the creation of the economic commission for Africa proposed by Brazil, which only reached the United Nations through our efforts. With the raising of living standards the African populations may attain the development necessary for their liberation. We have also cooperated fully with these African peoples in increasing commercial relations, in order to strengthen in Africa economies which might later purchase our manufactured products. We can hardly avoid the development of Africa, and it would be better right now to chart a policy for that market.

Brazil's Foreign Policy
Toward Latin America*

Luis Bastian Pinto

It has been customary for those who study and interpret Brazil's continental policy to set forth a series of basic principles which are supposed to represent traditional Brazilian lines of action in the hemisphere in a general way. These principles may be stated as follows:

1. Rejection of war, and especially wars of conquest, as a means of solving a conflict. This principle is written into the Constitution and is believed by many to derive from the peaceful nature of the Brazilian people and from their adherence to the cause of international justice.

2. Recourse to arbitration as a means of solving international disputes, with such zeal and steadfastness that many have come to regard this as a "typically Brazilian institution."

3. Uncompromising defense of the principle of juridical equality of states.

4. Strict adherence to international juridical instruments.

5. Maintenance of the status quo on the continent, which includes preservation of existing frontiers and opposition to the formation of any blocs, whether political, economic, or military, among countries of Latin America, even with the participation of Brazil.

These are the principles which are stated time and again to be

* This article was originally published in Portuguese as "A Política Exterior do Brasil na America Latina," in *Revista Brasileira de Política Internacional* 2(8):51–64, Dec., 1959. Translated and printed by permission.

those that guide our actions on this continent. However, I believe that this enunciation of principles is incorrect in that it is
unduly theoretical and does not really represent historical facts
as recorded throughout the centuries, nor does it correspond to
a deeper investigation of reality. These principles have undoubtedly given rise to our most moving speeches, but several of them
will not stand up under close scrutiny. Suffice it to say that rejection of war, defense of the juridical equality of states, and respect
for treaties have all been enunciated as fundamental principles
of action by practically all countries, including the Soviet Union.
Moreover, the first two are natural means of defense for all weak
countries.

As for arbitration, I want to point out that during the nineteenth century there were 212 cases of arbitration, 84 of them
among American nations, but Brazil was a party to only 5 of
these. Moreover, throughout our history as an independent
country we have been a party to barely nine arbitration cases,
some of them of very minor importance; therefore, I cannot see
how arbitration can be called a typically Brazilian institution.
The fact that in this way we solved three important boundary
disputes (with Argentina and with the French and British
Guianas) in less than ten years must have given rise to this idea,
which we have been repeating for half a century without subjecting it to fresh scrutiny or considering whether it does not already
belong to the past. I believe that admiration for the work of Rui
Barbosa at The Hague has also been a factor in giving rise to the
conviction that the principle of juridical equality of states is
ours exclusively.

Therefore, I believe that this way of stating the basic principles governing our political orientation on the continent is in
reality the result of an excessively theoretical and superficial
appraisal; this was mainly due to the fact that until a few years
ago we in Brazil, self-contained within our enormous territory
and almost exclusively preoccupied with our own internal
growth, were barely aware that other countries existed and that
we lived in a world made up of many nations. Foreign policy
was left to a small group of initiates; the rest of the country did

not permit what happened in other parts of the world to affect it, except occasionally, and then it reacted in an emotional manner.

It was only after World War II that Brazil awoke to international problems. Its awakening was very sudden. The whole nation now has become aware that today our great domestic problems are all in one way or another closely related to international life; the ruling classes now take great interest in foreign affairs, and for the first time domestic policy and foreign policy matters are linked. I think we have a long way to go in this respect: opinions are not always based on solid foundations, and emotions color the attitude of many toward foreign affairs. But we are making progress, and the truth is that we can already see the beginnings of full national participation in international life.

It seems to me that here we find a very important difference between Brazil and the rest of Latin America. While we within our great territory concentrated on ourselves and were almost indifferent to what was going on outside, the other Latin American countries much smaller, and consequently having their power centers much closer to each other, had constant and intensive contact with neighboring countries, established economic and personal relations, and were subject to many rivalries, serious frontier conflicts, and even numerous wars. Foreign policy was something which affected the life of the people much more than in the case of Brazil; this led to the development of a more deeply rooted international consciousness than among our own people.

Undoubtedly it was this isolation from the rest of the continent that gave rise to the conviction, very popular at the beginning of the century and still having many adherents, that we are different from the people in neighboring countries, that we are not part of Latin America, and even that we are a part of Europe transplanted to this side of the ocean. This strange idea, for which I see no foundation, pervaded our international policy during the first half of this century, and even now we can see vestiges of it, especially in the personal attitudes of our representatives abroad. For instance, this has led to the habit (which up to now we have been unable to change) of having our delegates to great international conferences speak in French or English, but never in Spanish.

Fortunately we are rapidly correcting an attitude which is so senseless and, especially, so harmful to our policy within the hemisphere.

II

Among the frequently mentioned principles to which I referred above, perhaps the one considered of greatest consequence is that of maintaining the status quo in South America. In fact, Brazil, as the largest country in the southern part of the hemisphere, occupying half its area and with half its population, throughout its history has tended to refuse to accept basic changes in the existing structure which might decrease its superiority. An example of the application of this principle has been Brazil's resistance whenever Argentina showed signs of expansion, whether by acquisition of territory in the past or by attempts at economic domination, as during the Perón era. We could also cite our official declaration to Bolivia in 1938 that we would guarantee its future territorial integrity.

However, more careful analysis of this policy reveals that it was not strictly and unremittingly relied on in the past and that it cannot serve as a safe guide for future action. We have already seen some examples of this in territorial questions. In the War of the Pacific the Empire did not oppose the conquest by Chile of great areas of Bolivian and Peruvian territories. In 1928, when Peru unexpectedly ceded Leticia to Colombia—by a treaty which broke the exclusively Brazilian-Peruvian possession of the banks of the Amazon River and which presaged unavoidable future conflicts—we contented ourselves with demanding guarantees that our frontiers would be respected. Then in 1932, when we arbitrated the Leticia conflict, we did not try to return to the historical status quo, but, on the contrary, we exerted a realistic pacifying action and returned the territory to the spurious, but no longer avoidable, sovereignty of Colombia. We did not oppose the recent attempts to reestablish Great Colombia by means of wide-ranging agreements (which, by the way, were ineffective) between Colombia, Venezuela, and Ecuador, and, indeed, we could not very well oppose them.

What does the future hold? Let us mention that at a recent Economic Commission for Latin America (CEPAL) meeting in Santiago at which the formation of a South American regional market was being studied, the question arose whether it would not be preferable to begin by establishing groups of countries within the same zone, as, for example, those in the southern part of South America, in order to find formulas later which would embrace the whole continent. Brazil is considering this matter realistically and does not oppose it on the ground of mere theoretical principles which in practice have been shown to be inapplicable.

Now, if even this, undoubtedly the most basic and the most often quoted principle of all, means so little, it seems to me that what we must do is to examine our continental policies conscientiously in the light of present conditions and of the tendencies we can already foresee for the near future—and especially to set aside any considerations of a more theoretical or rhetorical nature which are out of date in relation to the present situation. I am attempting, not to define here a policy which in many ways is still uncertain and fluid, but only to set down some basic elements which have already been ascertained, and to make a modest contribution toward the study of the solutions which are open to us.

III

There is no room here for a history of our territorial development, but it is well to recall that in this matter we uphold the principle of *uti possidetis de facto*, already included by Alexandre de Gusmão in the Treaty of Madrid in 1750. This doctrine of ours differs from that held by the Hispanic American countries for fixing their boundaries, that of *uti possidetis juris*, based on the right of possession according to the old subdivisions of colonial America.

Rio-Branco ended the task of fixing our boundaries by deciding the last important cases pending. The work of this great chancellor was perseveringly and patiently continued by his successors, who have striven to solve the minor disagreements which will inevitably arise on our very extensive boundary lines, and to that end various agreements have been entered into, such as the treaty of 1928 with Bolivia. We must emphasize here the truly heroic work of our boundary commissions that for many years have labored tirelessly, and sometimes under the most precarious conditions, and whose efforts deserve to be better known in Brazil.

The fixing of our boundaries still has not been completed, and Itamaraty* is striving to fix the last open sectors. Minister José Carlos de Macedo Soares only recently succeeded in concluding an agreement with Bolivia settling certain differences which were impairing our relations with that country because of the acute sensibility of Bolivian public opinion. The settlement arrived at may be considered brilliant, since we came to an agreement which fully satisfies our neighbor and, at the same time, completely protects our rights.

Throughout our history from colonial times through the era of the Republic, Brazil has expanded into adjacent territories, and almost all the treaties we concluded sanctioned our territorial acquisitions. For this very reason certain neighboring countries retain a trace of resentment, and some of them continue to harbor a latent fear of the possibility of Brazilian expansion. It is only in Bolivia that this fear is strong, which is understandable since the Acre question is still recent enough to be remembered. But for this very reason it behooves us to guide our policy with the greatest care in order to quiet these feelings and avoid any action which might revive them, while at the same time we attempt to secure the frontiers which may be subject to eventual pressure from adjacent countries.

IV

The actual or potential antagonism between Brazil and Argentina has been the most powerful and persistent of the factors

* Translator's note: Itamaraty Palace houses the Brazilian Foreign Office.

determining our continental policy. It is unnecessary to recall
the military conflicts of the past, during both the colonial and
the Imperial eras, which determined the present political structure of the River Plate region, by fixing its frontiers and creating
the buffer states of Uruguay and Paraguay. At the end of the
long period of the wars this antagonism (which resulted from
the proximity of two relatively powerful countries that had
clashed so many times already) continued. The material wealth
of Argentina naturally influenced the economies of the other
countries and allowed it at times to bring very strong political
pressure to bear. Results were positive at times; several of the
adjacent countries lived for years in more or less political and
economic dependence on Buenos Aires. Quite recently this
policy was carried to such lengths by the Peronist authorities
that it caused very strong reactions.

However, in recent years the circumstances which determined
the relative political position of Brazil and Argentina have
changed radically. Moreover, the rapid development of Brazil,
particularly in the field of industry, has wiped out the difference
in economic power which existed (or which at least we had
thought existed) between the two countries. Therefore we no
longer need fear or distrust their attitudes. On the other hand,
the profound social, economic, and political crisis in which
Argentina is presently floundering seems to have appreciably
modified the thinking of its ruling circles; everything now seems
to indicate a decrease in Argentine public opinion favoring a
foreign policy which does not coincide with our interests.

Also, the intensification of international activity after the war
and the present interdependence of the great domestic problems
of each country and its foreign relations tend to decrease the
relative importance of the problems which separated Brazil from
Argentina. On the contrary, they have brought to the fore those
matters in which we have common interests to defend before the
rest of the world. These circumstances make it evident that we
must formulate a new policy with relation to Argentina, one
which will lead to a profitable, open, and cordial understanding
with our neighbor. We should ignore all factors that no longer

represent the reality of the moment and try to eliminate any vestige of that mutual distrust which still sometimes seems subconsciously to color relations between the two countries.

President Frondizi's tenure was barely the beginning of a new government, but still it was an episode in the far-reaching revolution through which that country is passing. Though perhaps no more sweeping than what we are undergoing in our own land, it is certainly more violent and for that very reason more crucial. Consequently, this is the moment when our attitude toward Argentina may have the greatest influence in determining its future foreign policy. We must carefully observe the tendencies of the new Argentina. These are not yet quite clear, but the main outlines are already discernible. There is no longer any serious talk about the "third position" of Perón; Argentina has accepted alignment with the Western world, but it will attempt to orient its foreign policy in a highly hemispheric sense, this being understood to mean bringing about closer understanding in the political and economic relations between Latin American nations. This would not only be operative with regard to our potential enemies but it would also increase our effectiveness in negotiations with friendly nations such as the United States and those of Western Europe.

In fact, there is now a widespread belief in Brazilian and Argentine ruling circles that the main interests of both countries are closely related rather than in conflict. Therefore, the time has come for us to achieve the type of cooperation that will benefit us as well as the rest of the continent. Though as a conclusion this statement may seem too general and too vague, it assumes crucial importance because it represents the key to Brazilian policy on the continent.

V

Paraguay and Bolivia, as weaker neighbors (in comparison with whom we seem giants), both of which have had serious complaints against Brazil in the past, are the testing ground par excellence for the line of action we may follow as the greatest and strongest of the countries of the continent. Let us also not forget that the interests of the frontier regions are intimately bound together and that the development of one side of the frontier can only benefit the other. Even more, Bolivian oil is an example of the opportunities offered by a solid cooperation with our smaller neighbors.

In Paraguay in recent years Brazil's activities have been among the most intensive, through economic and technical cooperation for development of that country; the construction of superhighways to help counteract its landlocked position; effective cooperation in the cultural field; training of its armed forces; the conclusion of commercial and investment agreements, etc. These activities have been, with some exceptions, well coordinated and efficient, and have earned us great esteem and gratitude in Paraguay.

As for Bolivia, after a long period of uncertainty and disagreement which was beginning seriously to affect our prestige and was arousing latent distrust, we finally reached agreements making possible an era of close and profitable cooperation. But the task is not complete; these agreements will not be implemented automatically, and they require a careful effort on our part. We cannot repeat the mistakes of the recent past which included negligence in carrying out our obligations and lack of understanding of what our true rights and duties were.

With reference to Uruguay, a well-organized country, jealous of its independence but necessarily linked to its neighbor on the River Plate by strong bonds, our efforts in the past have been directed toward discreetly helping it to retain its autonomy. We have followed a similar line in our historic relations with Chile, a country with whom we have many very cordial ties (despite the distance which separates us), since Chileans, because of their conflicts with neighboring countries, look to Brazil as a potential ally.

Up to the present time we have remained even more distant from Peru despite our extensive common frontier. But in this case, too, political ties are quite strong, for the same reasons as with Chile. Here, perhaps, we come upon a new factor, the future importance of which is already becoming apparent, that is, the development of the Amazon Basin. The Brazilian government has already decided to undertake this and has even set aside a considerable percentage of the federal budget for the purpose. I want to emphasize that the problems of the Brazilian Amazon regions are common to the other neighboring countries of this great valley and that Itamaraty has reached the conclusion that Brazil, as a great Amazonian power and the one chiefly responsible for the future of the area, could not neglect taking the initiative in the survey, settlement, and economic exploitation of that immense region.

One of the factors that we should not overlook is that it is no longer a very remote possibility that Brazil may lose some areas of geopolitical influence which historically and geographically belong to it within the hydrographic basin comprising, or tributary to, the Amazon region. Or, what is even worse, that Brazilian populations or territories in the region may in the future, because of quickened development of adjacent areas, come to be subjected to overpowering economic influence by neighboring countries. An example of this is the "East" of Peru, which promises to develop quickly due to the influx of immigrants from the already overcrowded Peruvian coast, the construction of roads to the Pacific, and exploration for oil; it may come to be a center of attraction, ceasing to be tributary to the Brazilian Amazon region.

We cannot fail to cooperate with neighboring countries in their efforts toward development, since such a neglect would be equivalent to abdicating the role that is reserved for us as the largest Amazonian nation, but we must take precautions to make sure that the Brazilian Amazon will not become simply an exit channel for the goods of other countries and that these activities will become an effective factor in our development.

With this object in view, in 1958 we concluded various agreements with Bolivia, Peru, and Ecuador, and we expect to conclude others with Colombia and Venezuela. Several of these agreements provide for the formation of mixed commissions to study ways and means of obtaining effective cooperation on this matter. In addition, Itamaraty is organizing an official Permanent Work Group to study and weigh, on the level of the economic and political relations of Brazil with its Amazon Basin neighbors, the real national interests we should protect. Let us hope that guidelines for effective action may come from the work of these various organizations. The essential thing, however, is that we are now conscious of the problem.

VI

It can never be repeated too often that World War II radically changed the international political system by giving the relations between even the most distant peoples an importance and intensity unthought of a few years ago. It is within this new framework of international relations that we must examine the policies of Brazil in Latin America, without disregarding the lessons of the past, but, rather, adapting them to present circumstances.

In my opinion the first factor we must take into account, the most important one and the one that ought to determine the general outlines of our policy, is the fact that the world has been inexorably advancing during the last few years toward regionalism (or continentalism), that is, not only toward the predominance of nation-continents but also toward the political, economic, and military grouping of states according to their common interests and their geographical location.

It had become clear even before the end of the last war that those states smaller in area and population tended to disappear as great powers and that in their place the great masses of the nation-continents were rising irresistibly. At the end of the conflict those few men who then controlled the world at their discretion attempted to lead us to universalism through the creation of the United Nations and its related organizations. That idea was presented in such an Utopian manner that only a world disturbed by war could have accepted it, and now we have come to doubt the common sense or the good faith of those men. This is not because we think that the United Nations is likely to disappear; on the contrary, we are convinced that it and the other universal organizations will endure, but not as the absolute and exclusive panacea for all evils they were originally represented to be.

The Latin American nations, which were aware of the deficiencies of the United Nations from its inception, insisted upon saving the Organization of American States (OAS) and with great effort were able to preserve it with its full attributes, thus to establish a precedent for the subsequent creation of other regional organisms. Within a few years it became apparent that it was impossible for the United Nations to take care of all the objectives for which it had been created, especially because the organization itself unavoidably reflected the inevitable divergencies of its members. During this period all nations became progressively aware that few among them had sufficient power to solve by themselves their most pressing internal problems or even to endure as isolated entities in today's troubled world. Those nations which felt bound together by common interests and objectives gradually united and gave rise to the present innumerable groupings which variously have taken shape either as international organizations or military pacts, agreements for cooperation, or simply periodical meetings for the discussion of various subjects. The list of these groupings is already very long, but the most solid ones and those most likely to endure and become firmly established are the ones which are based on geographical proximity, that is, those formed among countries within the same region which are also united by other bonds.

The most impressive example of that tendency is the integration of Western Europe, which has been making great strides in recent years. It is indeed impressive to see how the peoples of Western Europe, who had fought one another from the dawn of history, became convinced of the need for regional union after the most bloody of all wars. Earlier, in 1946, Churchill had proposed the creation of a "United States of Europe," to be based on a Franco-German rapprochement. We have not gone that far and perhaps we never will, but after a time regional organizations—such as the European Council, the Western

European Union, the Coal and Steel Community, and several other organizations of an economic nature which culminated in EURATOM and the Common Market—started springing up in the Old World. The movement also spread to the rest of the world: the Arab League, the efforts at union among the African countries, and the Colombo Plan; Bandung, now especially based on political and economic interests, was also founded on a regional basis. We could cite many others.

Pan Americanism, although the oldest of the regional movements and already embodied in the OAS, has remained relatively static. The progress made by the OAS in the political field has been great, but certain factors tended to limit its greater development. The various differences between Latin America and the United States constitute one of these factors, especially because the latter nation wields much greater politico-economic power than all the other countries put together. Another one is the fact that Pan Americanism has always lacked an economic sense, its greatest development being in the political field.

But all that I have just said leads us to only one conclusion: the advisability and necessity of a more intimate union, of a true integration of the countries of Latin America. Such an integration would be based not only on the physical unity of the continent; it would confirm the deep roots of history, origin, religion, social and political background, language and racial admixture which are common to almost all the countries. It would also be based on the relatively similar stage of social and economic development, as well as on their aspirations for rapid and effective progress.

It is the reality of these common values that constitutes the essential element in the movement toward regional integration. These values have all been present from the beginning of our independent life as nations, but now the impulse toward integration is becoming irresistible. The one element that was still lacking, that of economic solidarity, is beginning to take shape. We find an example of this in the studies and projects for a future Latin American regional market. In Mr. Garrido Torres' definition, this means the gradual and progressive establishment of an area within which free trade in goods and services may eventually be carried on, to result in the optimal use of the human and natural resources of the region.

The realization is becoming widespread in our countries that we must move toward such unification. This will permit these nations to give each other mutual help, to resist possible adversaries with greater strength, and, especially, to negotiate more effectively even with their friends, such as the United States and Western Europe. This idea pervades *The Anti-Imperialist Struggle*, the book written by President Frondizi of Argentina, and in Chile the candidates for the presidency of the republic recently were promising in their campaign platforms to fight for the creation of the regional market.

In view of these facts, what should be the position of Brazil? Would it not be preferable for Brazil, which is already almost a continent in itself, to remain in an isolationist attitude? Everything indicates that the efforts at unification will continue with or without our support, and any negative attitude, or even any limitation on our part, will appreciably weaken our political position and would amount to renouncing our historical destiny on the continent. We are the ones naturally designated for this role. Our greater political and economic power, our greater area and population, our relative political stability, the absence of quarrels with our neighbors, our tradition of nonintervention in the internal affairs of others, and, in short, a variety of other factors, make us so.

In our opinion a desire to support a Latin American integration movement, to be carried out gradually and by successive stages, is the real motive for the present Itamaraty policy of rapprochement with our sister nations. This must also be true of all our foreign policy. In the context of a world tendency toward regionalism, Brazil finds itself in the privileged position of fulfilling all the conditions for influencing the destinies of Latin America as long as it continues to act in this respect with ability and persistence, and as long as it tries to defend the interests common to all more than its own. Such a policy will enable us to play, before both friends and foes, the significant part that is reserved for us in the world.

Brazil's New Foreign Policy*

Jânio Quadros

The interest shown in the position of Brazil in international
affairs is in itself proof of the presence of a new force on the
world stage. Obviously my country did not appear by magic, nor
is it giving itself momentarily to a more or less felicitous exhibi-
tion of publicity seeking. When I refer to a "new force," I am
not alluding to a military one, but to the fact that a nation, heretofore almost unknown, is prepared to bring to bear on the play
of world pressures the economic and human potential it represents, and the knowledge reaped from experience that we have
a right to believe is of positive value.

We are a nation of continental proportions, occupying almost
half of South America, relatively close to Africa and, ethnically,
having indigenous, European and African roots. Within the next
decade, our population will amount to close to 100 million inhabitants, and the rapid industrialization of some regions of the
country heralds our development into an economic power.

At present we are still beset by the evils of underdevelopment
which make of the greater part of our country the scene for
quasi-Asiatic dramas. We have poverty-stricken areas which are
overpopulated, and we have vast regions—the largest in the
world—still unconquered. And yet, great cities are becoming
industrial and trade centers of major significance.

* Reprinted by special permission from FOREIGN AFFAIRS, 40(1):
19–27 (Oct., 1961). Copyright © by the Council on Foreign Relations,
Inc., New York.

If Brazil is only now being heard of in international affairs, it is because on taking office I decided to reap the consequences of the position that we had achieved as a nation. We had been relegated unjustifiably to an obscure position, while—even in our own hemisphere—there were accumulating errors and problems in our way that jeopardized our very future. We gave up the subsidiary and innocuous diplomacy of a nation aligned with worthy though alien interests and, to protect our rights, placed ourselves in the forefront, convinced as we were of our ability to contribute with our own means to the understanding of peoples.

Before I undertake an objective analysis of Brazil's foreign policy, the reader will, I hope, bear with me in a somewhat subjective statement of views. It will serve to clarify the underlying reasons why we have taken particular positions on world issues.

To be genuine, a nation's foreign policy, as such, must be the embodiment of the ideals and common interests that govern its existence. Idealistic aspirations are defined by the explicit or implicit establishment of the goals aimed at. They reflect the common interests and all those economic, social, historic and political circumstances that at a given moment influence the choice of immediate aims and the selection of ways and means of action.

The ideals of the community are the backdrop against which the national drama unfolds, and are the constant source of inspiration of true leadership. They generally permeate the means and resources for the enforcement of political decisions. A national policy—as a tool for action—seems at times to turn against the fundamental impetus that gave it birth, in order the better to serve it; but in terms of the very essence of that policy, the truth of certain realities cannot be refuted. In order to ensure that the formulation of a national strategy is viable, popular desires and ideals cannot be ignored; but the truth of the matter is that very often the tactics must be neutralized and divested of idealistic or sentimental content in order to meet urgent interests and strengthen the ideals of the community itself.

There are two moments in the life of nations when complete freedom is permitted in the expression of what might be called a national ideology: when they are undergoing dire poverty, as the sole romantic consolation left to the people; and when they are thriving in abundance, as a duty imposed upon the nation by the multitude of interests asserted but never entirely satisfied.

A nation which no longer is so poor or unprotected as to be able to indulge in the luxury of dreamy consolations, yet is struggling against mighty odds to achieve the full possession of its wealth and to develop the potentialities of its own nature, must ever remain in the arena—alert, aware and vigilant. Such a nation cannot lose sight of its objectives, yet must avoid jeopardizing them by submitting to policies which—though in keeping with remote ideals—do not, at the moment, satisfy its true interests.

There can be no doubt that Brazil—thanks to a tremendous national effort—is making gigantic strides toward breaking the barrier of underdevelopment. The rate of national growth speaks for itself, and I am convinced that at the end of my term of office the country's rate of progress will be such as to make the population explosion no longer a somber prospect but rather an additional and deciding factor for advancement in the process of economic development.

We have no right to dream. Rather it is our duty to work—but at the same time to trust and hope—and work with our feet firmly on the ground.

In time, the foreign policy of Brazil will reflect the craving for developmental progress. Obviously, underlying the decisions which we are compelled to take in order to meet the problems of material growth inherent in the desire of the Brazilian people for economic, social, political and human freedom lies the interweaving of the country's material needs. Keeping our aims ever in mind, we must choose those of our country's sources of inspiration that can best be mobilized to assist the national effort.

II

Because of our historical, cultural and Christian background as well as our geographical situation, ours is a predominantly

Western nation. Our national effort is directed toward the achievement of a democratic way of life, both politically and socially. It may not be idle to stress here that our dedication to democracy is greater than that of other nations of our same cultural sphere. We have thus become the most successful example of racial coexistence and integration known to history.

Common ideals of life and organization draw us close to the major nations of the Western bloc, and on many issues Brazil can, in a leading position, associate itself with this bloc. This affinity is underlined by our participation in the inter-American regional system, which entails specific political commitments.

However, at the present juncture, we cannot accept a set national position exclusively on the basis of the above premises. It is undeniable that we have other points in common with Latin America in particular, and with the recently emancipated peoples of Asia and Africa, which cannot be ignored since they lie at the root of the readjustment of our policy, and on them converge many of the main lines of the development of Brazilian civilization. If it be true that we cannot relegate our devotion to democracy to a secondary place, it is no less true that we cannot repudiate ties and contacts offering great possibilities for national realization.

The closeness of Brazil's relations with neighboring countries of the continent and with the Afro-Asian nations, though based on different reasons, tends to the selfsame end. Among these, in the majority of cases, are historical, geographic and cultural motives. Common to them all is the fact that our economic situation coincides with the duty of forming a single front in the battle against underdevelopment and all forms of oppression.

From all this, naturally, certain points stand out that may be deemed basic to the foreign policy of my government. One of these is the recognition of the legitimacy of the struggle for economic and political freedom. Development is an aim common to Brazil and to the nations with which we endeavor to have closer relations, and the rejection of colonialism is the inevitable and imperative corollary of that aim.

It is, furthermore, in the light of these political determinants that today we consider the future of the inter-American regional system of first importance. The growth of Latin America as a whole and the safeguarding of the sovereignty of each nation of the hemisphere are the touchstones of a continental policy as the Brazilian government understands it.

The mistakes created by an erroneous equating of continental problems are only too well known. Insufficient or misdirected aid has increased regional disagreements. Nations at grips with grave problems in common—that is, all the countries of Latin America —must take stock of their needs and plan accordingly. Latin Americans are interested not in the prosperity of the small, leading groups, but in the national prosperity as a whole, which must be sought at all costs and regardless of the risks.

The United States must realize that today it confronts a challenge from the socialist world. The Western world must show and prove that it is not only Communist planning that promotes the prosperity of national economies. Democratic planning must also do so, with the assistance of those economically able, if the political system of a perplexed two-thirds of the Western world is to avoid the risk of bankruptcy.

We cannot too often stress the extent to which poverty separates us from North America and the leading European countries of the Western world. If by their success these represent, in the eyes of underdeveloped peoples, the ideal of achievement of the elite of European cultural origin, there nevertheless is taking root in the minds of the masses the conviction that this ideal, for a country without resources and hamstrung in its aspirations for progress, is a mockery. What solidarity can there be between a prosperous nation and a wretched people? What common ideals can, in the course of time, withstand the comparison between the rich, cultivated areas of the United States and the famine-ridden zones of the Brazilian Northeast?

Thinking of this sort irrevocably creates in us a sense of solidarity with those poverty-stricken peoples who, on three continents, are struggling against imperialist interests which, under the umbrella of democratic institutions, mislead—if not destroy —attempts to organize popular economies. When nations competing with the democratic group make demonstrations of real or pretended and disinterested economic help, this problem seems more acute under the pressure of the conflict of interests.

At this point it might be appropriate to refer to the ideological prejudices of the capitalist democracies, ever ready to decry the idea of state intervention in countries where either the state controls and governs economic growth—which has become a question of sovereignty—or nothing at all is achieved. We are not in a position to allow the free play of economic forces in our territory, simply because those forces, controlled from outside, play their own game and not that of our country.

The Brazilian government is not prejudiced against foreign capital—far from it. We stand in dire need of its help. The sole condition is that the gradual nationalization of profits be accepted, for otherwise it no longer is an element of progress but becomes a mere leech feeding on our national effort. Let it be known that the state in Brazil will not relinquish those controls that will benefit our economy by channeling and ensuring the efficiency of our progress.

III

Economic imbalance is doubtless the most critical of all the adverse factors that beset the inter-American regional system, and from it almost all others stem. My government is convinced that it is fighting for the recovery of Pan-Americanism and that this must start with the economic and social fields. Politically we are trying to give shape and content to the imperative principles of self-determination and nonintervention, and it is these principles that guide us in relation to the Americas as well as to the rest of the world.

The still dramatically present question of Cuba convinced us, once and for all, of the nature of the continental crisis. In defending with intransigence the sovereignty of Cuba against interpretations of an historical fact which cannot be controlled a posteriori, we believe we are helping to awaken the continent to a true awareness of its responsibilities. We stand by our position on Cuba, with all its implications. Surely the Brazilian attitude has been understood by other governments, and as it gains ground, the entire regional system shows signs of a regeneration in the assessment of the responsibilities of each member nation.

The government of the United States, through its recent aid programs, took an important step toward the revision of its classical and inoperative continental policy. We hope that President Kennedy, who is not lacking in the qualities of leadership, will carry the revision of his country's attitude to the very limit and will sweep away the considerable remaining obstacles on the road to a truly democratic, continental community.

As to Africa, we may say that today it represents a new dimension in Brazilian policy. We are linked to that continent by our ethnic and cultural roots and share in its desire to forge for itself an independent position in the world of today. The nations of Latin America that became politically independent in the course of the nineteenth century found the process of economic development delayed by historical circumstances, and Africa, which has only recently become politically free, joins us at this moment in the common struggle for freedom and well-being.

I believe that it is precisely in Africa that Brazil can render the best service to the concepts of Western life and political methods. Our country should become the link, the bridge, between Africa and the West, since we are so intimately bound to both peoples. Insofar as we can give the nations of the Black continent an example of complete absence of racial prejudice, together with successful proof of progress without undermining the principles of freedom, we shall be decisively contributing to the effective integration of an entire continent in a system to which we are attached by our philosophy and historic tradition.

The attraction exerted by the Communist world, by Communist techniques and by the spirit of Communist organizations upon the countries but recently freed from the capitalist yoke is common knowledge. Generally speaking, all underdeveloped countries, including those of Latin America, are susceptible to that appeal. It must not be forgotten that whereas the independence of the Latin American nations was inspired by a liberation movement rooted in the French Revolution, the autonomy obtained by the new Asian and African nations was preceded by a wave of hope aroused by the socialist revolution in Russia among the oppressed classes and peoples all over the world. The Afro-Asian liberation movement arose against the domination by nations that compose—if not lead—the Western bloc.

These historical factors are of decisive importance and must be borne in mind when gauging the role that a country such as Brazil can play in the task of reappraising the dynamic forces that are at work in the new world of today in Asia and Africa.

For many years Brazil made the mistake of supporting European colonialism in the United Nations. This attitude—which is only now fading—gave rise to a justified mistrust of Brazilian policy. Misinformed circles, overly impressed with European patterns of behavior, contributed to a mistake which must be attributed more to a disregard of the deeper commitments of our country than to political malice. Our fraternal relationship with Portugal played its part in the complacency shown by the Ministry of Foreign Relations of Brazil in this matter.

Therefore, everything points to a necessary change of position with regard to colonialism, which in all its guises—even the most tenuous—will from now on meet with the determined opposition of Brazil. This is our policy, not merely in the interests of Africa, nor for the sake of a platonic solidarity, but because it is in keeping with Brazilian national interests. These to a certain extent are still influenced by the most disguised forms of colonialist pressure, but call for a rapprochement with Africa.

I might add that the raising of the economic standards of the African peoples is of vital importance to the economy of Brazil. Even from a purely selfish standpoint, we are interested in seeing the social betterment and improvement in the production techniques of Africa. The exploitation of Africans by European capital is detrimental to the Brazilian economy, permitting as it does the fostering of commercial competition on the basis of low-salaried Negro workers. Competition on a civilized and human level must be found to replace that of enslavement by underpayment of an entire race. Here and now, the industrial growth of my country guarantees to the Africans a most important source of supply, which could even serve as the basis for arrangements for the linking together of our respective production systems.

We are setting up regular diplomatic and trade relations with several African countries, and my government's emissaries have visited that continent to study concrete possibilities for coöperation and exchange. In time, the potentialities of this closer relationship, destined to be a milestone in the history of human affairs, will be fulfilled.

IV

Here I must underscore another important aspect of the new Brazilian foreign policy. My country has few international obligations: we are bound only by pacts and treaties of continental assistance which commit us to solidarity with any member of the hemisphere that may become the victim of extracontinental aggression. We have not subscribed to treaties of the nature of NATO, and are in no way forced formally to intervene in the Cold War between East and West. We are therefore in a position to follow our national inclination to act energetically in the cause of peace and the relaxation of international tension.

Not being members of any bloc, not even of the neutralist bloc, we preserve our absolute freedom to make our own decisions in specific cases and in the light of peaceful suggestions at one with our nature and history. A group of nations, notably of Asia, is also careful to remain on the sidelines in any clash of interests which are invariably those of the great powers and not necessarily those of our country, let alone of world peace.

The first step in making full use of the possibilities of our position in the world consists in maintaining normal relations with all nations. Brazil, either through misinterpretation or distortion of its better political judgment, spent many years without regular contacts with the countries of the Communist bloc, even to the point of having only roundabout and insufficient trade relations with them. As a part of my government's program, I decided to examine the possibility of renewing relations with Rumania,

Hungary, Bulgaria and Albania; these have now been established. Negotiations for the reopening of relations with the Soviet Union are in progress, and an official Brazilian mission is going to China to study exchange possibilities. Consistent with this revision of our foreign policy, my country, as is known, decided to vote in favor of including on the agenda of the U.N. General Assembly the question of the representation of China; this initial position will, in due course, have its logical consequences.

The possibilities of trade relations between Brazil and the Orient are practically *terra incognita*. Even in the case of Japan, to which we are bound by so many ties, our barter relations are far from complete. China, Korea, Indonesia, India, Ceylon and all of Southeast Asia provide room for the development of our production and commercial endeavors, which neither distance nor political problems can discourage.

The world must be made aware of the fact that Brazil is intensively increasing its production, looking not only to the domestic market, but specifically seeking to attract other nations. Economically speaking, my government's motto is "Produce everything, for everything produced is marketable." We shall go out to conquer these markets: at home, in Latin America, in Africa, in Asia, in Oceania, in countries under democracy, and in those that have joined the Communist system. Material interests know no doctrine, and Brazil is undergoing a period when its very survival as a nation occupying one of the most extensive and privileged areas of the globe depends on the solution of its economic problems. Our very faithfulness to the democratic way of life is at stake in this struggle for development. A nation such as ours, with 70 million inhabitants and with the world's highest rate of population growth, will not permit even a slowing down of its movement toward the full utilization of its own wealth.

Without fear of error I can say that the experiment in democratic progress being carried out in Brazil is decisive both for Latin America and for all the underdeveloped areas of the world. Therefore, this experiment is of deep interest to prosperous nations which are also proud of being free. They will remain so to the extent that success crowns the efforts for economic emancipation of the underdeveloped nations living under the same system. Freedom once again becomes the outgrowth of equality.

It must be pointed out that the idea behind the foreign policy of Brazil, and its implementation, has now become the instrument for a national development policy. As part and parcel of our national life, foreign policy has ceased to be an unrealistic academic exercise carried out by oblivious and spellbound elites; it has become the main topic of daily concern. With it we seek specific aims: at home, prosperity and well-being; elsewhere, to live together amicably and in world peace.

There is no need to spell out to Brazilians what we are in the world today. We are fully aware of the mission we must accomplish—and can accomplish.

The Revolution and Foreign Policy*

Nicolas Boér ,

The Brazilian Revolution represents a decisive turning point not only in the history of the country but also in the evolution of the world community, so analyses of our foreign policy before and after March 31, 1964, since they are made from different points of view and presuppose a wide spectrum of critical attitudes, color conclusions which are surely parallel and complementary, rather than divergent. However, if after the Brazilian Revolution a study written on the future outlook of our foreign policy, or even of current international relations, should ignore this historical event (which according to the statement by Ambassador Lincoln Gordon, a qualified intellectual and expert on international relations, constitutes "one of the critical turning points in the history of the world around the middle of the twentieth century"), as though it had never happened or as though it had only slight political importance, it would constitute an admission of a lack of scientific objectivity or of historical perspective. The first (lack of objectivity) would be the consequence of an ideological *parti pris*—the forced or spontaneous acceptance of the Soviet concept of "peaceful coexistence"—which was characteristic of the adherents of the foreign policy which formerly called itself "independent." The other (lack of historical perspective) would be the result of an anti-ideological *parti pris*, which being led into wishful thinking by noble intentions or by ignorance

* This article was originally published in Portuguese as "A Revolução e a Política Externa," in *Cadernos Brasileiros*, 6:16–26, May-June, 1964.

of some of the more characteristic aspects of the world community in the 1960's, sees only the survival of expansionist imperialism, either explicit or masquerading in ideological terms. Both
betray apologetical attitudes.

Science and apologetics, in the case of political science and
political apologetics, involve opposite mental processes, since
the first studies facts in order to discover their consequences,
while the second tries to interpret the facts in accordance with
its own principles or with a priori categories. Furthermore, there
are additional complications when we deal with the case of
Brazilian apologists for the so-called "independent" foreign
policy, who, in order to justify their own position, may claim
that they have not been influenced in their analyses by any ideological *parti pris*. Thus these apologists leave their critics in
doubt as to the real significance of their attitudes, since, under
present conditions of the Cold War as it is being waged in
the so-called "third world," these may indicate either tactics
attempting temporarily to cover up a perfectly defined ideology
—the Marxist-Leninist—or a lack of national ideological definition which is both tolerant and liberal.

In addition, the lack of ideological definition which is adopted
for Machiavellian tactical reasons (disguised Marxism-Leninism)
or through temperamental bias (an attitude which is being encouraged by Marxist-Leninists) makes it difficult to understand
the typical mental processes of the apologists and followers even
by using correctly interpreted facts. They judge international
realities in the light of preconceived critical attitudes and postulates in order to justify positions adopted a priori.

Substituting noble and sophisticated postulates for facts also
explains the lack of perspective of those who, following the dic-
tates of an anti-ideological *parti pris*, believe that the Cold War
has passed its bipolar phase (characterized by expansionist imperialism and defined in ideological terms) and has resolved itself
into the phase of the polycentric conflicts which have arisen
within the two ideological blocs of the previous phase. If we
were talking about a postulate which outlines the requirements
of an "open" world, organized on a regional basis, with diffuse

(non-nuclear) power guaranteeing mobility on an international scale, analogous to "open" democratic societies, with great social mobility and circulation of the elites, we would recognize the image which we too project for the future. We may even catch a glimpse of the outlines of an international order which would structurally guarantee the success of Brazil's efforts to realize all its potential as a power destined to take its place among the greatest. However, when we project this image in terms of present international reality, stating that it reflects this reality, we are guilty of one of those grievous equivocal interpretations which distort the environment of the great international events taking place in the contemporary world. Facing the broad and deep international repercussions awakened by the Brazilian Revolution, which substantially modified power relationships in this hemisphere and stopped, we might say reversed, the aggressive strategy which was designed to disturb the balance of power in what is known as the "third world," we can only view this Revolution as one of the high and decisive points of the Cold War, which was displaced from the centers toward the peripheries of world power. To overlook this fact after the Brazilian Revolution, which also resolved *via facti* the "great debate" on the meaning of the independence of our foreign policy, would be equivalent to an admission of a lack of objectivity or mean being left at the mercy of the faulty perspective of an imaginary international view.

The foreign policy of a power is established on the point of coincidence between the perspectives open to the country abroad and the perspectives of the world community, which, starting from a global point of view, assigns each country a place in the system of states. The formulation of this is known as international policy. It is a constant confrontation of the imperatives of national interest, expressed by means of national power, and the possibility of its realization in terms of international power relations. By national interest—the basic concept of any foreign policy—we understand the imperatives of the existence and growth of the body politic within the integrity of its territory, including political, social, and economic conditions, and its full realization, that is, the achievement of all its material and spiritual potentialities, the self-determination of its people, the sovereignty of its state, and the integration and prosperity of all its population. And as the liberty of an individual within a society organized according to rational criteria can only be limited by the liberty of all the other citizens, in the same way national interest, in a world order of states organized according to international law and morality, may only be limited by the national interest of all the other states, as well as by agreements and treaties freely entered into and not denounced. As the liberty of each individual is interdependent and cannot be satisfactorily assured in any other way, national interest is also interdependent and cannot be guaranteed satisfactorily in any other way.

The concrete formulation of the national interest, besides its constant factors, also presupposes a critical evaluation of what is necessary and desirable at any given moment for the existence of the nation and of what is possible within the reality of international power relations, considering the availability of power at the disposal of those who are charged with administering it. Such a concrete formulation of national interest, since it constitutes a norm for action, is hardly susceptible to ideological interference, but is necessarily and properly subject to the influence of ideologies to the extent that this formal term embodies a nation's fundamental values, its character, and its style. Within this concept of the undisputed primacy of the national interest in defining the foreign policy of a country we cannot accept the validity of any ideology which contradicts or might frustrate the realization of its objectives or threaten the national interests of other states merged in the world balance of power. This is what the ideology of imperialism intends. But when ideology enters the plane of positive and empirical proof within the real community and real power relations, the conclusions which would lead to the concrete formulation of the national interest are rendered unreal and utopian.

The other basic concept of foreign policy, but subordinate to national interest as the means is subordinate to the end, is national power. Power in international relations is defined as the potential which a country is capable of bringing to bear in order to make its sovereign will (that is, its national interest) prevail within the community of nations, in relation to other states, and within the systems of states, whether allies or opponents. This power, however, is not shown merely in material, physical terms, that is, military terms; its components are the economic and cultural potential of a nation and its political evaluation, the cohesion and the vitality of its social structures and of its spiritual forces, the quality of its political leadership, the appeal of its personality and of its national message, and, last but not least, how and to what degree the state knows how to benefit from the system of alliances in which it participates. Naturally, in an era like ours when the balance of terror establishes a truce at the power centers, precluding the classical solution of international disputes which would involve the atomic superpowers in a nuclear encounter, the potential of a diplomacy employing nonmilitary power in an increasing degree will rise again.

However, these potentialities are still limited. The example of Cuba is typical and illustrative of this in many ways. It was there that the last expansionist imperialist attempt to subvert the nuclear power balance was thwarted because it came up against the decision of another superpower, with relatively greater nuclear power at its disposal, to maintain the status quo. But if, for example (as a pure supposition), the same imperialist superpower had transformed a newly independent island of Corsica (again this is a pure hypothesis) into a nuclear logistic base, France alone, even with its *force de frappe*, would never have been able to impose the withdrawal of the offensive rockets. It might have duplicated the North American accomplishment by relying on the military power of the Atlantic Alliance. In the same way, though acknowledging the imaginative force of De Gaulle's diplomacy (whose chances of success increased during the nuclear truce period owing to the weakening tactics it applies to both systems of alliances, whether the one to which he belongs or the one to which he is opposed), it is obvious that he can only gather apparent satisfactions which cannot do more than substantiate that he has independent opinions in international relations. However, if he is able to weaken the status quo, he will only complicate the situation, with consequent dangers to peace.

That is why we are in agreement with all those who proclaim the idea of cooperation and the idea of a greater participation in the system of alliances to which they belong—because of the natural imperatives of geography and of history or because of ideological choice determined by national traditions, values, sentiments, and style—as the most effective way of advancing the national interests. Such advancement necessarily requires not only the attainment of specific national objectives (development and integration) but also the equalization of forces within the system of alliances. This equalization also naturally presupposes efforts to overcome *organically* the technological gap between the underdeveloped and the developed sectors of the system by the distribution and propagation of know-how and by the more rational and just reorganization of the international division of labor and commerce.

Moreover, if we accept the idea that a rational foreign policy is a matter of outlook, determined by the intersection of the nation's view of the outside world and the view the world community holds regarding each country's place in it, then the two main historical merits of the Brazilian Revolution become evident, both nationally and internationally. The Brazilian Revolution restored the conditions for a rational foreign policy—national, independent, and realistic—by placing this foreign policy at the point referred to above; in other words, at the intersection of Brazil's view of the outside world and the view held by the latter regarding Brazil's place in the world. In Foreign Minister Vasco Leitão da Cunha's felicitous phrase, correct foreign policy "consists in the creation of perspective in the setting up of concentric circles which progressively increase their dimensions, first turning naturally and immediately around the policies of the Rio de la Plata, then those of South America, then of the hemisphere, and, finally, turning to the West." And, making his thought more explicit, he added: "Independence is first employed to give greater emphasis to our relations with our neighbors on the continent. Then, in the second place, with traditionally friendly countries of the West, within which we are situated by geographical, historical, and cultural determination. It is a question of perspective which in no way invalidates the universalist vocation of Brazil's foreign policy."

The second great historical merit of the Brazilian Revolution is that it correctly evaluated the world outlook, in which the country is assigned an eminent place. In other words, its great historical merit is to have justly interpreted the true nature of the present stage of the world conflict, that is, the challenge to national existence and to world peace, and to have contributed positively to overcoming it by maintaining—and, potentially, by its non-nuclear power widening—the sphere of the democratic and open world, ever more diffuse and polycentrically organized.

The world conflict known as the Cold War really entered into a new phase. This phase is characterized in the first place by a displacement of the principal battlefronts from European centers to the peripheries of world power in the hope of being able to avoid a nuclear accounting, which had been banished by the balance of terror. In the second place, it is characterized especially by indirect action, which might not absolutely exclude recourse to direct action such as the wars of "national liberation" or local wars to decide territorial disputes. By these means the imperialist power attempts to increase its sphere of influence by extending it to the so-called "third world" (including countries in the Asian, African, and Latin American continents), with the intent of there subverting the status quo in its favor. Third, it is characterized by the progressive liberation within the two world systems of centrifugal forces that had up to now been effectively counterbalanced by the centripetal forces, the latter functioning under the pressure of direct threat of armed contact between the two blocs. However, just as the polycentrism of power in democratic alliances is not only a natural phenomenon but also a rule and a desired end—at least to the degree in which this does not divest the alliance of its own *raison d'être* and does not endanger its operation—so the bipolarization of power in an alliance which declares itself "monolithic" (an euphemism to avoid saying "totalitarian") means that the tendencies to hegemony and imperialism tending to the overturning of the status quo in the world divide into two currents, indeed parallel and rival, but also complementary and mutually stimulating.

A two-pronged challenge does not imply paralysis; on the contrary, it revives the missionary expansionist spirit inherent in it. As we see the world conflict become more fluid and complex, that in itself (especially in the case of the less cautious, of the uncertain, of the uncommitted) represents the greatest danger, since it is more subtle than in situations where the positions are clearly fixed along frontier demarcations and ideological lines, in terms of "have" and "have-nots," of "black" and "white," so pleasing to the simplists.

This phase of the Cold War is comparable to the expansionist phase of European history in the sixteenth and seventeenth centuries, in which European nations interested in the exploration and penetration of the world overseas more or less tacitly agreed to maintain the status quo in Europe and to give a free hand to adventurers, corsairs, trading companies, and other representatives of a brutal competition for the possession of territories for expansion. Peace and the status quo in Europe, but "no peace beyond the lines," was the formula for this policy. It was also the way to promote the undermining of the European status quo and attacking it through the peripheral flanks. And since the meaning of "peaceful coexistence" in accordance with the official interpretation of the Soviet Communist party (October, 1961) is "to facilitate the struggle of colonial and dependent peoples for their liberation" along the lines which the People's Republic of China and Cuba have already experienced, and since, according to Khrushchev's thinking as revealed in an interview which he gave in October, 1958, to Walter Lippmann, the "social and economic revolution now going on in any part of Asia, Africa, and Latin America is the status quo, the USSR stands ready to incorporate all the dependent countries of Asia, Africa, and Latin America into its sphere of influence and to consecrate both the expansion now in process and that already consummated under the name of the status quo." In view of this strategy no one is entitled to ignore that in an essentially interdependent world any sort of change in world power relations (political, economic, or social) taking place in any part of the globe (at the center or at the periphery) affects the equilibrium of the whole world and all its component elements.

To encourage that transition from capitalism to socialism in the developing continents, which would mean the incorporation of the so-called "third world" into the world system of the socialist states, one of the Communist imperialist powers, the USSR, would prefer indirect action, "revolution from above," the control of the state being accomplished by a "single front" under firm Communist leadership and composed of elements of the "national" bourgeoisie (anti-American and anti-Western), the progressive intelligentsia (favoring socialization and statism), and the proletarian masses organized by union leadership controlled by the Communist party. A "national and democratic state" based on its own ideological assumptions would be channeled inexorably into the "world system of socialist states." Thus, in the process such ideological assumptions as "nationalism," "progress," and "socialism," besides having a vague theoretical but emotionally dense and explosive content, would be nourished by the tellurian passions of xenophobia, resentment, and discontent under the impact of international dialectic. This concept does not exclude a beginning by an armed revolution or a revolutionary war; on the contrary, it includes them in cases where the relations of social forces make them possible or where violent resistance by existing institutions do not permit the forces for "progress" to avoid them. All this philosophy and strategy is being explained clearly and in great detail in the program of the Soviet Communist party and in the letter which the Central Committee addressed to its Chinese counterpart on July 14, 1963. This does not influence the arguments of those in our midst who, adopting the terminology of the "Chinese line," believe that "the Soviet Union fears the reappearance of revolutionary Communism as much as it does the United States."

A concept categorizing the Soviet Union as a "conservative and imperialist nation" (contradiction in terms) combines not only the Chinese view of the world but also what might be called

"Europocentrism." In fact, an "Europocentric" conception of the world, which was peculiar to Great Britain and France during the last five centuries and according to which history is made in Europe and through Europe, so that world power relations are decided in the Old World, justifies concepts which attribute a conservative character to the international action of the Soviet Union. Europe, thanks to the Marshall Plan and the Atlantic Alliance, was saved from the Communist danger; the unimagined prosperity, which is being consolidated within the framework of the Common Market, excludes even the most remote possibility of internal subversion; its military security, under the North American atomic shield, is today better guaranteed than during any other era in its history. This optimistic outlook, undoubtedly justified within its narrow context, is projected by Europeans to the three continents—Asia, Africa, and Latin America—whose history in the past was made through Europe. Those continents, however, as the danger of Soviet imperialist expansion disappears in the countries which remained within the West European camp after the first Soviet expansionist impetus, are experiencing the same impact in a different, but no less real and acute, manner than that which Europe felt during the first years following World War II.

However, that "Europocentrism" is nonetheless responsible for numerous failures in international outlook. It believes that because Soviet imperialism has lost its revolutionary and expansionist character in Europe, it cannot be rekindled outside Europe. Consequently, it believes that the revolutionary processes which sweep the so-called "third world" may, and indeed should, be interpreted in the sense of European socialism or agrarian reform. We may discount the possibility of revolutionary Communism taking over, to the advantage of Soviet imperialism, which has absolutely not abandoned its objective of subverting the status quo of world power in its own favor. It was within this Europocentric context that a large part of the European press analyzed the events preceding and following the Brazilian Revolution. They did not recall the lessons of the Chinese Revolution, which at the time were interpreted with a simplistic outlook (both shocking and partisan) as an agricultural reform movement.

Within this "Europocentric" concept the Sino-Soviet conflict has only one meaning. It represents the diffusion and hence the diminution or paralysis of Communist power. Within the simplistic Marxist econo-deterministic imaginary view it "does not differ from the other conflicts between have and have-not nations." And even if those concepts offered valid and useful standards for analysis, still, in their unilateral withdrawal they cannot encompass the crux of the complicated problem. The problem is political, the central point is hegemony with its economic, ideological, racial, cultural, and territorial ramifications. The fact is that both nationalisms attempt to transform the world into their fief, the "monolithic" unity of which (a "closed" world and a "unipolar" power) would be assured by the same ideology applied to the cultural and social conditions of its own society. In this context, it would be useless to become involved in esoteric ideological considerations, the essence of which is that the Soviet Union accuses Communist China of practicing methods "very well known since the time of the Roman Caesars and the Emperors of China," that is, imperialism—and Communist China accuses the Soviet Union of practicing the "chauvinism of a great power," that is, imperialism. What matters is that for the perspectives of the nations of the so-called "third world"— the common object of both ambitions of hegemony—it would make little difference whether they are included in the closed world of "unipolar" power of a Russian or a Chinese cast.

Still, from the point of view of those nations the struggle for hegemony between the Communist imperialist powers in the "third world," instead of paralyzing, intensifies the proselytizing and aggressive spirit of international Communism. Khrushchev, Mao Tse-tung, Tito, and Fidel Castro, despite their ideological differences, competed in the communization of Brazil, almost cooperating and thus stimulating each other. The same thing happens in Egypt and in Algeria, in Ghana and in Guinea, in Laos, in South Vietnam and in Cambodia. First, it is necessary to communize; afterwards it is possible to Sovietize or Sinoize.

Over against that "monolithic" image of the world projected by Communist reality to the extent that between Russian and Chinese totalitarians there is barely a difference in nuances and that no country, on accepting Communism, can dispense with the initial phase of Stalinization, we have the image of an "open" and "pluralist" world. In this world the leading power, the United States, represents the role of *primus inter pares* with its global responsibilities of a subsidiary nature, ready and even anxious to abandon them as soon as the regional centers of pluralist power are judged qualified to assume their own responsibilities to their own advantage and that of the whole system. In a private conversation with the author of this article, held in July, 1962, Walt Whitman Rostow, then head of the Policy Planning Staff of the United States Department of State, declared: "Here in the United States we can live comfortably in a pluralist world of independent nations, each one assuming its modern personality, because our domestic life is based on the principle of cooperation among dignified and responsible equals, while the Communists are impelled by their methods of organizing their domestic power to violate the integrity of individuals and of nations in the same manner." Brazil can attempt to achieve and realize its true national independence and personality, in accordance with contemporary conditions of production and technology, only within the framework of an "open" and "pluralist" world.

If one accepts the conclusion that the cause and historical meaning of the Cold War, even in its present phase, continues to be the unchanging imperialist determination to continue to snatch new countries from the "open" and "pluralist" world, in order to include them in their "closed" world and thus alter the world's power distribution, he will also value the significance of the Brazilian Revolution. For Brazil occupies in the world community a place as the first decisive victory of democracy over Communism in the so-called "third world."

Naturally, this conclusion will not be accepted by those who are disposed to ignore the de facto existence and the conditions of the Iron, Bamboo, and Cane curtains, and ostensibly are more impressed by the at present rather fictitious nightmare of the

Monroe Doctrine. Undoubtedly, the Monroe Doctrine has represented, from the point of view of Latin America, a somewhat mistaken principle. At the moment, however, for the United States the Alliance for Progress has much greater significance than the Monroe Doctrine. The fact that the Charter of the Alliance for Progress was inspired mainly by Latin American suggestions considerably aided the United States in overcoming intellectually those ambiguities and dilemmas not cleared during the century and a half the Monroe Doctrine has been in effect, which in the last analysis were the underlying causes of the growing misunderstandings between the north and the south. It was ideological (democratic and republican) and strategic concepts that led President Monroe to proclaim his doctrine in order to prevent the Holy Alliance powers from reimplanting their colonial domination and their monarchical and aristocratic *Ancien Régime* ideology in this hemisphere. The strategic concepts which placed the whole hemisphere under North American military protection might externally manifest themselves in the defense of Latin America against European interventions, but internally in the exercise of patterns of paternalism or policing of which the nations of Central America were especially victims, but never Brazil. This is not the place to go into details of the history of the relations between the United States and Latin America, among other reasons because our continent is too extensive and heterogeneous to be viewed through only one prism.

As for the democratic crusade which the Monroe Doctrine implied, there were many inconsistencies which were only increased by the Good Neighbor policy substituted for it at the time of Franklin Delano Roosevelt. It so happened that the most liberal North American president, the author of the New Deal, and one of the great leaders of World War II adapted himself too easily to Latin American fascism, maintaining very friendly relations with a Somoza in Nicaragua or with a Getulio Vargas in Brazil. Unfortunately, even within the era of the Alliance for Progress this situation has remained practically unchanged. Unfortunately, too, it is not the dictatorial, totalitarian temperaments, the fascist sympathizers, and the Communist fellow travelers, or even less the uncommitted, who can raise questions about the application of the ideological implications of the Monroe Doctrine, but the true democrats do have very grave complaints against the excessive accommodation of the United States with the dictatorships of the right upheld by the oligarchy and with the Pelego-Goulartian regimes representing the rather antidemocratic collusion between established corruption (native oligarchic variety) and officially sanctioned communization. In this way—historians will have something to say about this in the future—the Brazilian Revolution concerns itself, not at all with endeavoring to vindicate the Monroe Doctrine, but rather with openly challenging the constant application of what is most mistaken in the Good Neighbor policy.

However, if someone continues to harbor completely unfounded fears with respect to the Monroe Doctrine, which in reality belongs to the historical archives, and insists on the "necessity of clearly defining the conditions-limitations of the application of the Doctrine," it must still be acknowledged that the Brazilian Revolution in this respect also fulfilled a high historical task. Its lesson is universal, but especially valid for this hemisphere. It expressed the determination, we might say the self-determination, of this country and of the whole hemisphere to stay with the open and pluralist world and in constant, free, and fertile intercommunication with all the powers and currents of the contemporary world. Through these contacts Brazil and all the nations of this hemisphere can enrich and develop themselves materially and spiritually, on condition that those nations and currents be disposed to respect the foundations of our open and pluralist society and not to undertake any action intended to enclose this hemisphere within a new totalitarian curtain. Such currents are not only the "noncapitalist totalitarian regimes," the "experience of militant Chinese-type socialism," but also all those national-progressive-socialist currents (entirely different from the labor and socialist currents of Europe) which are ready, because of their own composition and their objectives, to take paths that lead inevitably to incorporation in the "world system of socialist states." Whoever sincerely professes loyalty to the

West cannot absolutely discard the idea that the Latin American part of the open and pluralist world is prepared to attain self-determination by the introduction of regimes which, though making internal changes within the framework of Western power, in reality, instead of preserving their professed loyalty to the ideals of the Western world within the hemisphere, intend to destroy the framework of that power. Plots of the "Trojan horse" type are already outdated in this second half of the twentieth century.

It is in this sense that the Revolution will have to orient the course of our foreign policy. After its Revolution Brazil will have to emerge as a great power which on the basis of its historic experiences will define the means adapted to present Cold War conditions that the countries of the Western world, especially those called "the third world," will have to employ in order to overcome the subtle challenge of Communist imperialism. By making its own foreign policy dynamic and missionary Brazil will be able to give new life to all Western international policy by creating conditions that will permit the ideal of the open and pluralist world finally to prevail. That is the way in which Brazil, in the very midst of its process of integration and development, may project itself as a new great power on the international scene.

Brazil's New Foreign Policy: From Nonalignment to Solidarity with the West*

Vladimir Reisky de Dubnic

The Brazilian Revolution of April, 1964, represents a turning point in Brazilian foreign policy. The governments of Presidents Quadros, 1961, and Goulart, 1961–1964, were characterized by a policy of nonalignment, neutralism, and ambiguity, while the present Brazilian government has clearly returned to the camp of the inter-American defense system. Even on questions which do not immediately concern the Western Hemisphere, Brazil has adopted a decidedly pro-Western position. From a statement by Foreign Minister Vasco Leitão da Cunha, elicited by the events in Southeast Asia, it was clear that in the United Nations Brazil concerned itself just as intensely with the conflict as the United States, and would "go to war in the event that the war in Southeast Asia should develop into a worldwide conflict."[1]

In the course of the election for the presidency in 1960, which ended in an overwhelming victory for Quadros, an entirely different position was outlined for Brazil in the event of a war between the big powers. So far as the election of 1960 gave a clue to the course of foreign policy, everything seemed to point to the fact that Brazil set out to play the role of a third power. Quadros' program in foreign policy was a conglomeration of neutralist, pro-Cuba, and anticolonialist utterances to which he added, as

* This article was originally published in German as "Brasiliens neue Aussenpolitik: Von der Blockfreiheit zur Solidarität mit dem Westen," in *Europa-Archiv*, 20(3):91–100, Feb. 10, 1965. Translated and printed by permission.

an afterthought, that an open-door policy would be adopted toward foreign investors.

THE NONALIGNMENT EXPERIMENT

The Brazilian concept of foreign policy during the administration of Quadros was, in its main features, the following: Brazil would deal with the East and with the West; it was no longer oriented toward the United States or the inter-American point of view, but rather toward a global point of view. It would enter into ties without regard to the line of demarcation between the ideological or power politics groups. Quadros had declared that Brazil must be kept out of the present political struggle for supremacy in the world and would not remain allied to any of the major powers. However, this declaration of neutralism was counteracted to a certain extent by his statement that his government would remain within the inter-American system.

It was not only his conviction that Brazil should outgrow its role as a supernumerary on the outer fringes of world politics that caused him to develop a new line for Brazilian foreign policy, but also his knowledge of public opinion. The development of Brazil into a representative democracy and the growing national consciousness of each social class, stirred from lethargy by the process of industrialization, brought with them another element to add to the military hierarchy and the professional diplomats, namely, the political Left, which could make its influence felt with the President in his formulation of a new foreign policy. With his new foreign policy Quadros naturally offended leading military leaders, but he thought that in this way he could bring about an indispensable national consensus among the different political and social groups. The Left, which had been disappointed by Quadros' internal economic measures, found a certain consolation in the change in Brazilian foreign policy and allowed itself to be stirred by it to a position which was advantageous to the government. The political center was inclined to approve any policy which seemed to raise the prestige of Brazil in the world. Thus everyone—Communists, nationalists, and moderates, each for a different set of reasons—believed that a true multilateral foreign policy would insure a better future. In an atmosphere of exaggerated national expectations in the face of a desperate economic situation a novel, bold foreign policy could not help but divert attention away from the bitter reality in the country. It was generally noticeable at this time, at least up until the Chinese attack on India, that among countries with parallel levels of development the ones which adopted a neutralist position enjoyed greater international prestige than the ones which committed themselves to either superpower. It was the universal opinion of the influential political leaders under Goulart that a globally oriented Brazil which would remain out of Cold War confrontations as far as possible could, in spite of its domestic difficulties, gain international prestige which would be internally welcomed.

Between Brazil and the developing countries of the world there arose a certain community of outlook, whose basis remained outside the sphere of influence of the major powers; its source was the desire to change their common socioeconomic situation through rapid industrialization. This community of interest caused Quadros, six months before his election, to undertake a trip (for information-gathering purposes) which included India, Egypt, Yugoslavia, and Cuba, countries which a few years earlier had only a secondary interest for Brazil. His itinerary included only two industrial countries: Japan and the Soviet Union. Clearly as a result of this trip, Quadros concluded (and stated) that Latin America needed a Nasser.

The neutralist countries attempted to get Brazil in their camp. Brazil's presence would have, in their opinion, helped them in obtaining economic support from both East and West, thus relieving their isolation. But neutralism, to that time, did not have any precedents in Latin America. Up to 1962 the Brazilian government had hoped that Castro's Cuba would be able to control its revolution so that it could adopt a neutralist position. For Jânio Quadros the revolution was of great interest, because he saw in Castro a symbol of independence from foreign influence. But later it appeared that Cuba was wholly dependent on the Soviet Union, a fact which was brought home during the "missile crisis" in a very humiliating manner, when the Soviets withdrew their rockets without consulting Castro. Thus the hope of the Brazilian government for the establishment of a truly neutralist regime in Latin America sank. The illusion that Cuba could play the East against the West in the interest of its own development had been skillfully maintained. And therefore the fact that Cuba belonged to the Soviet camp and became a base from which the proliferation of Communism in South America was carried on was an unpleasant surprise to every neutralist who had hoped that Latin America would join together against the United States and thereby have a basis for negotiation. The Latin American countries' basis for negotiation had, on the one hand, become better during the early stages of Communist penetration into the area, but, on the other, many Latin Americans were disturbed by Khrushchev's announcement (and the acceptance of this announcement by the United States as an acknowledged fact) that the Monroe Doctrine had come to an end.[2] Nor did the manner in which all scruples had been thrown aside please those Latin Americans, since it was not they who had brought about the end of the Doctrine.

Since Latin America was directly threatened for the first time by the conflict between the superpowers, many Brazilians found the opinion held by neutralists, to the effect that international Communism constituted no real danger for Latin America, paradoxical. It would seem that this viewpoint could not be maintained for a very long time. And yet one could hear the theory that a country like Brazil could, under able leadership, move closer to the Soviet bloc in the interest of more rapid development without running the danger of being completely drawn into the Communist camp. Many Brazilians considered their ties with the United States as insufficient for an accelerated development of Brazil and were looking for relations outside the Western Hemisphere.

The attempt by Quadros to modify Brazilian foreign policy had been attributed to the general international situation. In view of the possibility of a nuclear war, espousing a neutralist policy was an instinctive reaction, a most logical path, of the countries which were on the periphery of the event. Quadros knew the importance of Brazil for the Latin American continent and for Africa, and he would not allow its being exploited to the advantage of one power or the other in the Cold, or even a hot, War.

The Brazilian public was no longer disturbed by Quadros' "harmless" neutralism; many of the backers of the nonalignment policy became aware, however, of the Communist infiltration of the bureaucratic system under his successor, João Goulart (1961–1964), as well as of the revolution which had been intended to come from the top, because neutralism began to serve the extreme Left as an opening wedge for a policy of friendship toward the Soviet Union and Cuba. The extreme Left tried to persuade the Brazilian public that Latin America had no real cultural affinity with the West and that Brazilians were tied to the West by neither social nor ethical standards, nor by the international security system, but rather that they could better afford an alliance with the countries that find themselves in a similar stage of development, although they are different from Brazil.

The government of Quadros had neutralist tendencies principally to compensate for the internal difficulties which had been manifested in Brazil. However, the ideological attitude of the extreme Left under Goulart was entirely hostile to the West. Brazil could surely have no interest in exchanging its peripheral position within the Western world for a similar position in the Eastern world, but it could easily have come to this under Goulart because the extreme Left pressed the presidency more and more for political decisions.

Significantly, the government had to strive against a break with the United States and for the establishment of good relations with Great Britain, Germany, France, Japan, countries which could afford her some help in her development. But nothing of the kind happened under Goulart. Furthermore, the Soviet bloc took immediate advantage of the strained relations existing between Brazil and the United States and entered into closer economic relations with Brazil.

Even Jânio Quadros, in spite of his unprecedented national and
international prestige, could not afford a policy which would
contribute to neutralism. When Goulart set about completing
this policy, he could only depend on a weak parliamentary system
and a divided public opinion. In view of the great social and
economic revolution confronting Brazil a neutralist policy was
then no longer feasible because in this situation it could no
longer be presented as a patriotic policy.

The open-door policy which Quadros had initiated in 1961 to
draw capital into the country and to promote commerce did not
bring about the hoped for results, not only on account of the
unfavorable economic and insecure political situation in Brazil
but also because the ambiguous Brazilian foreign policy made
the United States uneasy—without securing compensating advantages from the Soviet bloc. The Brazilian effort to bring a
Latin American Free Trade Association (LAFTA) into existence could not possibly have any success that would make up,
even in part, for the difference between American and Common
Market capital and that of a Brazil alienated from the West.

There was no place in Goulart's strategy for the American
instrument for development aid, the Alliance for Progress, because his government could not conform to the economic and
political conditions set up by the United States, for example, in
areas such as inflation and tax reform. A further hindrance was
the position taken by Brazil regarding compensation for expropriation of American companies; the American provisions stated
quite clearly that a country that did not pay an adequate compensation could receive no aid. More unfortunate than these
technicalities was the political resentment of Goulart's government toward the Alliance; had it not been for that, a solution
would have been found in regard to the technical provisions.
Thus, a Brazilian policy inclined toward the Alliance would have
meant that the power of the professional politicians would have
been curtailed and that of the economic planners and experts
increased. The fact that Goulart threw out the "three-year-plan"
and dismissed Celso Furtado and San Tiago Dantas, who were
its authors and executors, was characteristic of a political leader

who was not ready to share his power with economic planners. Finally, we should mention the Communists and the Communist-influenced nationalists in whose eyes the Alliance would only serve to protect the interests of the United States in Latin America, and who, for this reason, turned down this building and development program, because it was not inspired by them and because it would not promote a revolutionary climate.

THE LAST ATTEMPT AT A NONALIGNMENT POLICY

The position taken by Brazil at the Inter-American Conference of Foreign Ministers of the American States, held at Punta del Este in January, 1962, was scarcely understandable in the light of its own national interest. The goal of the Goulart government was to keep Castro's Cuba in the Organization of American States (OAS) and to hinder economic sanctions, a goal which had no relation to Brazil's domestic or foreign interest, since between Brazil and Cuba there existed practically no trade. The stand of the Goulart government against an isolation of Cuba was not only diametrically opposed to the goals of Brazil but also opposed to the opinions of many Brazilians. Democratic groups raised a protest against the stand taken by their country in Punta del Este, and the Brazilian Congress subjected Foreign Minister Dantas to a sharp cross-examination and severe criticism.[3] Washington avoided denouncing the position taken by Brazil as being against the letter and the spirit of the Inter-American Defense Treaty (Rio Pact) in order to draw general attention as little as possible to the disunity of the Western Hemisphere on the question of Cuba.

If Brazil trifled with its ties with the Soviet Union by its abstention from voting on the question of the suspension of Cuba's membership in the OAS, it was not, as Dantas declared, because one could hope to keep Cuba in line—for this Cuba was already too deeply involved—but because the government wished to pursue a policy of nonalignment. And this it could certainly not admit in view of the opposition of a considerable portion of public opinion and its ties to the Inter-American

Treaty of Reciprocal Assistance. The argument of easing the international situation and furthering coexistence was also used, and Dantas boasted that by successfully hindering the sanctions against Cuba he had contributed to peace. But this success was obtained at the cost of United States backing for his regime and of hemisphere security. It was only as a result of the indecision at Punta del Este on the part of the major nations of the Western Hemisphere in regard to the Cuban question that the Soviets were able to hit upon the idea of placing nuclear weapons in the form of middle-range missiles in Cuba without the accompanying risk.

The abstention from voting by the government of Goulart on the matter of the expulsion of Cuba from the OAS strengthened the prestige of the extreme Left, which held that Brazilian policy was the result of a reenforcement of anti-imperialistic national consciousness. However, Goulart, as well as Foreign Minister Dantas, underestimated the anti-Communist feeling in a considerable portion of the Brazilian nation. After the conference at Punta del Este he was no longer successful in maintaining the support of the Brazilian center.

The policy of the Goulart government was contradictory: sometimes an open-door policy toward all countries was proclaimed; at other times it approached the countries of the Soviet bloc which could not be useful to the rapid development of troubled Brazil. This policy could be considered as autonomous since it could not be traced to pressure from the outside. In reality its backers were people who subscribed to outside ideologies. It should not be forgotten that Hermes Lima, Dantas' successor as Foreign Minister during the presidency of Goulart, had stated —probably under pressure from the extreme Left—that the Cuban experiment in the area of socialism should not be allowed to come to an end. This ideologically founded neutralism had no longer anything in common with the nonalignment ideas of Quadros and his Foreign Minister, Arinos. It only insulted the United States without opening up the substantial resources of the Soviet bloc, simply because they were not available, as it happened in 1963 when the Soviet Union was asked to sell grain to

Brazil; it may be remembered that shortly thereafter the USSR had to turn to the United States to remedy its own grain deficiency. If Goulart's foreign policy of nonalignment had brought tangible advantages to Brazil, he would have been able to strengthen his position inside Brazil. However, that was not the case because the international situation was not propitious to playing off one side against the other. The Brazilian nonalignment policy from 1960 to 1964 proved useful only to Soviet and Cuban interests. That had certainly not been in the mind of Quadros, the initiator of this policy, but that was clearly the result.

THE FOREIGN POLICY OF THE REVOLUTIONARY GOVERNMENT OF 1964

The revolt of April, 1964, against the economic and political anarchy of the Goulart regime brought to power a government which put an end to the fruitless neutralist policy of the Quadros-Goulart era. The new government under the presidency of Castelo Branco departed from the policy of Goulart on three points: first, with regard to the position of friendship toward Castro; second, with regard to the goals of merging the underdeveloped countries as a third force against the developed countries; and, third, with regard to the effort for a stronger economic and cultural tie with China and the Soviet bloc.

This alone effected a climate favorable to relations between the United States and Brazil.

At the Ninth Inter-American Conference of the OAS held in Washington in July, 1964, Brazil introduced the outline of a statement to the Cuban people which expressed the hope that Cuba would rid itself in the near future of the oppressive tyranny of the Communist regime and would establish in the country a government freely elected by the people that would guarantee respect for basic human rights.[4] With this Brazil reversed itself completely and accepted a leading role in the effort to obtain a vote for an inter-American diplomatic and economic quarantine of the Cuban regime. Many observers were of the opinion that without the Brazilian initiative no vigorous sanction against Cuba would have been concluded. The Brazilian Foreign Minister emphasized that the sanction by the OAS against Cuba was binding for all member states. Brazil's interest in strengthening the prestige of the OAS led to its again becoming a champion of inter-American solidarity.

With the example of Brazilian foreign policy and its development during the last four years, from the presidency of Quadros to that of Castelo Branco, it became apparent how the idea of nonalignment and of neutralism had gone out of fashion for developing countries of Latin America, so that it is no longer a practical alternative for them because such a policy does not suit their need in the area of economics and of national security.

The first concrete and immediate measures of the revolutionary government were[5]

1. willingness to negotiate over the repayment of foreign debts,

2. resumption of normal relations with France,

3. resumption of the great dialogue with the United States,

4. reorganization of the diplomatic relations with Portugal, and

5. initiation of economic negotiations with West Germany and Sweden.

To be sure, the deterioration of relations with France resulting from the "Lobster War" was not attributed to Goulart. But the dialogue with the United States had been thoroughly sabotaged by the Goulart regime. The friendly relations which had for a long time existed with Portugal had been disturbed by the position of Quadros and Goulart, who had given preference to friendship with the African nationalists. The economic relations of the Goulart government with the Western European countries could not have had satisfactory results because the socializing and ultranationalistic tendency of Goulart did not create a climate favorable to foreign investment. The effort of Quadros and Goulart to take up economic relations with East Germany prejudiced a deeper economic relation with West Germany. In short, the most significant foreign policy goal of the Castelo

Branco regime was to end Brazil's isolation from the Western powers.

Today Brazil wants friendly relations with all countries, but it has no particular military, political, or economic reason for forming a closer alliance with the Soviet bloc, with Yugoslavia, and with the neutralist countries; the present government entertains no illusions about this. The Foreign Minister of the Brazilian Revolutionary government, Vasco Leitão da Cunha, has even taken a position against international Communism which seems, strangely enough, more resolute than many utterances of foreign policy spokesmen for the United States. Perhaps this odd state of affairs can, in the long run, be looked upon as all for the good, because a Latin American country cannot be expected to show too much enthusiasm in the fight against Communist infiltration if the offensive in this fight comes from a foreign country, namely, the United States. If the defense against Communism and a demand for social reform arise out of an indigenous national effort, as today in Brazil, it is of far more lasting value.

Brazil felt the need for self-development in the area of international relations. It wanted to follow its own ideological beliefs exclusively, which were based on an independent turning away from international Communism, regardless of the form. This became evident in the hostility and coldness which were shown to Marshal Tito during his state visit of 1963. Brazil's quest for a new model in the sense of an imitation of Nasserism (under Quadros) and of Titoism (under Goulart) did not only prove unprofitable from the standpoint of economics and prestige but also could find no response in the cultural and ideological background of this largest Catholic country in the world.

So it may be that the foreign policy of the present military government of Brazil will have a stability beyond the new state elections for President and for Congress in 1966. The Castelo Branco regime has a special interest in laying a firm ideological foundation for Brazilian foreign policy, because by means of a revolution it has, among other things, set itself the goal of eradicating Communist and extreme Left influence from the government. To be sure, the short-range goals of Brazilian foreign policy are based on the principle that foreign policy has to be of service to the development of Brazil, since the new ideological orientation of the Revolution is a decisive factor in the formation of an outline for foreign policy. Any foreign policy which met with the approval of the extreme Left would internally strengthen the enemy of the Revolution.

Thus the new government is committed to an anti-Communist foreign policy and will try to lay the foundation for a Brazilian foreign policy which is foresighted and global. This is determined, not so much by the subjective character of the currently powerful nations or by last-minute developments in the Cold War, but much more by the evaluation of inherent possibilities and internal political interests. Brazil would welcome the interest which De Gaulle or any other Western European country might take in Latin America because it does not want to be directed exclusively toward the United States. The foreign policy of Brazil is designed first of all to serve a rapid economic upturn. Any support of this plan from outside costs a price in the form of economic concessions and price reductions to the trade interests of the participating country. Thus the negotiating position of Brazil becomes stronger the more countries there are interested in development projects in Brazil.

The new Brazilian foreign policy can only be profitable to the extent that internal social, political, and economic reforms are successful. Should the latter fail, then the former would be largely meaningless. If, however, the Brazilian Revolution should effect a rapid social and economic improvement, then Brazil would be a shining example to the rest of Latin America; and the Free World would be richer for the partnership with 80 million Brazilians who want to develop a territory which is almost as large as the United States. However, more than half of the population is not yet incorporated into a modern production society.[6] The intensive collaboration of the Western democracies to attain a realization of the Brazilian potential is the lesson of Brazil's foreign policy. It was fortunate for the West that Brazil did not become a second China, which would have seriously shaken the balance of power in the world. Considered from the standpoint of world politics, the Brazilian preventive Revolution of April, 1964, was a contribution to world peace, which the government of Goulart had disturbed when it stepped into the stream of international Communism.

The new course of Brazilian foreign policy could be the beginning of a productive relation between Brazil, the United States, Western Europe, and the rest of the Free World. Brazil is too large to remain confined to relations inside the inter-American system. An Atlantic triangle of interest is the more appropriate need and goal. The policy of nonalignment has proved unfruitful for Brazil; it does not serve its national interests. The policy of solidarity with the West makes for better prospects. Also, if the present revolutionary government is distinctly pledged to this policy and follows it with particular firmness, then future Brazilian governments will also value the policy which yields practical advantages to the country. The orientation of Brazilian policy to the broad view stands or falls with the response which it finds in the world.

NOTES

1. *Boletím Informativo* (Brazilian Embassy in Washington, D.C.), No. 152 (Aug. 7, 1964), quotes from the *Diario de Noticias.*

2. The Cuban rocket crisis of 1962 was, to be sure, solved in favor of the United States. Yet, politically, Cuba remained in the Soviet camp, so that the principles of the Monroe Doctrine were not reestablished.

3. A statement of the opposition against the stand taken by Brazil in Punta del Este is found in the explanation of San Tiago Dantas himself in his *Politica Externa Independente* (Rio de Janeiro: Editora Civilisaçao Brasileira S.A., 1962).

4. *Boletím Informativo*, No. 29 (July 22, 1964).

5. According to the television interview of Foreign Minister Leitão da Cunha, communicated in *News from Brazil*, No. 28.15 (July, 1964).

6. Compare the statistic of illiteracy in *Contribuçao para o Estudo de Demografia do Brazil* (Rio de Janeiro: Conselho Nacional de Estatistica, 1961), according to which 48.35 percent of all Brazilians could read and write. Yet a great portion of the reading and writing population cannot be considered incorporated into a progressive production process because of their insufficient technical training.

Section IV

The Foreign Policy of Argentina

Introduction

Geography has been as important to Argentina as it has been to Mexico (see Section II), but in the opposite sense. Sharing with Chile the southern portion of the Western Hemisphere, Argentina is one of the two Latin American countries located farthest from the regional superpower; unquestionably, this distance has influenced and, regardless of modern technologies, will continue to influence Argentina's foreign policy. However, geography has not been the only factor which until recently has made Argentina's foreign policy clearly distinguishable from that of the rest of the area. The heavy influx of European immigrants during the period 1880 to 1930 was reflected in a ratio of one foreigner for every three inhabitants by 1914; if only the economically active population is taken into account, 40 percent of them were foreign-born.[1] The other crucial factor which has influenced Argentina's foreign policy was the interest demonstrated by Great Britain in the River Plate region, which can be traced back to the direct invasion attempts of 1806 and 1807. As an indication of economic interest, by the year 1913 Great Britain had 10 billion dollars invested in Argentina; this figure represented 42 percent of the total British investment in Latin America.[2] Needless to say, these monies, which went into railroads, public services, meat-packing plants, and the like, led to very close political, as well as economic, ties with the British Empire.

When faced with the growing ambitions of the United States toward Latin America, the traditional upper class which controlled Argentina until 1916 did not hesitate to utilize this relationship with Great Britain as a counterbalancing force. Both the middle-class Radical party administrations (1916–1930) and the Perón regime (1946–1955) attempted essentially to continue this type of foreign policy. A careful analysis of Perón's

289

"third position" shows that it was only a fruitless attempt to provide an ideological framework and a new name for the old game of threatening Great Britain and the United States with each other in order to act more independently of both. While commercially the British markets were paramount, at least until World War II, culturally and emotionally the countries of Western Europe occupied an important place. The former Argentine Foreign Minister José María Cantilo put it quite well in 1938 when he said:

> the interests, and not Argentina's alone, held by the River Plate countries in the European markets are in opposition [to those of the United States] and do carry weight in their national and international politics. But here economic reasons are not necessarily of paramount importance in determining the course of Argentine international policy. We feel a close solidarity with Europe through the immigration we received from that continent, an element that has contributed so much to our greatness; also to European capital we owe the development of our agricultural production, of our railroads and industries. . . . From Spain came our race and religion, while from France, Great Britain, and the United States came the doctrinal orientation of our democratic institutions. If to the mother country we owe the basis of our literature, then to French culture we owe the basic formation of our intellectual life and to Italy and Germany all the vital aspects of our evolution. . . .[3]

For reasons which cannot be discussed here, *brevitatis causa*, this traditional foreign policy, which gave Argentina substantial freedom of action, as well as steady and rewarding markets for its traditional exports (meat, grains, and the like), lost its validity after World War II when one of the key elements, Great Britain, could no longer be played against the then nearly hegemonic superpower. It took Perón and his "third position" approximately six years to discover this, but the price was extremely high and Argentina may still be paying it. Great Britain's loss of stature as a world power made Argentina's traditional foreign policy of "pragmatic independence" no longer viable.

However, it would be inaccurate to claim that Great Britain's political decline was solely responsible for the Argentine failure in the late 1940's and early 1950's. The fact is that during and after World War II the United States had grown from one among the world powers to one of the two superpowers. Unquestionably, with its increase in power came a desire to increase its control over the South American countries which had heretofore shown a certain degree of independence, and naturally Argentina was the most conspicuous candidate.

During the second half of Perón's dictatorship his "third position" had become an attractive slogan used mostly for domestic consumption. When economic difficulties ensued, neither Great Britain nor the nations of Western Europe were able or willing to assist. One of the first signs of surrender was the ratification of the Inter-American Treaty of Reciprocal Assistance, signed in Rio de Janeiro in 1947. It was ratified in 1950 by a congress in which the *Peronistas* had a two-thirds majority. The *quid pro quo* was a 125-million-dollar loan granted by the United States and used almost exclusively to pay Argentine debts to American exporters. One observer commented, "The price, then, for which the State Department obtained from an Argentine government in 1950 what all previous ones had refused to do during more than half a century was extremely reasonable."[4] This change was reflected at the United Nations, where the *Peronista* delegations shifted to the support of the Chiang government and refused to vote for condemnations of the policy of "apartheid" followed by the Union of South Africa, as well as to sanction its retention of the mandate territories. Argentina thus inched closer to American foreign policy.[5] The surrender was to have culminated in the year 1955, when Perón was preparing the country to subscribe to agreements with the Atlas Corporation and the California Argentina de Petróleo (a Standard Oil subsidiary), granting them extensive concessions. When seen in this light, the feeble attempts to organize an economic and political bloc which was to include Chile, Paraguay, Nicaragua, and possibly others, and the abstention in the Dulles-sponsored resolution condemning Communism and the Arbenz regime, are nothing but expressions of independence without substance. The ambivalent attitude toward the pro-Arbenz Guatemalans who took refuge in the Argentine embassy and who were granted political asylum in Argentina provides further evidence of the nonapplicability of the "third position."[6]

The Frondozi administration, elected in 1958 with *Peronista* support, made the only serious attempt to return to a foreign policy of pragmatic independence which would take into account the fact that Great Britain could no longer be counted on for counterbalancing support against American influence. Under these conditions Frondizi realized that the only possibility of diminishing the trend toward a quasi-satellite status was through a general understanding with Brazil, which toward the end of the Kubitschek administration was already showing clear signs of restlessness and annoyance at its role as a "safe ally" of the United States.[7] One of the architects of this new approach, Carlos A. Florit, who was Frondizi's first foreign minister, has been unusually clear in presenting his thinking. He wrote:

> The political and economic resources already mentioned imply a firm understanding, without *arrière pensées*. Because of their level of evolution, Brazil and Argentina should be essential participants; the objective should be adequate coordination of the international attitudes of both countries, first in relation to the inter-American system and second in relation to the rest of the countries of the world. . . . A solid and concrete understanding, such as the one we have just described, would immediately and automatically become the necessary platform on which both countries, and through them other countries of Latin America, could hope to develop a *relatively independent international position*.[8]

However, Brazil's willingness to reach such an understanding materialized only when Jânio Quadros became President (see Section III). Argentine sponsors of this understanding with Brazil were aware of what Quadros' victory meant; shortly after it took place, Florit stated:

> With Jânio Quadros the national popular movement has triumphed in Brazil; the integrationist will which encompasses both the geographic and the social has triumphed; the concept of harmonic economic development as the foundation of political free-

dom and the strengthening of democracy has triumphed; the permanent and obstinate exaltation of legality for everybody and the conscious and energetic repudiation of all violence as a means of political or social action have triumphed; the people, and therefore the nation, has triumphed.[9]

For the Frondizi administration, however, foreign policy was only one of the vehicles to carry out a national policy of development, and was not really an end in itself.[10] This view was in general similar to the one held by all previous governments up to 1943, but the definition of development was substantially different. As Dardo Cúneo points out clearly in his article, the Frondizi administration understood development in terms of petroleum, steel, and industrial goods; development meant industrial development—if need be at the expense of the traditional exports. This implied, to a certain extent, that development was to be achieved at the expense of the established upper class, which benefited primarily from the traditional exports. On the other hand, this definition would articulate the interests of the industrial upper class, the modern middle class, and, to a certain extent, the urban lower class. Frondizi himself defined his terms quite precisely when he stated:

> The evil of the Latin American oligarchies did not consist in their defending and increasing their wealth, but in their being unable to foresee the future. They did not understand in time that the scheme of the international division of labor between industrialized countries and agricultural and mining countries was doomed to disappear. This scheme is no longer useful to either side. . . . The only possible and stable customer for an industrialized country is another industrialized country. In view of that, and because our peoples are not willing to continue having low levels of living, both culturally and socially, Latin America has irrevocably started on the road toward development.[11]

Essentially, then, Frondizi's concern was to combat the trend shown in the international terms of trade against the raw-material-producing countries by making Argentina become an industrialized country and thus able to behave toward the under-

developed countries of Latin America and elsewhere as industrialized countries were then behaving toward Argentina. Trade
was to be directed to the Latin American Free Trade Association
and, if necessary, to the Soviet bloc and Communist China.
Aware of the fact that this policy was going to produce adverse
reactions in the Western bloc, the Frondizi administration also
offered important advantages to American and Western European investors, including major concessions to their oil companies. But internal and external pressures made trade with the
Communist bloc politically impossible, in spite of the fact that
the European Economic Community was closing its members'
markets to Argentine meat and grain and that the British market
was curtailing its purchases.[12] Finally, Frondizi was overthrown,
and his plan to revitalize the foreign policy of "pragmatic independence" was abandoned, together with the Uruguayana agreement and the attempt to organize a southern bloc which would
jointly face American influence. This agreement was intended
to coordinate the foreign policies of Argentina and Brazil
through a series of regularly scheduled meetings at various levels,
on the assumption that the other countries of the southern part
of South America would have no choice but to follow the joint
decisions of the "big two." It should be noted that, by implication, this organization recognized the extension of American
influence from Central America and the Caribbean to Venezuela, Colombia, and Ecuador.[13] As events demonstrated, the
Uruguayana agreement was too little and too late.

The alternative foreign policy, followed by the military government from 1955 to 1958 and by the various administrations
since 1962, is a return to the traditional exports as the first objective of Argentina's foreign economic policy and, in the absence
of a nation able and willing to undertake the role played by
Great Britain up to World War II, a reliance on the inter-
American system. This foreign policy, presented in the article
written by Professor Hechen, proposes to fight the adverse trends
in the terms of trade by better marketing, more contacts, superior diplomatic personnel, and requests directed essentially to
the United States to cease subsidizing agricultural exports. This
foreign policy assumes that Argentina will have, within today's

inter-American system, enough flexibility to achieve its objectives and that long-term markets will in fact be found without contradicting the senior member of the regional system. These assumptions have not yet been confirmed or fully denied.

Naturally, this foreign policy, which could be called one of "minimum dependence," admits varying degrees of commitment to the inter-American system and to the dominant superpower. Thus, the Illia administration (popularly elected in 1963) opposed the inter-American military force and refused to contribute men and matériel to the 1965 Dominican Republic operation, in spite of the demands made by the United States and pressures exercised by the Argentine military establishment.[14] On the other hand, the military government which replaced President Illia in 1966 has become the most active sponsor of such a force, going beyond the position of the United States in its eagerness to press for it. The Onganía regime also showed its commitment to the inter-American system by opening the door to new concessions to oil companies and by further curbing Communist activities. Recently, however, it has shown a desire to move away from this position, at least in the area of military supplies; the army has recently decided to purchase sixty French-made tanks and to negotiate the establishment of a plant which would assemble them in Argentina.

This foreign policy of "minimum dependence" runs counter to the traditional attraction exercised by Europe on most Argentines; this feeling has been identified as a "mental style" which transcends political philosophies, ideologies, and principles.[15] While it is too early to proclaim it a failure, it seems clear that such a foreign policy would have to produce extremely convincing concrete returns in order to counterbalance the tendency of most Argentines to look toward Europe and disassociate themselves from the rest of Latin America, the influence of the United States, and the inter-American system as it exists today. In calling for this policy of "minimum dependence," Vicente Pellegrini told his fellow countrymen:

> Consequently, some serious thinking is required toward the abandonment in international gatherings of the naïve pretense of trying

to explain to the Europeans that we are different from the others. Our land is also Latin America, and our arguments against that reality fail to convince the Europeans and engender a sour feeling among the sister countries.[16]

This policy, however, does have the advantage of making it possible to return to the traditional competition with Brazil for influence within the inter-American system and the neighboring countries; this competition has now been extended to include each country's relationship with the United States. Consequently, those Argentines (and there are many) who measure the national interest in terms of what Brazil does or does not do will tend to feel more comfortable with this type of foreign policy.[17] Those who favor a coordination of policy with Brazil *against* American influence, "Europeanism," and industrialization at any cost will tend to reject the foreign policy followed by Argentina since 1962 and will favor some sort of a return to Frondizi's policy of "pragmatic independence."

The policy of "pragmatic independence" failed to achieve its objectives in the 1958–1962 period for various reasons, among them the fact that its sponsors were restricted in their moves by important power elites, such as the military and the traditional upper class, and were finally overthrown. Therefore, unless these power elites change their minds, a redistribution of power in Argentine society becomes a prerequisite for the return to "pragmatic independence." Furthermore, the overwhelming power of the United States creates further doubts regarding the feasibility of such a foreign policy.

On the other hand, there is no indication yet that Argentina's present foreign policy is in fact providing solutions for national threats such as the trend in the terms of trade, the closing of the markets of the European Economic Community members to Argentina's traditional exports, and the constant deterioration of the country's influence in the inter-American system. On the contrary, there are indications of diplomatic isolation, which has been fought by active and direct contacts at the level of the minister of foreign relations and of the ranking military officers.

It is difficult at the time of this writing to predict the future course. The Onganía regime seems to be fully committed to a policy of "minimum dependence," although domestically it gives the impression of, and in fact claims to be, following an independent course. This duality may be an implied recognition of the greater popular appeal of something close to "pragmatic independence," although the military regime does not seem to be interested in subjecting itself to a popularity contest. But one should not rule out the possibility of drastic changes if the present policy does not bring about the assistance and the international improvement which important sectors of the military establishment have requested.

NOTES

1. See Gino Germani, *Política y Sociedad en una Época de Transición; de la Sociedad Tradicional a la Sociedad de Masas* (Buenos Aires: Editorial Paidos, 1962), p. 212.

2. Aldo Ferrer, *La Economía Argentina; las Etapas de su Desarrollo y Problemas Actuales* (Mexico: Fondo de Cultura Económica, 1963), pp. 104–5. For a comprehensive, if negativistic, view of British influence in Argentine politics and economics see Raúl Scalabrini Ortíz, *Política Británica en el Río de la Plata* (Buenos Aires: Editorial Reconquista, 1940).

3. As quoted in Alberto Conil Paz and Gustavo Ferrari, *Argentina's Foreign Policy, 1930–1962* (Notre Dame: University of Notre Dame Press, 1966), pp. 45–6.

4. Sergio Bagu, *La Realidad Argentina en el Siglo XX. III, Argentina en el Mundo* (Mexico: Fondo de Cultura Económica, 1961), p. 110.

5. On this point see John A. Houston, *Latin America in the United Nations* (New York: Carnegie Endowment for International Peace, 1956), *passim*.

6. The Argentine embassy in Guatemala City is known to have encouraged pro-Arbenz politicians to seek refuge in it. Those who did so were fully protected from Castillo Armas' repression. However, many of those who decided to go to Argentina were jailed upon their arrival and later interned in small towns, far away from Buenos Aires.

7. For changes in Brazilian foreign policy see Section III. An interesting, if somewhat naive, view of the United States interest in Brazil is expressed by Henry Albert Phillips, *Brazil: Bulwark of Inter-American Relations* (New York: Hastings House, 1945).

8. Carlos A. Florit, *Política Exterior Nacional* (Buenos Aires: Ediciones Arayú, 1960), pp. 43–4 (emphasis in the original).

9. *Ibid.*, p. 96.

10. This point was made quite clearly by Frondizi. See, for instance, Arturo Frondizi, *La Política Exterior Argentina* (Buenos Aires: Transición, 1962), pp. 40–6. Also see Florit, *op. cit.*, p. 55.

11. Frondizi, *op. cit.*, p. 99.

12. Commercial relations with Communist countries were suggested by Frondizi in the 1958 electoral campaign and endorsed by writers from different schools of thought, particularly in view of the threat posed by the European Economic Community. See Vicente Pellegrini, *Argentina y el Mercado Común Europeo* (Buenos Aires: Editorial Sudamericana, 1963), passim.; Julio Notta, *Crisis y Solución del Comercio Exterior Argentino* (Buenos Aires: Ediciones Problemas Nacionales, 1962), pp. 98–104 and 113–26; and Ricardo E. Olivari, *El Comercio Exterior Argentino; Reorganización Necesaria* (Buenos Aires: Edinorte Editores, 1963), pp. 82–8 and 153–252.

13. For opposing opinions on the Uruguayana agreement see Roberto Noble, *Satelismo contra Soberanía* (Buenos Aires: Ediciones Arayú, 1966), pp. 120–32, and Conil Paz and Ferrari, *op. cit.*, pp. 201–22.

14. While it is true that the Argentine alternate delegate to the Organization of American States voted in favor of the inter-American military force, this action should not be considered indicative of the position taken by President Illia, who resisted strong pressures to contribute to the force. In fact, the bizarre episode of the Argentine vote has been clouded by intrigue; for a view of the episode and its implications see Osiris Troiani, *Dominicana: Solo para Adultos* (Buenos Aires: Editorial Jorge Alvarez, 1965), pp. 113–25.

15. The expression belongs to Julio Mafud, *Psicología de la Viveza Criolla* (Buenos Aires: Américalee, 1965), p. 254n.

16. Pellegrini, *op. cit.*, p. 85.

17. For an illustrative example of this type of thinking see Alfredo Kölliker Frers, *Pasado, Presente y Futuro de la Política Económica Argentina; Gobierno y Economía* (Buenos Aires: Ediciones Theoría, 1964), pp. 133–7.

Argentina's Foreign Policy*

Dardo Cúneo

I

The Argentine government surprised the foreign ministries of the Western Hemisphere on March 5, 1961 (weeks before the frustrated invasion of Cuban beaches by contingents of United States trained Cuban exiles) by offering its good offices to Washington and Havana to seek ways of solving the conflicts pending between those countries.

At the Conference of Foreign Ministers at Punta del Este in January, 1962, Argentina, Mexico, Brazil, Chile, Bolivia, and Ecuador did not participate in the vote that excluded Cuba from the inter-American system.

These facts can only be understood in the context of Argentine domestic politics.

II

On February 23, 1958, the Argentine people made Arturo Frondizi President of the Republic. It was not the triumph of a party. The electoral majority of the country, denied the right to run their own candidates, opted to support the slate of the *Unión Cívica Radical Intransigente*. A national movement was formed around that slate; it was endorsed by four million votes,

* This article was originally published in Spanish as "La Política Exterior Argentina," in *Cuadernos Americanos*, 23(2):7–20, Mar.–Apr., 1964. Translated and printed by permission.

the greatest number ever carried by an Argentine president. The significance of the movement transcended the mechanics of voting and the electoral processes. Basically, it was a step taken by the people toward rescuing their sovereignty; it represented the unanimous desire of the people that their country move forward.

For the Argentine people the *Revolución Libertadora* had meant the restoration of the oligarchy. History will confirm the way the people judged the replacement of General Lonardi's *neither vanquished nor victors* attitude by a campaign unyieldingly opposed to the popular foundations of the nation. The *Revolución Libertadora* attempted to take an impossible step backward when it restored the already discredited structures of an Argentina exclusively devoted to agriculture and cattle-raising and attempted to send the former peons who had already been transformed into industrial workers back to the country, to an area without electricity, without mechanization. The immediate consequence of this was the restriction of foreign trade—and with it, foreign policy—to a market adapted to the old imperial patterns which England still maintains in the Río de la Plata region. It meant becoming again an agricultural region for the imperial metropolis, a colony with the appearance of a nation.

The result was a theoretical democracy for the benefit of minorities along with the exclusion of the people. This primitive philosophy was clearly retrograde in character and showed an attempt to force the nation to continue as a British supply depot, subject to the colonial business routines of delivering meat and grain at uncertain prices, and of acquiring manufactured goods and fuels at ever-rising prices. These were backward steps for the country. But the Argentine people were already transcending such a subsistence-level economy, and their instincts, their needs, their energies, attested to the powers of a sovereign country, a developing nation with industries and unions; in other words, a country and a nation impelled to complete its social, economic, and cultural processes. The first alternative was a policy of civil war by a minority against majorities; of an oligarchy against a country and a nation. The answer given by the majority and by the country at large was the vote which elected Arturo Frondizi President.

The appearance of such a candidacy represented a new radical alteration of no-longer-viable structures. His was a national slate, not a party one, not a predetermined list made up of party members and nonparty members; it was the emerging of majority decisions; it was the Argentine people. In the name of the people organic methods of developing the nation were proposed: industrialization, with basic industries, so that no part of the country should lack the essentials for its particular production requirements; to include all the country in an orderly effort, so that the energies of the nation should not be restricted to plans for the coast, for the port. This is the sort of thing that happens in underpopulated colonies but should not occur in countries that are searching for their own identity, mobilizing all their resources, developing all their potential. For this purpose a dynamic state, daring entrepreneurs, technicians with an understanding of the nation as a whole, and a centralized labor movement are needed. For this purpose, also, the unity of all Argentines belonging to productive sectors should be achieved in order to meet the technological needs of the nation. That is, we need a forward-moving country, a nation which fulfills itself.

When between February and March, 1958, Arturo Frondizi, President-elect, and Rogelio Frigerio, the future incumbent of the Bureau of Socioeconomic Relations of the presidency, analyzed the econo-financial framework within which they must act, they noted that the nation, which had just expressed the ambition of being propelled energetically forward, must have not only the means with which to begin this great adventure but also what was required to meet its daily obligations, to pay for even the most necessary imports, to buy the fuel essential to keeping its factories running. The outgoing government left the state on the verge of bankruptcy. It was the logical result of the policy of returning to the oligarchy. The outgoing executive was still to be there in the wings, contemplating military anarchy. And the new national movement government was to be conditioned, pressured, hammered; in other words, it would not be allowed to govern. These were the new tactics which the oligarchy would adopt to restrain, frustrate—and at times, too many times, straightjacket—the country and its popular government.

It was within this inhibiting wall that the government would have to attempt to initiate basic reforms and appropriate strategies and techniques. Any move to make possible self-sufficiency in fuel, development of the iron and steel industry, and enlargement of the nation's own resources gave rise to charges of immorality. And this resulted from the propensity of the oligarchy to identify majorities and progress with immorality. Having been culturally dependent on the income of a primitive economy, it had long sanctioned as the moral law what was in use among the *decent part of the population* and took for granted that decency was based on its own traditional social position or a corresponding appropriation of property. Nothing could therefore be more natural than that the uprisings in support of Colonel Dorrego* and the later mass labor movement should have been branded indecent and immoral. Morality and minority were equated. The moral concept defined static societies; therefore innovation and majorities were immoral. When power was transferred from the minority sectors to the more populous sectors, the fears of the former made them insist on referring back to their own idea of morality when voting on changes in the traditional equilibrium. They had little interest in correcting the abuses of officials who might have been guilty of fraud or malfeasance. What they desired was to label all the processes of transformation and popular expansion immoral so as to obstruct and resist them. In doing this the oligarchy is usually successful in making alliances with frustrated sectors of the middle class, and thus gives the latter a channel for expression of their resentment and keeps them under the influence of the traditional society.

For four years President Frondizi endeavored to maintain at all costs constitutional legality as an instrument for economic development and yielded all he could yield in the face of his

* Colonel Dorrego in 1825 demanded the vote for day laborers, that is, for the Argentine masses who in their day voiced the need for the same opportunity for expansion and progress and sovereignty for the common people as was later achieved by the middle class, which through the vote became part of the fabric of the state in 1916.

united enemies: he yielded as far as the formal aspects of his own proper presidential authority were concerned, but the country moved forward. Each military crisis meant disturbance of all order, loss of national patrimony, loss of prestige abroad; but in spite of it all the country moved forward: more industries; more petroleum; full employment. The capacity of the country to rise above the minorities which attempted to curb it strengthened a foreign policy in harmony with national history and with the times. A stagnant, curbed country has little or no place in a world swept along by the stream of technological progress which, on the one hand, imposes peace as an alternative to total annihilation and, on the other, opens the way for new nations and decrees a permanent end to colonialism. A country in the process of development hopes to take its place in the world as a complete nation, fully sovereign, without any restrictions; that is, it places itself on the side of peace and assimilates technological progress to emphasize its own identity, to be more of a nation, to insure its own sovereignty, to do away with the last vestiges of colonial servitude. For that reason the enunciation of a domestic economic policy of self-sufficiency, of iron, steel, and petroleum production, of road and airport construction, was the basis of a foreign policy of self-determination, of nonintervention, of Latin American integration, of world peace.

III

The offer of good offices made by Argentina to the United States and to Cuba had a precedent: the good offices that in April, 1914, were offered to the United States and Mexico by the ABC countries—Argentina, Brazil, and Chile—with the understanding "that internal affairs—according to the criteria accepted by the parties—should be the subject of an accord between representatives of the parties that are fighting in Mexico, without outside interference." These good offices persuaded the United States in June of that year not to insist on demanding war indemnities and to agree to recognize the government that the Mexican parties might give themselves. The precedent being so remote, the news of the new offer surprised the foreign offices. However, there was one that should not have found President Frondizi's attitude surprising: the Vatican's Foreign Office. The policy of John XXIII coincided with the attitude of the Argentine government at the time when Arturo Frondizi (in his third year in office) was gathering his strength to pursue his own policy between the unsuccessful attempts at coups d'etat and the pressures and persecutions he had succeeded in eliminating. At that moment Argentine foreign policy returned to its traditional line, adapted to modern developmental requirements; it was the most representative foreign policy in the last few years. While the Vatican's Foreign Office, inspired by the ideas of harmony and peaceful solutions of John XXIII, instructed the Cuban bishops not to abandon their flocks, the Argentine President declared himself against breaking relations and recalling ambassadors, because he understood that the latter had work to do in Havana in preventing the most unfortunate aspects of the conflict. Yet the offer of good offices was also based on the belief that the Cuban problem was an acute expression of an underdevelopment crisis. The Castro Revolution is in truth the result of the underdevelopment in which Cuba has been maintained. The solution does not lie in police systems or in punitive measures. What matters is that the underdevelopment of the aggregate of Latin America should not promote and encourage crises with the characteristics of the Cuban one and will instead find democratic outlets and methods of improvement. Arturo Frondizi declared in a message to the Argentine people when he gave an account of the points of view he had expounded in his first conversation with John F. Kennedy in September, 1961:

> Billions of dollars came out of the pockets of the North American taxpayer to equip the armies that fought and are still fighting against Communism in China, Indochina, Korea, Laos, Vietnam, and other countries. . . . But war is the explosive phase of a process which antedates it and which can be foreseen and prevented. Because of that, it is necessary to satisfy the needs and desires of the people by developing their national economies. Legal order and respect for human rights are inseparable from social well-being.

On that occasion he emphasized:

> The true danger of Communist aggression lies in its offering a hope of escape from poverty. If the West does not offer that escape from poverty by deeds and not by words or good intentions, the enemy will continue to exist and grow stronger. There is little time left to show people that liberty is not incompatible with material improvement and with raising the standard of living. This is the dilemma that confronts Latin America and this is the challenge presented by the Cuban case, to which we should respond by demonstrating that democracy, development, and social peace offer the best road for the solution of our common problems.

When the Inter-American Economic Conference met at Punta del Este in August, 1961, President Frondizi instructed his country's delegation to obtain rapid implementation of the Alliance for Progress and to direct it toward basic structural answers to solve Latin America's underdevelopment. A highly developed country may at certain times, when motivated by the urgencies of the balance of power and political strategy or by the existence of surpluses, provide social measures for a retarded country. But would not the retarded country prefer to receive, instead of loans for education or for housing development or grain from surplus stocks, modern techniques and long-term capital loans that would permit it to develop itself in its own way and provide social measures of its own? This is the Argentine point of view which has already been presented by the delegation that attended the economic conference held in Bogotá in September, 1960, and which was debated during the last months of that year in the press and government circles of Washington and New York, immediately after the statements made by Rogelio Frigerio, President Frondizi's assistant. *The Journal of Commerce* said in its editorial of September 20:

> But the real question is this: if the United States can distribute 500 million dollars a year, and perhaps 600 million next year, for this type of social aid, will the best return on that money be achieved in this way? Would it not be possible, as was suggested last week by Rogelio Frigerio, to hope for better results from the

loan of an equivalent amount applied to productive works? We feel inclined to state our agreement with the latter. Economic aid offers at least the prospect of reducing, if not eliminating, the most acute problems of other countries, both in the social and in the economic order. And we fear that the New Deal or social approach will only succeed in creating more problems.

Plans for sanitation, for housing, for education, though all very necessary, will not lift a country out of stagnation and paralysis; they will not give dynamic impetus to the realization of its needs and desires. Through this system one would achieve a well-dressed colony that would always require new and infinite quotas of aid; it will not put instruments into the hands of the community that will permit it to work out its own proper national destiny. Without economic development, social development programs will be mere imports that countries have to accept, not a result of raising national cultural levels. This approach leaves in effect—and functioning—the old patterns of the international division of labor; though with apparent generosity it at once corrects the deficiencies in the living conditions of the people through an immediate program, it does not remedy the causes that gave rise to those deficiencies. Under those circumstances social development without economic development is only charity from rich countries to poor countries that will not stop the latter from being poor. This method will not affect the interests of the monopolies that control and benefit from the output of the single-product countries which are subject to the uncertainty—and oppression—of single markets. On the other hand, the economic development method will permanently affect the traditional economic structure of a backward country; it should act on it with enough order, energy, and depth to assure that the backward nation can dredge up from its own foundations the possibility of blazing its own trail as a complete and independent country. Integrating itself in harmony with its own potentialities and with the technical and financial assistance that it receives, such a nation will fit itself to grow and administer its wealth, its commerce, its national patrimony.

Remodeled structures and dynamic processes in action will result in social justice; that is, such social justice will be, not merely an occasional import of health services and schools, but rather the result of the community becoming a modern nation. When the colonial forms which cause the social deficiencies disappear, justice will be the work of its own national abilities, it will be the product of its own endeavors and will encompass all aspects of the life of the community. Arturo Frondizi said to the Associated Press in October, 1960:

> It will be no use for the United States to help us construct a hospital or a highway without first helping us to develop our economy, which in turn will enable us to build our own hospitals later.

If we consider the Alliance for Progress as a joint operation of the progressive sectors of both the United States and of Latin America in their struggle against the backward sectors of both the United States and Latin America, its task is to pour into Latin America the most technical assistance and financial aid possible, and to make sure that they are applied to permanent, creative works. Ample assistance and help will prevent the necessary transformation from being carried out outside the framework of the democratic order. A sufficiently subsidized transformation will facilitate the mobilization of all the resources of the community—geographic and human—in a disciplined and orderly effort. Also, the rhythm of change today requires overcoming any delays. The way to avoid chaotic trends is to give timely help and to encourage the processes of expansion. In the process of economic development, order is nurtured by plentiful and timely aid.

IV

This conviction was basic to the conversations of Arturo Frondizi with Adlai Stevenson, with Hubert Humphrey, and with John F. Kennedy.

Ambassador Stevenson visited Buenos Aires during 1961 as President Kennedy's special envoy, to compare opinions about

Cuba. On Frondizi's part the conversation was a continuation of the one his assistant Rogelio Frigerio (who spoke for him) had started with Stevenson in New York. One of the subjects the Argentine President referred to in plain language dealt with the pressures President Kennedy had to withstand within his own country which threatened to disrupt his proposal to speed a policy of greater progress. Frondizi said:

> To the extent that this policy of progress does not overcome these pressures within the United States and does not at the same time establish itself on a secure and coherent continental basis within the Latin American countries, the conflict between the Latin American development parties and the old oligarchic factions, the conflict between economic development and democracy on the one hand, and backwardness and anarchy on the other, will become increasingly more acute. To the extent that the United States appears before the world with a foreign policy impaired by actions such as the frustrated invasion of Cuba, such impairment reacts on those pressures which President Kennedy must withstand. The immediate answer lies in a restatement of inter-American policy based on these two premises: to aid basic development and to give greater participation in the conduct of the general policy of the continent to the countries which have reached a high level of development, such as Mexico, Brazil, Chile, and Argentina.

Ambassador Stevenson took with him a memorandum to this effect from the Argentine President, in which the latter proposed an immediate meeting of the presidents of the United States, Mexico, Brazil, Chile, and Argentina to consider this agenda: the Cuban question, the nature of aid for development, and the restatement of inter-American policy with the freezing of the problems of the Caribbean.

Ambassador Stevenson also took with him in his portfolio a letter that Rogelio Frigerio sent him when a proposed meeting did not materialize because of unforeseen circumstances. It read:

> The present historical juncture precludes any attempt at political hegemony and dependency within a bloc or group of nations. The United States cannot replace Great Britain in the dominant role

that the latter played in the nineteenth century. The examples of Asia and Africa prove it. In the case of Latin America, the concept that the United States should be an associate and not a master is accepted unanimously.

With regard to Cuba:

A strong and democratic Argentina, friendly to the United States, can initiate joint action to reintegrate Cuba into the Western camp. The Communist bloc itself will pressure Cuba so that it will negotiate its reintegration into the American family, because for Communist policy it is not convenient—within the rules of the game of negotiating coexistence—to provoke the United States in its sphere of influence beyond predetermined limits. . . . One must keep in mind the lesson of the Congo, of Laos, and of Algeria; it is useless to attempt to crush nationalism by force.

About the middle of 1961 there were military crises, and the government of Frondizi was on the verge of falling. From Punta del Este, where he had gone for the meetings of the Inter-American Economic Conference, Guevara, then minister of economics of Cuba, asked the President of Argentina to receive him. The Argentine President, exercising his constitutional powers, established the manner in which this interview would take place. It would afford him an opportunity to gather information on the Cuban crisis through one of its principal participants. However, if the possibility of direct information moved him to accept the interview, it was not the sole motive. Perhaps the principal one was that of finding a way to reorient Cuban policy within an inter-American framework: to reopen the doors to an understanding between Washington and Havana. The President who received Castro's minister was the same one who had offered, months before, the good offices of his Foreign Office for a rapprochement between the countries involved. Had no new conditions arisen since then? Had the failure of the invasion not proved that the procedures recommended and carried out by extremists in the United States led to nothing—being the product of counsels of frustration, they led only to frustration? Would it not perhaps be more propitious to the new currents

inspired by John F. Kennedy to have an opportunity for negotiations that would avoid new expressions of extremism?

Under those circumstances the President of Argentina was
bound to explore, directly, all avenues that might lead to negotiations which would save the United States and Cuba—and
consequently the whole continent—from new dangers under the
existing lack of understanding. But within the environment of
the military commands the presidential decision gave rise to
expressions of disagreement, which were echoed by politicians
without votes and by the reactionary press. The President explained the reasons for his attitude at conferences with the
military. The misunderstanding still persisted. Then the President addressed himself directly to the people.

> A serious and responsible nation should not practice the policy of
> an ostrich, which consists in avoiding problems or in pretending
> to ignore them. A Cuban problem exists and it is the obligation
> of all the American states to consider it and to search for a solution
> that will be suitable to the American community and to its demo-
> cratic ideals. . . . Satellites contribute nothing to the principles
> we are trying to preserve. Independent nations, involved and allied
> in the defense of the great causes of humanity, contribute the
> political and moral force of their own commitment. . . . If instead
> of acting like an independent country exercising its full sovereignty,
> we act like satellites, not only would we be setting aside our na-
> tional dignity but we would also be guilty of leaving the country
> unprotected from reaction and extremism.

Once again a military crisis was averted, but again it left the
prestige of the country impaired abroad.

The following month the President of Argentina held a meeting with the President of the United States in New York, at a
time when the Assembly of the United Nations was in session.
In their conversation the former said to the latter:

> For the cause of America, tomorrow is too late. Vigorous develop-
> ment, directed toward basic objectives, is work for today, a task
> which cannot be postponed, deferred, or excused. Cuba is a warn-
> ing signal.
>   There is no alternative but to prove by concrete and immediate

examples that democracy is capable of liberating people from poverty and ignorance, without subjecting them to any dictatorial oppression.

And he insisted that:

Cuba and Argentina constitute the two national alternatives in the foreseeable processes of Latin America. Argentina is proceeding to the transformation of its economic structure; Argentina's way is that of progress within liberty and of respect for human beings. But those values are menaced when democracy is incapable of guaranteeing everyone access to culture, to a healthy life, to sanitary housing, and to adequate nourishment, to full employment, and to increased training of the labor force. These values are menaced when democracy is incapable of guaranteeing full enjoyment of civil liberties, a regime based on the free expression of the popular will, and full exercise of national sovereignty, without interference or foreign dictation.

In November of that year Senator Hubert Humphrey, one of the most representative figures of modern political thought in the United States, visited Buenos Aires. In conversations with President Frondizi they found they were in complete agreement. Why not have the President of Argentina return the visit and meet with United States foreign policy makers after his trip to Canada? Senator Humphrey himself telephoned to make arrangements for the meeting. The Conference of Foreign Ministers, which was to meet at Punta del Este, had already been convened, and it was necessary again to present the views of the President of Argentina to them. Humphrey brought to bear much energy and all his common sense to secure a hearing in Washington for these views. After all, were not the same views held by the "party of progress" in the United States? As a typical representative of this party, Humphrey thought so. An agreement between the United States and Argentina on methods for Latin American development, on the nature of the relations between the members of the inter-American system arising from consideration of the Cuban case, might provide avenues to possible coherent solutions for that conference, convened so hastily and without proper justification.

Who would profit from driving Cuba away from the inter-American organization, when to accomplish this both the letter of the bylaws of the organization and the juridical principles on which it rests must be violated? Cuba, driven out, separated, would go its own way, while within the inter-American system a sort of schism would develop between the countries of marked growth—Mexico, Brazil, Chile, Argentina—zealous of safeguarding the principles of inter-American organization, on the one hand, and, on the other, a majority of the small countries suffering from stagnation and easily controlled by the old oligarchies. Senator Humphrey had already got in touch with Washington, and Frondizi's new meeting was to be with Stevenson and would take place during the former's stopover at Trinidad. There Frondizi repeated the Argentine view, stating that Argentina supports the way of development, that is, the way of prevention, not that of police control; and that it supports the trend toward full, speedy, and vigorous technical and financial assistance for Latin America. Such assistance should start in the countries of marked development and lead to the transformation of the basic structures in such a way that the assistance will result in productive development, not being used up immediately, but on the contrary flowing dynamically throughout all the territory of Latin America and including all social sectors, thus to create the basis for full democracy and lasting social justice.

At the end of November, on his return trip from Japan, the President of Argentina stopped in the United States, again meeting with President Kennedy. The place was Palm Beach, and the subject, Cuba, Punta del Este. Frondizi said to Kennedy:

> The Cuban question, despite its importance, is drawing us away from the search for suitable solutions to the problem of underdevelopment, which is the one that causes problems like that of Cuba on our continent. The punitive measures proposed are distracting us from the consideration of the general preventive policies which are the most important ones, and the ones which can lead to permanent solutions.

When Frondizi reported on this meeting in a message to the Argentine people, he said that there had been agreement as to zealously respecting the principle of self-determination and nonintervention and safeguarding the American community from the infiltration of ideas and procedures foreign to its traditional way of life. Both governments share fully the concept that there is no better way of strengthening American ideals than to base them concretely on the spiritual and material well-being of their peoples and that this will be the result of the rapid development of their internal economies, of regional cooperation and integration, and of the unrestricted flow of investment and commerce between Latin America and the developed nations of the West, without neglecting commercial exchanges with other regions of the world.

On January 2, 1962, Frondizi repeated these concepts in a letter to Kennedy, and based his opposition to the application of measures against Cuba on those concepts. In the letter he contended:

> if an American nation subordinates its sovereignty to an extracontinental power, the independence of the American nations is to be considered endangered, but the principles of the American nations cannot be effective if one does not at the same time foster economic development and social progress at an unprecedented pace and in accordance with a mobilization of resources of exceptional magnitude with the purpose of multiplying the riches of the continent and spreading it throughout all social sectors, on the basis of the nation's own effort and the cooperation of the countries which have reached the highest living standards.

The same concepts were set forth by Frondizi in a letter to the President of Colombia, Lleras Camargo; he also decided that the author should travel from Washington to Caracas to present them personally to the President of Venezuela, Rómulo Betancourt.

V

The government of Arturo Frondizi was faced with a new military crisis before the deliberations of the Conference of Foreign Ministers were brought to a close. This was a renewal of

the strategy of procuring the overthrow of the government or of
paralyzing its effectiveness; it was crisis number thirty-odd. . . .
From the moment of his election, Frondizi had to waste a great
deal of his energy on neutralizing those who attempted his overthrow or those who tried to pressure, harass, or constrain him.
The coup strategy had two goals, two methods, two purposes.
The first method was that of military uprisings which had as
their goal the overthrow of constitutional order. The second did
not depart too greatly from the intent of the first, but its key element was pressure, its timing depended on making the most of
the conditions created by the other, and its purpose was to prevent the functioning of the government. The first strategy had
numerous actors who succeeded each other and disappeared in
the course of the crisis. The other has been represented more or
less constantly by General Aramburu. The two strategies had
been planned from the time Frondizi was elected. Under the
first, an attempt was made to ignore election results; under the
second, the vote count was recognized, but pressures were to be
applied to the government elected.

The country moved forward during those four years only by
skirting these two enemy lines, by overcoming coups and pressures. In spite of them, the country produced more petroleum,
more iron. In petroleum it attained self-sufficiency and even
managed exports. In iron the 200,000 tons that were produced in
1958 became nearly a million, and if plans are not interfered
with, the annual production for 1964 will be 4 million, which
will mean 200 kilograms per capita, that is, the highest production rate in Latin America. In 1961, manufacturing production
surpassed that of 1958 by 13.2 percent. If in 1958 we used a
third of our foreign exchange holdings to import fuel, today
we can use a greater proportion, 50 percent of our total hard
currency, to import industrial equipment. Two hundred thousand unnecessary bureaucrats have been removed from public
administration and more than seventy thousand from the railroads, without changing the full employment picture. The General Confederation of Labor is guided by its own leaders as a
result of democratic procedures. The conspiracies have inter-

rupted progress, but they have not completely paralyzed the country. Will they do so now, using the vote of Argentina at Punta del Este as a pretext?

At Punta del Este, Foreign Minister Carcano, an old conservative with the acumen of a modern man, conducted the negotiations in the name of his country in the courteous, unruffled, and loyal manner of a diplomat and a patriot. At times the president of the Argentine delegation was the center of complicated negotiations intended to secure a unanimous vote of the conference within the principles and the bylaws of the inter-American system. The instructions that he had been given by President Frondizi were scrupulously precise.

> As I said to you then and as I repeat now, we have to be absolutely clear and precise. In spite of the Cold War and the selfish interests that hide behind them, in spite of repeated attempts at penetration by international Communism, it is up to us Argentines to establish clearly that what is being discussed in America is, not the lot of an extremist leader who has declared himself in favor of a political order which has no bearing on the realities encountered in our countries, but rather the future of a group of underdeveloped nations that have freely decided to attain high levels of economic and social development. If this sovereign decision is not respected, if an attempt is made to hide or distort it by extremist ideological juggling, then it will be truly difficult to avert the danger; an entire continent will be the prey of political and social convulsions. We wish to save the unity of the inter-American system, and for that reason we will abstain from voting for sanctions that can endanger the principle of nonintervention and that aggravate present political conditions and lend themselves to the continuation of the activities of extremists of the Right and of the Left.

The military crisis did not respond to such language; it is a decisive crisis; the one that would occur within the next two months would be but the capping of this one. Frondizi fell because of Punta del Este. As he confronted the crisis, he foresaw his political demise. How did he confront it? By an address to the people.

Let us consider that the principles of nonintervention and self-determination are the only ones capable of safeguarding the sovereignty of nations, especially that of the small nations of the continent. History will prove that the nations which refused to infringe these principles saved the inviolability of America against any eventual open or hidden aggression. And when the passions and the impatience of today are quieted, the same ones who did not listen to the calm warning represented by this attitude will recognize that it agreed with the highest and most enduring interests of the liberty and sovereignty of the American nations.

Here ends the most representative and most mature chapter of Argentine foreign policy in recent years.

Argentina's Foreign Policy and Development*

Santiago Hechen

INTRODUCTION

Safeguarding the autonomy of the state in international affairs and defending the basic interests of the country in relation to other world powers normally constitute the frame of reference for the activities of the Ministry of Foreign Relations. These tasks are carried out subject to juridical principles which have survived the various stages of national and international evolution and remain in full force.

Usually the activities of the Foreign Service are confined to maintaining contact with other world powers, either in a bilateral manner, or through meetings of international organizations, or even through permanent representation in the latter, these activities being limited to safeguarding the position to which the state is entitled within the community of nations.

This interpretation of the duties of the Ministry of Foreign Relations, which focuses its activity exclusively abroad and confines it to maintaining relations, while traditional in Latin American countries and generally followed by ministers and presidents,[1] does not seem to be in accordance with the concept of the duties of the Ministry as set forth by the present Minister, Zavala-Ortiz.

In order not to fall into the very frequent error of repeating

* This article was originally published in Spanish as "La Política Exterior Argentina y el Desarrollo," in *Foro Internacional*, 5(20):489–510, Apr.–June, 1965. Translated and printed by permission.

significant but not fundamental concepts, or those which are not characteristic of or do not define the objectives pursued in the development of Argentine foreign policy, it is advisable to analyze in some detail the formulation of the same by the Foreign Minister and the measures which have been or are being taken.[2]

DEFENSE OF TRADITIONAL PRINCIPLES

Without immediately attempting to determine the main outlines, we can point out, as the majority of those who have studied the subject have done, that present Argentine international policy is based firmly on traditional principles and that self-determination of peoples, nonintervention, equality of states, and defense of sovereignty continue to be basic postulates which the executives of the nation have asserted personally or through their spokesmen on all suitable occasions.

An exhaustive study of the occasions on which they were first set forth, though interesting, would add nothing to a better understanding of the objectives sought by our effort in the international order; they are, as has previously been stated, traditional principles, not interpreted in exactly the same way everywhere in Latin America, but within certain limits common to the majority of states in that region.

Because of this diversity of interpretation, differences in application exist, not only in different states but also within the same country, owing to the change of administrations charged with the application of these principles. But these differences alter only slightly what have come to be known as traditional principles; their role is to determine in international affairs and to bring up to date domestically the modes of behavior which in due time will become part of this tradition, and which the men of the future will also seek to adapt. If it were necessary to point out a particular instance in which the present administration differed from the preceding ones with respect to the interpretation of one of the basic principles of Argentine international policy, we might mention the position taken by the Minister of Foreign Relations at the Ninth Meeting of Foreign Ministers in Washington with respect to the principle of nonintervention.

Until recently the official doctrine maintained by the Argentine Ministry of Foreign Relations did not accept the application of the right of legitimate defense provided for by Article II of the Inter-American Treaty of Reciprocal Assistance except in the case of armed attack, and its interpretation of armed attack was in accord with classical juridical literature.

In his speech Dr. Zavala-Ortiz stated with reference to the present government of Cuba: "by methods, and operations, and concrete objectives it has indoctrinated, mobilized, organized, and equipped a force for armed attack and for subversion within the territory of the nation attacked."

As he pointed out in another part of his speech, "Classical juridical literature generally gives an interpretation of armed attack based on the characteristics of conventional warfare, that is, direct invasion of territories or blockade of ports carried out by forces coming from outside," but he repudiated this interpretation, saying, "armed attack at the present time should not be interpreted in an exclusively military sense as by the state which formally initiates hostilities, since that is not the most common phenomenon in our era. The activities of a state that wishes to dominate or change the status quo of another by recourse to the use of material force is in reality armed attack."

In accordance with this new doctrinal interpretation, he concluded by saying, "The acts of the Cuban government, in accordance with this interpretation of the concept of armed attack, fall within the concept of intervention. It would be dangerously naive to classify all these acts as revolution instead of intervention. Considering the preponderantly revolutionary technique of modern warfare, they can only be classified as armed attack." This manner of treating the concept of intervention, which we will not analyze in this paper, but which equates certain types of aggression with armed attack, is changing former doctrinal statements but maintains in full force one of the basic principles of Argentine international policy.

We might give numerous examples of the unremitting efforts of the Ministry in defense of the basic principles which guide its foreign policy, but this would not add anything to clarifying the goals pursued by Argentina through the newly adopted policy. By studying the efforts made in the defense of permanent principles, we would only come to know these guiding principles, but we would learn nothing about the ends sought. Since the literature dealing with the former is ample, and there is none dealing with the latter, it is advisable to examine the activities which characterize the present administration in greater detail to ascertain whether there are in truth definite goals other than the well-established one of peaceful coexistence.

BASES OF PRESENT INTERNATIONAL POLICY

Besides reaffirming the traditional principles on which Argentine foreign policy has always rested, the Ministry of Foreign Relations since October, 1963, has considered the need of having this branch of the government undertake new responsibilities, to contribute positively to the development of the country.

The role normally played by the Argentine Foreign Service used to be almost exclusively limited to the political and juridical aspects of international relations, and not even the Consular Corps (whose essential function should be economic in accordance with the original purpose for which it was legally constituted) seemed able to depart from its official representative functions. This situation was widespread and not limited to the Argentine Foreign Service, being the result of an antiquated interpretation which it was hard to abandon.

The recent reactions in Argentina are up to now a proof of this, since it is just being put into practice. Any action to be taken in accordance with this new attitude must fall within the guidelines expressly set forth by the Minister of Foreign Relations and confirmed on the occasion of the Ninth Meeting of Foreign Ministers, when he said: "In the drafting of Argentine foreign policy only the national will is consulted. We recognize international responsibilities and obligations, but not foreign dependence. In the exercise of its full sovereignty and guided by its universalist and peaceful concepts, Argentina wishes to be friendly with all the countries of the world that are ready to respect it."

The greatest emphasis has been placed on pointing up the firm intention of proceeding with absolute independence within the international order, without ignoring corresponding responsibilities and obligations.

This affirmation of full sovereignty has been confirmed on various occasions. In his speech of October 13, 1964, one year after assuming his duties, Dr. Zavala-Ortiz stated: "It would be extremely dangerous for the independence and sovereignty of nations to have any of them fix for the others the interpretation which should be given to the concept or ideology concurrently expressed."

The fact of belonging to the Christian or Western civilization does not carry with it the obligation of accepting the imposition of interpretations set up by any country in this group, nor should it imply a restriction on dealings with nations that do not belong to it. This freedom of ideological interpretation and of dealings with all the countries of the world carries with it the possibility of considering democracy as a political system whose content has not been determined a priori. Thus the possibility of variations exists as long as the principles of a free community are followed: democracy cannot be associated with a given economic system. When this interpretation is accepted, it tends to eliminate obstacles in international dealings with nations of any sector of the world.

It is within the framework of these principles establishing a national, democratic, independent, universalist, and pacifist position adopted by consulting "only the national will" that the needs of the country are analyzed in order to act in accord with them.

THE SITUATION AND THE NEEDS OF THE COUNTRY

The present Argentine government acknowledges the existence of an internal crisis, yet at the same time points out that this is not limited to the Argentine nation, but is shared by the majority of developing countries. These crises are not created by internal causes; they are produced as a result of commercial relations with more developed countries.

According to the Argentine Foreign Minister development is a problem of income and markets, and it is affected when a fair price is not paid for the original product or when a proportionately higher price is charged for industrial products. In any of these cases financial assistance does nothing but make the situation worse by adding interest payments that depress the developing economy even more.

The solution to the problem, after rejecting financial assistance, lies in enlarging the market, and this can only be achieved if markets in the industrialized countries become available, but the latter can be helpful only after going through structural changes, which cannot be limited to the developing countries, inasmuch as national economies are related and interdependent.

This outline, as presented to the General Assembly of the United Nations at its Nineteenth Period of Sessions in 1964, sets forth the main points of the position maintained at the Alta Gracia Conference and subsequently at Geneva, and endorses commerce, and not aid as up to now given, as the only solution for the Argentine economy. Exports offer the opportunity of obtaining external resources without acquiring a debt or being under obligation, for special favors to any other country, and maintain freedom of choice as to the manner in which such resources are to be used.

INTERNATIONAL ECONOMIC POLICY

The present Argentine government, bearing in mind that international policy should be not only a means of communication between countries but also, and mainly, an instrument for contributing to the fulfillment of national needs, acknowledges development to be the basic need at this time, while it recognizes that foreign commerce is essential in order to attain a constant rate of growth, which it has decided to make a maximum effort to increase. However, it is not easy to solve the problems which arise when an attempt is made to attain a sufficient increase in exports under conditions which will produce a real benefit to the national economy. Foreign income is at present derived almost exclusively from the export of agricultural products, and the demand for these products on the international market suffers constant and unpredictable fluctuations due to climatic changes in other producing countries, changes in diet of the population of the world, and so on, but principally because the policy of the industrialized countries exerts a depressing effect.

There have been various kinds of protectionist policies such as quotas, shares, prohibitive prices, and such, and their purpose is to protect a less efficient domestic industry. Another aspect has been the subsidizing of a domestic production that is then dumped on the world market at an artificially low price and under gift-like terms of payment.

The effect abroad of the protectionist policy is the artificial decrease of world demand and the lowering of prices, and the effect on the agricultural countries is to discourage production.

In order to solve the domestic difficulties occasioned by the irregularity of demand and the low price of exports, the Foreign Minister proposes international attitudes favorable to the domestic conditions required to attain a sufficient increase in exports to encourage full development. Solution on the international scale is based on a triple effort: Latin American integration, a struggle against protectionism, and the opening up of new markets, which in practice means the planning of a wide and reasonably secure market, able to absorb an increasing production. But this solution should, in turn, be complemented domestically by an increase in agricultural production and diversification of exportable products through the processing of raw materials and the production of manufactured goods.

Latin American Integration

In the past, many attempts have been made to cement unions among the nations of the continent. They have all failed to the degree that the attempts have represented the slightest decrease in the sovereign attributes of states.

The ABC Pact by Argentina, Brazil, and Chile in 1915, after

protracted negotiations, was with difficulty put into final form, only to fail of ratification because of the doubts aroused as to its possible scope.

It became possible to form the Organization of American States only by sacrificing on the altar of sovereignty its effectiveness and the possibility of doing a constructive job, and all efforts made to change this situation seem foredoomed to failure.

While on a continental basis the presence of the United States may be considered an obstacle to integration, both because of historical differences and the level of development, the same should obviously not be true within the Latin American fold, yet the results obtained up to now are nil. The common factor in these misunderstandings has been a nationalism which rejects any situation which may lead to closer unions and weaken the sovereignty of the state within the international sphere. For this reason, regional attempts have proved even less workable, despite the greater affinity and the underlying historical circumstances which might have facilitated them, since in this case the threat to nationalism is greater because the conditions for integration are better.

Though the Argentine Foreign Ministry is cognizant of the difficulties existing in the way of attaining closer regional ties, it intends to overcome both domestic and international difficulties.[3] The Foreign Minister pointed out in his speech of October 13, 1964, that Argentine nationalism should be favorable to integration and that the national ideal could not be realized without regional cooperation. For this reason he considers it necessary to promote and achieve the union of Latin America, which will not mean substituting regionalism for nationalism, but that regionalism will serve nationalism.

For the purpose of achieving this integration, a system of preliminary consultation with the other Latin American countries has been set up to facilitate exchange of information and unanimity in international policies, and this procedure has been utilized on various occasions, especially in situations, such as the breaking of relations with the Cuban government and attendance at the Second Conference of Nonaligned Countries, that could have become obstacles to continental harmony.

The purpose of this system of diplomatic consultation is to maintain a certain unity of regional viewpoints on the international scene without setting up permanent organizations of a political nature which might cause any attempt at integration to miscarry. In this way it has been possible to envisage Latin American economic integration independent of the political unions to which Latin Americans have always shown themselves resistant, even though economic integration would in the end imply a certain degree of political coordination.

The international economic policy inherited from previous administrations is most fully expressed in the Montevideo Treaty. However, due to dissatisfaction with the progress achieved by the Latin American Free Trade Association (LAFTA) during its four years of existence, the creation of a Latin American common market is being proposed which, without ignoring LAFTA and the Central American Common Market, would include all the Latin countries of the hemisphere. The majority of the nations involved share this concern, and the favorable atmosphere in which the effort has begun affords hope for greater progress. This would not only benefit the economy of each of the nations of Latin America but would also help all the countries of the world, since according to Dr. Zavala Ortiz: "The unity of America will not mean withdrawing from the rest of humanity. It will mean contributing its own union to the union of the world, to the cause of peace, to the development effort, to the equality of peoples, and to the security of the human individual."[4]

THE STRUGGLE AGAINST PROTECTIONISM

Since agricultural production is basic to Argentine export policy, its protection is essential not only because of the foreign currency it may produce but also because it represents the only source of income for a great sector of the population.

The degree of efficiency attained in agricultural production, which has been improved until it has reached highly satisfactory levels, is affected by the protective tariff policy adopted by other countries because it limits the possibility of exports, and so discourages production to a degree which leaves meager balances for export.

This protectionist policy has been applied mainly in two ways. One of them has been adopted by countries whose production costs are greater and who protect their products by means of duties, quotas, and such. Industrialized countries which might benefit and generally do benefit through the sale of manufactured products to Argentina, but which are reluctant to modify their attitudes, belong in this category. Another method has been that of domestic subsidizing of production in order to throw agricultural exports upon the international market at very low prices, under easy payment terms, a practice which thus makes competition impossible. These government subsidies tend to favor agricultural production artificially, and this results in the raising of industrial production costs, since industry is forced to maintain the subsidies through taxation.

Subsidies for domestic production are used mainly by the United States, a highly industrialized country whose manufactured articles make up the most important sector of Argentine imports. This attitude has a twofold effect on the Argentine economy: first, it makes the placing of agricultural export products on the international market difficult, and second, it makes the manufactured articles it acquires from the United States more expensive.

As anyone can easily see, this sort of protection is one of the most burdensome for the economy of developing countries, and tends to increase existing imbalances vis-à-vis the developed countries. In accordance with what the Argentine Foreign Minister has said, this problem cannot be solved by financing, since its solution requires changes in the structure of the highly developed states.

Protectionist policy is more stringent in the case of processed products, so such a policy constitutes the main obstacle to the industrial growth of developing countries because it limits the market.

In order to achieve uninterrupted progress in development, we must have assured markets for our exports of agricultural and manufactured goods, but this requires the elimination of the various types of protectionist barriers.

OPENING UP OF NEW MARKETS

The need of assuring the sale of excess national products (which in turn will permit the acquisition of products not produced within the country) and the difficulties encountered in the countries with which traditional commercial ties have been maintained make it essential to search for new markets. The economic relations maintained with Western Europe and the United States leave increasingly less favorable balances because of the falling off of the prices of the raw materials we export as compared to the manufactured products which we import. The same Latin American raw materials, with slight United States or European processing, are sold to other nations with which until recently the majority of Latin American countries did not maintain commercial relations.

In the case of a country within the Communist orbit, the ideological reaction has been the principal obstacle to any attempt to change the situation. The Foreign Minister was explicit in his statement in this connection, saying "no ideological or political difference will stand in the way of negotiations advantageous to the country."[5] In accordance with this view, the Western and Christian position has been ratified, but trade has been established with the Communist orbit countries, to benefit greatly Argentina's economy.

The ideological division of the world is merely one of the problems which the present government encountered in endeavoring to enlarge the market for the products of the country. The emergence of a great many states in the last few years arouses the hope of obtaining new markets; however, it is very difficult to obtain these. The principal difficulty lies in the ties which those countries still maintain with their former metropolis. Commercial or financial ties are kept at present by channeling the majority of their transactions through the British Commonwealth, the New French Community, and the European Common Market. To these traditional ties we must add the lack of Argentine representation in the new nations, which makes it necessary to initiate a serious effort first to establish representation and then to achieve trade relations.

Although there are many obstacles to be overcome, there is no doubt that the effort made to open up new markets will offer advantages which will fully compensate for the sacrifice.

DOMESTIC CONDITIONS NEEDED TO TAKE ADVANTAGE OF THE EXPANSION OF THE FOREIGN MARKET

Analyzing the present situation and the intention of the present administration to enlarge the international market for Argentine products makes clear that to attain the objectives desired it is necessary to have domestic conditions consonant with the changes the new international economic policy is intended to make in international relations.

Any effort made to widen the market requires that domestic production be sufficient to cover the resulting demand; for this reason the Foreign Minister, at the time of initiating the present effort to gain markets, pointed out the reaction which he hopes will take place in the domestic sector.

Although production has not decreased, during the last decade a general retrenchment has taken place and growth has been paralyzed. Agricultural production reached a high technical level after World War II, and this made possible the achievement of higher yields. However, conditions abroad which acted as depressants on the domestic situation caused discouragement to become widespread among the producers. The situation has remained unchanged until now and has resulted in a paralyzation of industrial development. This industrial development may have been triggered by the euphoria produced by the great foreign demand for agricultural products at the end of that conflict, but because it had not had time to become firmly rooted, it came to a standstill, partly as the result of the reduction in agricultural production, which in turn decreased domestic purchasing power, and partly as a consequence of the lack of foreign markets to absorb increasing industrial production.

In order to profit truly from our proposed international economic policy, it will be necessary to base it on a greater agricultural production and on diversification of export products by processing raw materials and increasing industrial production.

GREATER AGRICULTURAL PRODUCTION

While this does not mean we are to attempt to limit the country exclusively to the role of provider of raw materials, it should be pointed out that the degree of development achieved up to now has been obtained by perfecting agricultural production, which is the main, if not the sole, traditional export of the country.

Although the capacity for domestic consumption is limited, the international market requires increasing amounts of foodstuffs. At present there is a marked deficit in the diet of a very high percentage of the population of the world, and it will grow worse as the population increases.

The disparity between the prices of raw materials and of manufactured products should disappear when the demand for these is normalized, and there is no doubt that this will come about, as restrictive policies and dumping succeed only in prolonging the situation.

But the possibility of taking advantage of the greater demand for agricultural products depends upon the existence of surpluses for export, and these should be obtained by increasing production and not by limiting domestic consumption, as it has been necessary to do previously to fulfill our commitments. Favorable conditions exist within the country which will permit increasing agricultural production until we attain figures which will in themselves be sufficient to maintain a favorable balance of trade, even allowing for the need to purchase what is required to revitalize the process of industrial development. This increase may be obtained by improvements in technology which would permit better use of the land already under cultivation and the use of others now cultivated hardly or not at all.

As a result of the new policy of commercial relations with all the countries of the world, whatever sacrifices are made to increase the production of foodstuffs are sure to produce immediate benefits because of the opportunity this policy will afford of placing the surplus left after domestic consumption on the international market. On the other hand, for various reasons we cannot maintain the artificial reduction of prices by means of subsidies for domestic products and the barriers erected against the products of other countries, this policy having seriously impaired the economy of the nation. First, this subsidized production would not be sufficient to supply the needs of the world market, and, second, it will not be possible to maintain the subsidy by increasing the price of industrial articles, because then the latter would no longer find purchasers due to the competition in price produced by the opening of new markets.

Because of the evolution taking place in the world economy, everything seems to point to the end of the stagnation suffered by Argentine economy for the past decade. Should the country be in a position to take advantage of a favorable opportunity to the fullest degree, it might attain the domestic development necessary to meet the critical situations which may occur in the future, without sacrificing the standard of living of the population.

PROCESSING OF RAW MATERIALS

Until now the placing of processed products on foreign markets has been very slight because of the resistance of the countries which have traditionally imported our agricultural products, but the availability of new outlets will make it possible to market packaged or somewhat processed foodstuffs, and the greater value of these will at least partially compensate for the disadvantages normally arising in international trade from the difference in price between the raw product and the manufactured one.

There are processing plants in the country capable of markedly increasing their production, but there are also favorable conditions for the construction of new plants to cover any increase in demand.

It may be possible to continue existing restrictions in Western European markets arising from the desire of those nations which are the traditional purchasers of our foodstuffs to protect their own production, but these restrictions do not exist in other markets which will be opened up by the new policy which applies to all the markets of the world. In this way, that is, by taking steps to eliminate protectionist barriers in those traditional markets which have exhausted the possibility of increasing their production but must meet greater food demands and consequently will be better disposed to negotiate on other terms, and by making efforts to achieve the conquest of new markets, there is no doubt that the demand for processed agricultural products can be increased. However, it will be necessary to prepare to meet that demand by increasing agricultural production and by building additional processing plants.

INCREASED INDUSTRIAL PRODUCTION

It is generally agreed that the industrial development of Argentina is a matter of markets. The basic conditions necessary for development, such as a high technological level, a skilled labor force, and entrepreneurial organizations qualified to meet the situation, exist, but the market is not sufficient for mass production. The naturally small domestic market has further been reduced by the retrenchment induced by low demand and low placement prices for traditional exports. The solution to this lies in expanding the market for agricultural products, but the domestic market continues to be insufficient to make possible industrial development on the level of that attained by industrialized countries, so that expansion by securing additional foreign markets becomes necessary to make possible large-scale production and to place us in a position to compete with the products of other countries. As we have already said, the basic requirement of high technical quality is present, and we have the added advantage of comparatively lower costs for skilled labor. However, our products must meet the quality requirements of the international market and do so at competitive prices.

The greatest difficulty to be overcome is the demand for well-known and highly regarded brands in the international market, but by displaying sufficient initiative in promoting our products and by maintaining stable sales channels in the expanded market resulting from our present international economic policy it will be possible to obtain satisfactory results.

The present efforts of the government are intended to achieve the proposed goals. To this end they are increasing their activities in the Latin American field and attempting to destroy protective barriers in traditional markets, while at the same time trying to establish contacts with the other countries of the world.

ROLE OF THE FOREIGN SERVICE IN
DOMESTIC DEVELOPMENT

To coordinate our international economic policy and our proposed domestic economic policy as suggested by the Foreign Minister will require a display of activity of a different sort than what is customary in the Argentine Foreign Service.

Up to now the Consular Corps has not acted with the efficiency necessary to carry out the mission which historically gave rise to the creation of our consular institutions. Nor has the Diplomatic Corps undertaken the protection of national commercial interests abroad, despite the modern tendency to have diplomacy direct an increasingly greater proportion of its efforts to the defense of commercial interests. This should be corrected, not only to benefit national interests but also to aid Argentine diplomacy itself, since the latter cannot act efficiently for the attainment of the goals of the nation entrusted to it if it is not buttressed by a solid economic situation in its own country.[6]

The laws and regulations governing the Foreign Service take into account the need of having its members cooperate with the private sector in various ways, but mainly by drawing up general reports that cover the many aspects of the economy of the country to which the mission is accredited. The reports, when made, accumulate in files, and it is difficult to put them to any profitable use. The other forms of cooperation have not been implemented, so we need not consider them.

The need of reorganizing the Foreign Service to enable it to achieve its present goals has been considered, particularly with a view to facilitating the duties relating to trade, such as carrying on preliminary market research, informing Argentine exporters of the opportunities offered by foreign outlets, or answering inquiries about the possibility of marketing Argentine products; in short, providing the means for bringing Argentine exporters and foreign importers into direct contact. All these activities are centralized in a Department of Trade Development which acts as the intermediary between the Consular Corps based abroad and entrepreneurs at home. A policy of answering specific inquiries and trying to solve each problem individually has been substituted for the former system of general reports and monographs.

The diplomatic missions also have their specific role within the new system, as they are entrusted with creating the conditions necessary to enable the Consular Corps to carry out their promotional activities. Their efforts are to be concentrated on solving existing problems in our economic foreign policy, so that Latin American integration will be achieved, protective tariff barriers eliminated, and new markets opened.

By this reorganization it is hoped to speed up the procedures necessary to publicize the opportunities existing in foreign markets and to take advantage of them to get the national economy moving again.

We should remember that the Minister of Foreign Relations has insisted on the necessity of developing foreign trade as the only possible way to achieve the objective of speeding up the rate of domestic evolution essential to attaining full development. The Foreign Service plays a very important part in this, since the success of the development program undertaken depends upon the effectiveness with which this service acts in fulfilling the new obligations imposed upon it.

CONCLUSIONS

Though in accordance with the traditional division of activities of the government, preoccupation with the domestic economic problems of the country does not pertain exclusively to the Ministry of Foreign Relations, it cannot be denied that at this time the activities of the latter in Argentina are oriented toward obtaining a degree of domestic development which will enable the country to surmount the crisis which has held it prisoner for over a decade. This approach is in contrast to the foreign policy of peaceful coexistence traditionally applied within an accepted and conventional international order, in which Argentine diplomacy confined itself to acting in defense of juridical principles that would permit peaceful coexistence within a system of mutual respect between nations. Thus, our foreign policy is now directed toward the definite goal of defense of Argentine interests within the world community in order to achieve the conditions necessary for domestic development.

There has been no abdication of the principles considered traditional in Argentine international policy; rather their application and defense have become automatic and the greatest effort is now directed toward the implementation of measures of an economic nature. According to the theories of the Ministry of Foreign Relations this should foster an effort in the domestic field leading to progressive evolution of the economic potential of the country.

Summing up, we can set forth the characteristic outlines of the present Argentine foreign policy as follows:

Argentine international policy is based on the traditional principles which have always been characteristic of the nation in its international relations.

The interpretation of these principles is subject to adaptation in accordance with the new doctrinal concepts made necessary by modern science and technology.

The Illia administration has not confined itself to performing Argentina's traditional role in the sphere of foreign relations, that is, to maintaining relations with other countries, but instead centers its activities around domestic needs and attempts to satisfy them.

The planning of the present international policy of Argentina is subject to the organic doctrinal principles systematically expounded by the Minister of Foreign Relations.

With the need to speed up economic development as the starting point, the inadequacy of the existing markets is indicated to be the cause of what may be termed the development crisis.

This inadequacy can be corrected, not by financing from abroad as has been done up to now, but only by foreign trade.

In accordance with these conclusions, Argentine international policy should pursue predominantly economic objectives in order to enlarge its markets.

This attempt to enlarge its markets is to be made through Latin American integration, elimination of protectionist barriers, and the opening up of new markets.

It is the firm intention of the present government to act with absolute independence in its economic relations and therefore to trade with all the countries of the world which may offer it favorable conditions.

In order to adjust to the true needs of the country, the activities of the Foreign Service must be directed toward achieving the objective sought.

The present objective of Argentine international policy is full domestic development.

NOTES

1. Decisions on foreign policy in Argentina are the prerogative of the executive branch. The President is the court of last resort, and in some cases he personally assumes the direction of foreign policy as Frondizi did, the Minister of Foreign Relations being charged with the execution of it; but in other cases, such as the present one, direction and execution are concentrated in the hands of the Minister, although always subject to final approval by the President.

2. Although on many occasions Foreign Minister Zavala-Ortiz has appealed to public opinion, outlining the activities of the Ministry of Foreign Relations and explaining the reasons for the attitudes adopted by the nation, his most significant speeches and those which point out most clearly the doctrinal bases of the present conduct of foreign affairs are those made at the Ninth Meeting of American Ministers; at the Nine-

teenth Period of Sessions of the General Assembly of the United Nations; the one of October 13, 1964 (made a year after having taken charge of the duties of the Ministry) to the Argentine people, whom, as he has himself stated, he wishes to keep properly informed; the one on the creation of the Department of Trade Development of the Ministry of Foreign Relations; and, finally, the one of March 10, 1965.

3. It should be remembered that although at present a very high percentage of the population of Argentina seems disposed to accept close union with the Latin American states and even to delegate sovereignty to international organizations, in 1915 it was precisely the Argentine Congress that refused to ratify the ABC Pact.

4. Speech given before the General Assembly of the United Nations during its Nineteenth Period of Sessions.

5. Speech given on March 10, 1965, for public information.

6. The dominant position which it occupied within the American community until the end of the decade of the 1940's and which it gradually lost during the decade of the 1950's cannot be regained through the individual action of its representatives. That position was solely and exclusively due to a degree of internal development relatively superior to that of the other Latin American states, so that the voice of its representatives carried all the weight of the relative economic potential of the nation.

Index

A

Act of Bogotá, 69, 92, 119, 121, 123, 124, 134
agrarian reform, 29, 49, 142, 145, 148, 163, 268
Alliance for Progress, see regional organizations
anti-imperialism, see imperialism
Argentina, 3, 4, 6, 10, 13, 15, 25, 26, 41, 43, 50, 55, 56, 84, 86, 126, 135, 143, 147, 156, 158, 171, 178, 202, 203, 208, 228, 237, 239, 241, 247, 287, 336
Argentine-United States Mutual Assistance Pact, 12
Atlantic Charter, 152

B

Baghdad Pact, 232
balance of trade, 329
banking, 86
Batista, Juan, 11
Bay of Pigs, 116, 117
belligerency, 96, 227
Bolivia, 7, 13, 126, 132, 135, 237, 241, 242, 243, 299
Brazil, 4, 6, 13, 14, 15, 25, 26, 30, 33, 41, 43, 49, 50, 54, 55, 56, 59, 84, 86, 126, 131, 132, 135, 143, 156, 158, 165–289, 292, 294, 299, 303, 308, 318, 323
Brazilian Workers' party, see political parties
"by country" studies, 70, 72

C

Calvo Doctrine, 13
capital, 60, 108, 138, 139, 207, 218, 224, 253, 255, 305
capitalism, 25, 47, 222, 267
Caribbean, 11, 14, 15, 190, 294, 308
Castelo Branco, Humberto, 172, 175, 188, 193, 282, 284
Castro, Fidel, 3, 6, 11, 41, 117, 170, 269, 276, 277, 280, 304, 309
caudillismo, 203
Central America, 11, 14, 15, 294
Central American Common Market, see regional organizations
Chaco War, 14, 180
Chile, 4, 13, 14, 15, 25, 32, 34, 43, 45, 51, 52, 126, 132, 143, 178, 205, 208, 237, 242, 291, 299, 303, 308, 312, 323
China, 19, 21, 101, 102, 112, 172, 190, 222, 230, 257, 266, 267, 269, 276, 282, 304
Christian Democratic party, see political parties
class, 31, 223, 275
bourgeoisie, 32, 47, 223
lower, 293
middle, 25, 26, 28, 33, 46, 47, 48, 50, 85, 183, 213, 289, 293

D

E

O

U

underdevelopment, 19, 100, 145, 186, 220, 221, 222, 225, 229, 250, 254, 264, 304, 305

United Nations, 61, 68, 90, 96, 98, 101, 112, 117, 152, 154, 170, 171, 172, 184, 190, 244, 245, 274, 291, 322

United States, 6, 8, 10, 13, 14, 15, 19, 20, 21, 23, 24, 33, 39, 40, 42, 43, 51, 52, 63, 81, 89, 90, 93, 95, 97, 100–110, 112, 126, 138, 158, 161, 169, 171, 172, 176, 178, 179, 180, 182, 184, 188, 191, 192, 197, 205, 206, 207, 208, 209, 210, 211, 222, 228, 233, 241, 247, 252, 270, 275, 278, 282, 283, 285, 289, 296, 299, 303, 307, 308, 309, 310, 311, 324, 327

"Uniting for Peace Resolution," 103

Uruguay, 3, 13, 25, 126, 172, 175, 202, 203, 240, 242, 294

V

Venezuela, 14, 15, 34, 39, 43, 45, 126, 158, 238, 243, 294, 313

W

West Germany, 101, 283

Western Europe, 19, 35, 228, 241, 245, 247

World War I, 147

World War II, 21, 23, 170, 236, 244, 268, 271, 290, 291, 294